Business Professional's For Dummies®

D1067029

International Telephone Codes

Country	Code	Country	Code
Argentina	54	Luxembourg	352
Australia	61	Malaysia	60
Austria	43	Mexico	52
Belgium	32	Morocco	212
Brazil	55	Netherlands	31
Chile	56	New Zealand	64
China	86	Nicaragua	505
Columbia	57	Norway	47
Czech Republic	420	Oman	968
Denmark	45	Pakistan	92
Ecuador	593	Panama	507
Egypt	20	Paraguay	595
El Salvador	503	Peru	51
Finland	358	Philippines	63
France	33	Poland	48
Germany	49	Portugal	351
Greece	30	Qatar	974
Guatemala	502	Romania	40
Honduras	504	Russia	7
Hong Kong	852	Saudi Arabia	966
Hungary	36	Singapore	65
Iceland	354	Slovakia	421
India	91	South Africa	27
Indonesia	62	Spain	34
Iran	98	Sweden	46
Iraq	964	Switzerland	41
Ireland	353	Taiwan	886
Israel	972	Thailand	66
Italy	39	Turkey	90
Japan	81	United Arab Emirates	971
Jordan	962	United Kingdom	44–
Korea, Republic of	82	United States	01
Kuwait	965	Uruguay	598
Libya	218	Venezuela	58
Liechtenstein	41	Yemen Arab Republic	967

For Dummies™: Bestselling Book Series for Beginners

Business Professional's Kit For Dummies®

Cheat Sheet

Reporting Lost or Stolen Credit Cards

Card	Dial from the U.S.	Dial Collect from Abroad
American Express	800-528-4800	910-333-3211
Diner's Club	800-234-6377	None
Discover	800-347-2683	Not accepted outside the U.S.
MasterCard	800-622-7747	303-278-8000
Visa	800-336-8472	410-581-7931

Toll-Free Airline Numbers

Airline	Toll-Free Number
Air Canada	800-776-3000
Alitalia	800-223-5730
America West Airlines	800-235-9292
American Airlines	800-433-7300
British Airways	800-247-9297
China Airlines	800-227-5118
Continental Airlines	800-525-0280
Delta Airlines	800-221-1212
Delta Express	800-325-5205
Finnair	800-950-5000
Iberia Airlines of Spain	800-772-4642
Japan Airlines (JAL)	800-525-3663
Korean Air	800-438-5000
Lufthansa	800-645-3880
Midwest Express	800-452-2022
Northwest Airlines	800-225-2525
Qantas Airways	800-227-4500
Sabena Belgian World Airlines	800-873-3900
Southwest Airlines	800-435-9792
Swissair	800-221-4750
Trans World Airlines (TWA)	800-221-2000
United Airlines	800-241-6522
US Air	800-428-4322
Virgin Atlantic	800-862-8621

IDG BOOKS WORLDWIDE®

The IDG Books Worldwide logo is a registered trademark under exclusive license to IDG Books Worldwide, Inc., from International Data Group, Inc. The ...For Dummies logo and For Dummies are trademarks of IDG Books Worldwide, Inc. All other trademarks are the property of their respective owners.

Cheat Sheet $2.95 value. Item 5273-2.

For more information about IDG Books, call 1-800-762-2974.

For Dummies™: Bestselling Book Series for Beginners

Praise for Business Professional's Kit For Dummies

"Business may not always be war, but it's certainly an endless series of skirmishes. The *Business Professional's Kit For Dummies* is an indispensable guide for start-up entrepreneurs as well as those managing established organizations. It neatly integrates hints, success stories, and common sense into an accessible and wide ranging package."

> — Jamie Rapperport, President and CEO, OfficeClick.com, Inc., Palo Alto, CA

"The *Business Professional's Kit For Dummies* is a true treasure. With clearly written tips and steps for action, the book is an invaluable tool for any entrepreneur or business owner. Whether one is just starting out in business or is "seasoned," there is much to be gained from this highly readable text."

> — Barbara A. Macaulay, UMass Center for Professional Education

"Sheryl has hit the mark again! For those who are looking for a concise and complete overview of the personal business process, this is your guide! It is written in a bright, straightforward manner that really communicates a host of wonderful ideas. For beginners it provides both encourgement and a vital checklist for getting started; experienced professionals will thoroughly enjoy this not-to-be-missed review."

> — William C. Noz, Jr., Principal, The ISO 9000 Network

"This fantastic reference book is the perfect tool for any business professional. It is the how-to manual for success in business."

> — Dr. Ivan Misner, author of *Masters of Networking* and founder of Business Network International (BNI)

Praise for Writing Business Letters For Dummies

"*Writing Business Letters For Dummies* is a life raft in a sea of bad communication. Sheryl Lindsell-Roberts has compiled a guide that everyone — from the anxious beginner to the seasoned pro — can use immediately. But what makes her book such a delightful read is its light-hearted approach to a process that intimidates most of us but shouldn't! This book is a comprehensive road map to getting noticed in business."

> — Bill Lane, Business Editor

"Great business letter writing has become a lost art — until now. Thanks to Writing Business Letters For Dummies, the art of letter writing has been resuscitated. Armed with creative tips and strategies set forth in this book, you will give your business letters — and your career — new life. Get the book!"

> — Evilee Thibeault, Senior VP/Publisher, *Network World,* Inc.

"Ms. Lindsell-Roberts has created a "must-read" work for anyone entrusted with the art of written communication. Written in a form that is both easy to read and easy to implement, this book flies in a real world setting. Whether expert or novice, this book will greatly enhance your ability to communicate your ideas and get results."

> — Dr. Tony Palermo, Chiropractor and Success Coach

Praise for Business Writing For Dummies

"*Business Writing For Dummies* is an important resource that will find its way to everyday use by the people in business today who intend to be the leaders in business tomorrow. It is an excellent blend of practical basics, advanced concepts, and skilled insight that will make better communicators of us all."

> — Gary Sullivan, electronic commerce consultant and university lecturer

"*Business Writing For Dummies* really means business. From job-hunting to sales-pitching, from e-mail to snail mail, Sheryl Lindsell-Roberts gives you the verbal tools to build your career with confidence and competence."

> — Richard Lederer, author of *The Write Way*

"Sheryl combines great knowledge and experience with a very readable style. This book will be an excellent resource for writers everywhere."

> — Bard Williams, Ed.D., author of *The Internet for Teachers,*
> *Web Publishing for Teachers,* and *The World Wide Web*
> *for Teachers*

 ™

...For Dummies™

References for the Rest of Us!™

BESTSELLING BOOK SERIES

Do you find that traditional reference books are overloaded with technical details and advice you'll never use? Do you postpone important life decisions because you just don't want to deal with them? Then our *...For Dummies*® business and general reference book series is for you.

...For Dummies business and general reference books are written for those frustrated and hard-working souls who know they aren't dumb, but find that the myriad of personal and business issues and the accompanying horror stories make them feel helpless. *...For Dummies* books use a lighthearted approach, a down-to-earth style, and even cartoons and humorous icons to dispel fears and build confidence. Lighthearted but not lightweight, these books are perfect survival guides to solve your everyday personal and business problems.

> *"More than a publishing phenomenon, 'Dummies' is a sign of the times."*
>
> — *The New York Times*

> *"...you won't go wrong buying them."*
>
> — *Walter Mossberg, Wall Street Journal, on IDG Books' ...For Dummies books*

> *"A world of detailed and authoritative information is packed into them..."*
>
> — *U.S. News and World Report*

Already, millions of satisfied readers agree. They have made *...For Dummies* the #1 introductory level computer book series and a best-selling business book series. They have written asking for more. So, if you're looking for the best and easiest way to learn about business and other general reference topics, look to *...For Dummies* to give you a helping hand.

IDG BOOKS WORLDWIDE ®

Business Professional's Kit

FOR DUMMIES®

by Sheryl Lindsell-Roberts, M.A.

IDG Books Worldwide, Inc.
An International Data Group Company

Foster City, CA ◆ Chicago, IL ◆ Indianapolis, IN ◆ New York, NY

Business Professional's Kit For Dummies®

Published by
IDG Books Worldwide, Inc.
An International Data Group Company
919 E. Hillsdale Blvd.
Suite 400
Foster City, CA 94404
www.idgbooks.com (IDG Books Worldwide Web Site)
www.dummies.com (Dummies Press Web Site)

Library of Congress Control Number: 00-106337

ISBN: 0-7645-5273-2

Printed in the United States of America

10 9 8 7 6 5 4 3 2 1

1O/QW/QZ/QQ/IN

Distributed in the United States by IDG Books Worldwide, Inc.

Distributed by CDG Books Canada Inc. for Canada; by Transworld Publishers Limited in the United Kingdom; by IDG Norge Books for Norway; by IDG Sweden Books for Sweden; by IDG Books Australia Publishing Corporation Pty. Ltd. for Australia and New Zealand; by TransQuest Publishers Pte Ltd. for Singapore, Malaysia, Thailand, Indonesia, and Hong Kong; by Gotop Information Inc. for Taiwan; by ICG Muse, Inc. for Japan; by Intersoft for South Africa; by Eyrolles for France; by International Thomson Publishing for Germany, Austria and Switzerland; by Distribuidora Cuspide for Argentina; by LR International for Brazil; by Galileo Libros for Chile; by Ediciones ZETA S.C.R. Ltda. for Peru; by WS Computer Publishing Corporation, Inc., for the Philippines; by Contemporanea de Ediciones for Venezuela; by Express Computer Distributors for the Caribbean and West Indies; by Micronesia Media Distributor, Inc. for Micronesia; by Chips Computadoras S.A. de C.V. for Mexico; by Editorial Norma de Panama S.A. for Panama; by American Bookshops for Finland.

For general information on IDG Books Worldwide's books in the U.S., please call our Consumer Customer Service department at 800-762-2974. For reseller information, including discounts and premium sales, please call our Reseller Customer Service department at 800-434-3422.

For information on where to purchase IDG Books Worldwide's books outside the U.S., please contact our International Sales department at 317-572-3993 or fax 317-572-4002.

For consumer information on foreign language translations, please contact our Customer Service department at 1-800-434-3422, fax 317-572-4002, or e-mail rights@idgbooks.com.

For information on licensing foreign or domestic rights, please phone +1-650-653-7098.

For sales inquiries and special prices for bulk quantities, please contact our Order Services department at 800-434-4322 or write to the address above.

For information on using IDG Books Worldwide's books in the classroom or for ordering examination copies, please contact our Educational Sales department at 800-434-2086 or fax 317-572-4005.

For press review copies, author interviews, or other publicity information, please contact our Public Relations department at 650-653-7000 or fax 650-653-7500.

For authorization to photocopy items for corporate, personal, or educational use, please contact Copyright Clearance Center, 222 Rosewood Drive, Danvers, MA 01923, or fax 978-750-4470.

is a registered trademark under exclusive license to IDG Books Worldwide, Inc., from International Data Group, Inc.

About the Author

I'm fortunate to be in a profession that would be my hobby if it weren't my livelihood. Between freelance writing assignments and business writing seminars, I've written seventeen books for the professional and humor markets (including *Business Writing For Dummies* and *Writing Business Letters For Dummies*), plus a host of magazine articles.

When my life gets more complicated than it needs to be, my warm-weather nirvana is my 30' sailboat — *Worth th' Wait*. My husband Jon and I are aboard every weekend that the temperature rises above 60 and the seas aren't too treacherous. (We've also been out there when they were too treacherous, but not by choice.) I don't bring my suitcase stuffed with clothes because there isn't room to put too much; I've learned to minimize. All I need is sunscreen, a few pairs of shorts, some T-shirts, and a good book. Columbus wanted to prove the world was round, Captain Kirk wanted "to boldly go where no man has gone before," Jon and I merely want to leave our obligations and harried lives on shore. Everyone needs a nirvana, even if it's a spot under a tree or the corner of a room.

When I'm not writing or sailing, I travel, paint (watercolors, not walls), garden, photograph nature, read, ski, eat tiramisu, and work out at the gym (after the tiramisu I really need to). I try to live each day to the fullest! Jon and I live in *Parnassus*, the incredible home in Marlborough, Massachusetts, that my son Marc designed.

— Sheryl Lindsell-Roberts, M.A.

ABOUT IDG BOOKS WORLDWIDE

Welcome to the world of IDG Books Worldwide.

IDG Books Worldwide, Inc., is a subsidiary of International Data Group, the world's largest publisher of computer-related information and the leading global provider of information services on information technology. IDG was founded more than 30 years ago by Patrick J. McGovern and now employs more than 9,000 people worldwide. IDG publishes more than 290 computer publications in over 75 countries. More than 90 million people read one or more IDG publications each month.

Launched in 1990, IDG Books Worldwide is today the #1 publisher of best-selling computer books in the United States. We are proud to have received eight awards from the Computer Press Association in recognition of editorial excellence and three from Computer Currents' First Annual Readers' Choice Awards. Our best-selling *...For Dummies*® series has more than 50 million copies in print with translations in 31 languages. IDG Books Worldwide, through a joint venture with IDG's Hi-Tech Beijing, became the first U.S. publisher to publish a computer book in the People's Republic of China. In record time, IDG Books Worldwide has become the first choice for millions of readers around the world who want to learn how to better manage their businesses.

Our mission is simple: Every one of our books is designed to bring extra value and skill-building instructions to the reader. Our books are written by experts who understand and care about our readers. The knowledge base of our editorial staff comes from years of experience in publishing, education, and journalism — experience we use to produce books to carry us into the new millennium. In short, we care about books, so we attract the best people. We devote special attention to details such as audience, interior design, use of icons, and illustrations. And because we use an efficient process of authoring, editing, and desktop publishing our books electronically, we can spend more time ensuring superior content and less time on the technicalities of making books.

You can count on our commitment to deliver high-quality books at competitive prices on topics you want to read about. At IDG Books Worldwide, we continue in the IDG tradition of delivering quality for more than 30 years. You'll find no better book on a subject than one from IDG Books Worldwide.

John Kilcullen
Chairman and CEO
IDG Books Worldwide, Inc.

Eighth Annual Computer Press Awards ≥ 1992

Ninth Annual Computer Press Awards ≥ 1993

Tenth Annual Computer Press Awards ≥ 1994

Eleventh Annual Computer Press Awards ≥ 1995

Dedication

To my awesome sons, Marc and Eric.

From the time Marc and Eric were little tykes, our house was filled with wall-to-wall children who turned our Currier and Ives snowfalls into a yard with footprints and snow mountains, and who turned our basement into a chemistry lab, a stage for a puppet show, a detective agency, and anything else for which they found an inch of space.

Marc and Eric grew up to be the most incredible young men on the face of this earth. They are truly wonderful people, successful professionals, and my good friends. Marc is an award-winning architect, who lives and works in San Francisco, CA (my favorite city). Eric is a dedicated chiropractor, who lives and practices in Columbia, MD. Marc and Eric truly illuminate the inner depths of my soul; I'm the luckiest mother alive!

Author's Acknowledgments

I express my heartfelt thanks to my family and my dear friends. Without their love and support, I wouldn't be the person I am today and wouldn't be realizing my dreams.

I want to praise all the "Dummies" (and I say that with the utmost respect) who made this book a reality. They're a wonderful group to work with. This is especially true of Karen Doran, Acquisitions Editor, who gave me sagely advice and laughed at my jokes. I also appreciate the wonderful support from Tim Gallan, Project Editor, who worked tirelessly to keep this project on the straight and narrow. I'd also like to extend a thanks to the following special subject-matter experts who kept me honest in several of the chapters:

- ✔ **Dr. Eric Lindsell,** Essential Family Chiropractic, Columbia, MD.

- ✔ **Robert E. Lajoie,** Operations Manager, Omega Collective Technologies, Inc., Worcester, MA.

- ✔ **Dr. Bard Williams,** author of many books in the Dummies series. His latest is *Web Publishing For Teachers* (IDG Books Worldwide).

- ✔ **Harry Pape,** Director of the Information Services Group, Windmill International, Inc., Nashua, NH.

And I can't forget my loving, wonderful, and patient husband. Jon was always there to help me with my computer problems — even when I got testy.

Publisher's Acknowledgments

We're proud of this book; please register your comments through our IDG Books Worldwide Online Registration Form located at `http://my2cents.dummies.com`.

Some of the people who helped bring this book to market include the following:

Acquisitions, Editorial, and Media Development

Senior Project Editor: Tim Gallan

Acquisitions Editor: Karen Doran

Copy Editors: Elizabeth Netedu Kuball, Ben Nussbaum, Kathleen Dobie

Acquisitions Coordinator: Jill Alexander

General Reviewer: Perrin Capell

Permissions Editor: Carmen Krikorian

Editorial Manager: Pam Mourouzis

Media Development Manager: Heather Heath Dismore

Media Development Specialist: Megan Decraene

Media Development Assistant: Marisa E. Pearman

Editorial Assistant: Carol Strickland

Production

Project Coordinator: Nancee Reeves

Layout and Graphics: Amy Adrian, Stephanie D. Jumper, Gabriele McCann, Tracy K. Oliver, Kristen Pickett, Jill Piscitelli, Brent Savage, Jacque Schneider, Brian Torwelle, Julie Trippetti

Proofreaders: Laura Albert, Corey Bowen, John Greenough, Susan Mortiz, Marianne Santy, Susan Sims

Indexer: John Sleeva

General and Administrative

IDG Books Worldwide, Inc.: John Kilcullen, CEO; Bill Barry, President and COO

IDG Books Consumer Reference Group

Business: Kathleen A. Welton, Vice President and Publisher; Kevin Thornton, Acquisitions Manager

Cooking/Gardening: Jennifer Feldman, Associate Vice President and Publisher

Education/Reference: Diane Graves Steele, Vice President and Publisher; Greg Tubach, Publishing Director

Lifestyles: Kathleen Nebenhaus, Vice President and Publisher; Tracy Boggier, Managing Editor

Pets: Dominique De Vito, Associate Vice President and Publisher; Tracy Boggier, Managing Editor

Travel: Michael Spring, Vice President and Publisher; Suzanne Jannetta, Editorial Director; Brice Gosnell, Managing Editor

IDG Books Consumer Editorial Services: Kathleen Nebenhaus, Vice President and Publisher; Kristin A. Cocks, Editorial Director; Cindy Kitchel, Editorial Director

IDG Books Consumer Production: Debbie Stailey, Production Director

IDG Books Packaging: Marc J. Mikulich, Vice President, Brand Strategy and Research

◆

Contents at a Glance

Introduction 1

Part I: The Road to Success Is Always Under Construction 7
Chapter 1: Surviving in an Ever-Changing World 9
Chapter 2: Telephone Talk 13
Chapter 3: Learning to Love Your Office Equipment 27

Part II: High Octane on the Information Superhighway 43
Chapter 4: It's a Bird! It's a Plane! It's E-M@il! 45
Chapter 5: Doing Business on the Net 59
Chapter 6: Be It Ever So Humble, You're Working at Home 79
Chapter 7: Oh, My Aching Back 97

Part III: Streamlining the Paper Trail 107
Chapter 8: Anatomy of a Letter 109
Chapter 9: The Great "Write" of Passage 127
Chapter 10: Purely Postal 139
Chapter 11: Cleaning Up the Infobog 147

Part IV: Minding Your Business Manners 155
Chapter 12: Getting to Know You 157
Chapter 13: Wining and Dining 171
Chapter 14: It's Better to Give 185
Chapter 15: When Worlds Collide: Men and Women in the Workplace 199

Part V: Be a Fearless Road Warrior 211
Chapter 16: Air Travel: Up, Up, and Oy Vey! 213
Chapter 17: Please Come Inn 225
Chapter 18: Getting Your Papers in Order 233
Chapter 19: When in Rome 241

Part VI: Conducting Meetings People Relish 263

Chapter 20: This Meeting Will Now Come to Order 265
Chapter 21: Presentations with Panache 277
Chapter 22: Hosting a Special Event 289

Part VII: The Part of Tens 299

Chapter 23: Ten Ways to Accommodate People with Disabilities 301
Chapter 24: Ten Hints to Conquer the Brave New World of Dress Codes 309

Appendix A: Geek Speak 317

Appendix B: Gulliver's Travel Terms 323

Appendix C: About the CD 329

Index 341

IDG Books Worldwide End-User License Agreement.....354

Installation Instructions.............................356

Book Registration Information.......................Back of Book

Cartoons at a Glance

By Rich Tennant

page 107

page 155

page 211

page 7

page 299

page 43

page 263

Fax: 978-546-7747
E-mail: richtennant@the5thwave.com
World Wide Web: www.the5thwave.com

Table of Contents

Introduction *1*

What's Your Business Survival Quotient? 1
How to Use This Kit 2
Preview of Coming Attractions 2
    Part I: The Road to Success Is Always Under Construction 3
    Part II: High Octane on the Information Superhighway 3
    Part III: Streamlining the Paper Trail 3
    Part IV: Minding Your Business Manners 3
    Part V: Be a Fearless Road Warrior 3
    Part VI: Conducting Meetings People Relish 4
    Part VII: The Part of Tens 4
Icons, Icons Everywhere 4
Don't Call the Gender Gendarmes 5
Answers to the BSQ Quiz 5

Part I: The Road to Success Is Always Under Construction *7*

Chapter 1: Surviving in an Ever-Changing World *9*

The One Constant Is Change 10
Managing Knowledge 11
In Their Infinite Wisdom 11

Chapter 2: Telephone Talk *13*

Putting a Smile in Your Voice 13
Handling Sticky Wickets 14
    Dealing with a grumpy caller 14
    Putting someone on hold 15
    Cutting a caller short 15
    Getting rid of telemarketers 15
    Dialing the wrong number 16
Answering the Phone for Someone Else 17
    Screening calls 17
    Dealing with telephone emergencies 18
Placing a Call 18
    Identify yourself 18
    A penny saved is a penny earned 18
Voice Mail Mania 19
    Superb outgoing messages 19
    Refreshing incoming messages 20

Spanning the Globe 21
Just For the Cell Of It 23
    Selecting a cell phone that's right for you 23
    Avoiding cell phone perils 24
    Take the sting from the ring 25
    Honing your cell phone etiquette 25
What's Hot on the CD-ROM 26

Chapter 3: Learning to Love Your Office Equipment **27**

Learning to Love Your Crabby Computer 28
    Avoiding the crash site 28
    Waking up a sluggish computer 29
    Searching for a missing file 31
    Protecting against outages: More power to you 32
    Avoiding viruses 32
    Speeding up Internet access 33
    Protecting your data 33
Getting Help Online 34
You Come from Alabama with Your Laptop on Your Knee 35
Loving Your Copy Machine When It Eats Your Original 35
    Finding a photocopier you can live with 36
    Preventing chewing 37
Just the Fax, Ma'am 38
    Oops! Wrong number 38
    The case of disappearing ink 38
    Save our forests 38
You Have the Whole (Computer) World in Your Hands 39
What's Hot on the CD-ROM 41

**Part II: High Octane on the Information
Superhighway** **43**

Chapter 4: It's a Bird! It's a Plane! It's E-M@il! **45**

E-Mail Gives You the Business Edge 45
    Breaking down barriers 46
    Accelerating teamwork 46
    Holding virtual meetings 46
    Sending corporate communications 46
Anatomy of a Message 46
E-Mail Pros and Woes 48
    Pros 49
    Woes 49
E-Mail Security: Not Exactly Snug as a Bug in a Rug 49
    Keeping your system safe 50
    Looking at a more secure future 50
Spam, Spam, No Thank You Ma'am 50

Cutting Information Overload 51
    As a writer of e-mail messages 52
    As the reader of e-mail messages 53
Showing a Little Emotion 53
Minding Your E-Manners 54
    Douse the flame 55
    Identify yourself 55
    Be aware of libel and copyright issues 55
    Say "hello" and "goodbye" 56
    Avoid mud in your face 56
    Use international dating 57
Create an Electronic Filing Cabinet 57
What's Hot on the CD-ROM 57

Chapter 5: Doing Business on the Net **59**
Internet Surfing 101 60
    Plain and simple 60
    Just one big global library 61
The Web 61
    Seek and ye shall find 62
    Getting to know the home page 64
Intranets with Emphasis on "Intra" 64
Going Paperless 67
    Access to knowledge replaces paper reporting 67
    Make knowledge available to people authorized to have it 67
    Make the owner/creator of the information its keeper 68
    Preserve lessons learned for the future 68
    No more wincing trees 68
Changing the Culture 69
    Who's who 69
    A commitment from the top down 69
    Stumbling blocks become stepping stones 70
    Keep the momentum going 70
    Remember the early e-mail days 70
    You can tell when the culture HAS changed 71
Click and Shop 71
    Shop 'til you bot 72
    Safety and security 72
    Become a cybermerchant 73
    Become a cybershopper 75
Going, Going, Gone: Online Auctions 77
What's Hot on the CD-ROM 77

Chapter 6: Be It Ever So Humble, You're Working at Home **79**
Don't Just Get Up and Go 80
Look Before You Leap 81
What's in a Name? 82
To Incorporate or Not to Incorporate: That is the Question 83

What You Need To Get Started 83
    The basics 84
    Computer issues 85
    Telephone issues 85
    Multifunction devices 86
Be Good to Yourself 86
Weaving a Web 87
    Deciding whether you need a Web site 87
    Putting your site together 88
Keeping the IRS at Bay 90
A Little Insurance Goes a Long Way 91
Planning for the Golden Years 92
    Setting up a SEP 92
    Crafting a Keogh 92
Expand Your Sphere of Contacts 93
    Join a Professional Association 93
    Become active in a service club 93
    Join a professional networking group 94
    Stay connected through technology 94
    Create your own infrastructure 94
What's Hot on the CD-ROM 96

Chapter 7: Oh, My Aching Back **97**
The Office Environment and the Running Shoe 98
Furniture Built for Comfort 98
    Choosing the ideal chair 99
    Desktop comfort 100
Computers and More 101
    Adjusting the monitor 101
    Mousing around 102
    Keyboarding with safety 103
Don't Be a Couch (Chair) Potato 103
    Take five 104
    Listen to your body talk 104
What's Hot on the CD-ROM 106

Part III: Streamlining the Paper Trail *107*

Chapter 8: Anatomy of a Letter **109**
Putting the Parts Together 109
    Date 110
    Mailing or in-house notations 110
    Inside address 110
    Attention line 112
    Salutation 113
    Subject line 113

Body (The message) 114
Complimentary closing 114
Signature line 115
Reference initials 115
Enclosure notation 115
Copy notation 116
Postscript 116
What's Hot and What's Not in Letter Styles 118
Multi-Page Letters 123
Memorable Memos 124
Signature or initials 125
Proper protocol 125
What's Hot on the CD-ROM 126

Chapter 9: The Great "Write" of Passage **127**
Step 1: Getting Started 128
Getting comfortable with the Start Up Sheet 128
Getting beyond writer's block 131
Step 2: Writing Headlines and Strategic Sequencing 131
Step 3: Writing the Draft 132
Step 4: Designing for Visual Impact 133
Step 5: Honing the Tone 133
Leave out unnecessary words 133
Be positive, not negative 133
Invoke the active voice, not the passive voice 134
Select reader-focused words 134
Avoid clunky *he/she* and *her/him* constructions 134
Step 6: Proofreading 134
What's Hot on the CD-ROM 137

Chapter 10: Purely Postal **139**
Understanding Domestic Mail 140
First class all the way 140
Special sending methods 141
Bar codes 143
Keeping Costs Down 143
Mailing Abroad 143
Special services 144
Special treatment 144
Standard regulations for mailing abroad 145
Addressing the envelope 145
Non-USPS Carriers 146
What's Hot on the CD-ROM 146

Chapter 11: Cleaning Up the Infobog **147**
Cleaning Up the Burial Ground 147
Phase 1: It's as easy as 1-2-3-4 148
Phase II: Divide and Conquer 149

Retaining Valuable Records 150
  Keep for all eternity 150
  Keep for seven years 150
  Keep for three years 151
  Keep for one year 151
Preventing Molehills from Turning into Mountains 151
  Identify the sources of your clutter 151
  Ditch magazines 152
  Empty your in-box and out-box 152
  Toss out old drafts 152
  Use electronic media 153
Save the Forests 153
What's Hot on the CD-ROM 153

Part IV: Minding Your Business Manners 155

Chapter 12: Getting to Know You 157
Introducing Others 157
  The pecking order 158
  What's in a name? 159
  Using titles 160
  Memory lapses 160
  Using first or last names 160
  Using nicknames 160
Introducing Yourself 161
The Golden Handshake 161
  Giving the right impression 161
  Handshake etiquette 162
  Rising to the occasion 162
The Art of Conversation 162
  Rating your conversational skills 163
  Speaking 163
  Listening, not just hearing 165
Body Language 167
  Being aware of the signals you send 167
Working the Room 168
  Do's and taboos for working the room 169
What's Hot on the CD-ROM 170

Chapter 13: Wining and Dining 171
Making Reservations 171
Checking Your Coat 172
Greeting Guests 172
Using Your Napkin, Not Your Sleeve 172
Placing Your Order 173
  Ordering cocktails 173
  Ordering wine 174

Minding Your Table Manners 175
    Reaching across the table 175
    Summoning a server 176
    Handling utensils 176
    Letting the server know there's a fly in your soup 176
    Dining do's and taboos 177
Paying the Check 178
    Dealing with an error in the check 178
    Tips on tips 178
Eating a Dinosaur 179
What's Hot on the CD-ROM 183

Chapter 14: It's Better to Give **185**

Putting On Your Creative Cap 185
    Cybershop 186
    Everyone loves books and magazines 186
    Seedlings grow up 186
    Just like grandma used to make 186
    Playing it safe 186
    For the traveler 187
    Giving the gift of "thank you" 187
    Gift for your supervisor 188
    Gift for your administrative assistant 188
Mixing Business and Pleasure 189
    It's a boy! It's a girl! 189
    April showers 190
    Here comes the bride — and groom 190
Sending a Gift through the Mail 191
When the Shoe Doesn't Fit 191
Giving to Foreigners 192
    Gift-giving do's 192
    Gift-giving taboos 193
Refusing a Gift 194
Thanks a Million 195
    You've got great taste 195
    Acknowledging an inappropriate gift 196
What's Hot on the CD-ROM 197

Chapter 15: When Worlds Collide:
Men and Women in the Workplace **199**

Say Goodbye to Stereotypes 200
    For men only 200
    For women only 201
Use Gender-Neutral Terms 202
Sticky Wickets 203
Sexual Conquistadors Need Not Apply 204
    What is sexual harassment? 204
    Responsibilities and procedures 205

Don't Be a Stupid Cupid 205
    Shaking hands or kissing 206
    Dealing with a roving eye 206
Supervisors and Assistants 206
    Do's for the male supervisor 207
    Taboos for the supervisor 207
    Do's for the female assistant 208
    Taboos for the assistant 209
The Good Old Girls' Network 209
What's Hot on the CD-ROM 210

Part V: Be a Fearless Road Warrior 211

Chapter 16: Air Travel: Up, Up, and Oy Vey! 213

Booking Your Flight 213
    Getting the best deal 215
    Safeguarding your tickets 216
    Avoiding the perils of electronic tickets 217
Avoiding the Big Bump 218
Fight Flight Delays and Cancellations 218
    Getting to the church on time 218
    Making the connection 219
Flight Etiquette 219
Working Out the Kinks 220
Overcoming Jet Lag 221
    Before the flight 221
    During the flight 221
You Can Get Something for Nothing 222
    Earning frequent flyer points 222
    Managing your miles 223
    Getting a free trip 223
Navigating International Airports 223
What's Hot on the CD-ROM 224

Chapter 17: Please Come Inn 225

Star Gazing 225
Using the Hotel's Toll-Free Number 226
    Getting the best deal 227
    Getting a room without a reservation 227
    Getting a room with a view 227
Check Out Before You Check In 228
    Shopping for safety before you book 228
    Staying safe after you arrive 229

Hotel Savvy 230
   Checking out your room 230
   Staying on the club floor 231
   Personalizing your room 231
   Concerning the concierge 231
   Talk is (not always) cheap 231
What's Hot on the CD-ROM 232

Chapter 18: Getting Your Papers in Order 233

Your Passport to Paradise 233
   If it's your first time, be gentle 234
   Renewals 235
   An ounce of prevention 235
Visitor's Visa 236
International Driving Permit 236
International Certificate of Vaccination 236
Here's to Your Health 237
Money Matters 238
   Foreign currency 238
   Credit cards 238
   Traveler's checks 239
What's Hot on the CD-ROM 240

Chapter 19: When in Rome 241

Notice the Rose in the Vase, Not the Dust on the Table 241
Unifying Languages 242
   Hablo Esperanto, monsieur? 242
   Computers to the rescue 242
You're an Ambassador 243
   Open doors with key words 243
   General do's 243
   General taboos 245
Mixing Business with Pleasure 246
   Asking for directions 246
Being Respectful of Holidays 247
Enjoying Europe 249
   Shake, bow, or hug? 250
   Topics of conversation 250
   Tips on tips 250
   Staying current on currency 250
   Looking like a native 251
   Minding your table manners 252
   Value-Added Tax (VAT) 252

Amazing Asia 253
    Pleased to make your acquaintance 253
    Dressing and blending in 254
    A yen for conversation 254
    Shop 'til you drop 254
    For your dining pleasure 255
    Tipping 256
    General business practices 256
Loving Latin America 257
    Naming names 257
    Confirming appointments 258
    Getting around 258
    Border crossings 258
    Eat, drink, and be merry 259
Mingling in the Middle East 259
    Mainly meals 259
    Cashing in on currency 260
    Getting down to business 261
Homeward Bound 261
What's Hot on the CD-ROM 262

Part VI: Conducting Meetings People Relish 263

Chapter 20: This Meeting Will Now Come to Order 265

The Proof Is in the Planning 266
    Your blueprint for success 267
    When to distribute the agenda 268
    Location, location, location 268
Banging Down the Gavel 269
    Getting started 270
    Staying on track 272
    Creating a paper trail 272
With Sensitivity and Justice for All 273
    Being sensitive to the customs of foreigners 273
    Being sensitive to people with special needs 274
Videoconferencing 275
    Lights, camera, action 275
What's Hot on the CD-ROM 276

Chapter 21: Presentations with Panache 277

Getting from Point A to Point B 277
    Learning all you can about your audience 278
    Knowing your purpose 278
    Identifying your key issue 278
    Checking out the environment 279

For Your Viewing Pleasure 279
    White boards and flip charts 280
    Transparencies and slides 280
Thrill 'Em, Don't Chill 'Em 282
    Opening do's 282
    Opening taboos 283
    Appearing natural 284
    Delivering the heart of your presentation 285
    Ending on a high note: The grand finale 285
    Making a list, checking it twice 285
What's Hot on the CD-ROM 287

Chapter 22: Hosting a Special Event **289**
The Registration Table 290
Your Badge of Honor 290
    Wearing your badge proudly 291
    For all the world to see 291
Native Tongues 292
    English as a second language 293
    Using an interpreter 293
Tricks of the Trade Show 294
    Come one! Come all! 294
    Walking the floor 295
Making Special Accommodations 296
    Before the event 297
    At the start of the event 297
    During the event 297
    At the end of the event 297
What's Hot on the CD-ROM 298

Part VII: The Part of Tens *299*

**Chapter 23: Ten Ways to Accommodate People
with Disabilities** **301**
What's Politically Correct 302
Working with People with Disabilities 302
    People who are vision impaired 303
    People with hearing disabilities 305
    People with speech impairments 305
    People with paralysis or loss of a limb 306
    People with AIDS 306
Dispelling Fears of Potential Employers 307
What's Hot on the CD-ROM 308

**Chapter 24: Ten Hints to Conquer the
Brave New World of Dress Codes** 309
    Opening the Fashion Envelope 309
    Understanding Business Casual 310
    Dealing with Jackets 311
    Tips for Men 311
    Tips for Women 312
    Getting Clad for Business Meetings 313
    Making a Good First Impression at an Interview 314
    Meeting with Foreigners 314
    What's Hot on the CD-ROM 315

Appendix A: Geek Speak *317*
    Learning the Language of the Locals 317
    What's Hot on the CD-ROM 322

Appendix B: Gulliver's Travel Terms *323*
    Terms of Endearment for Airlines 323
    Hotel Lingo 325
    Automobile Terms 326
    What's Hot on the CD-ROM 327

Appendix C: About the CD *329*
    System Requirements 329
    Using the CD with Microsoft Windows 330
    Using the CD with Mac OS 331
    What You'll Find on the CD 331
        Software Tools 331
        Chapter files 332
        Bonus Files 339
    Using the CD Files with a Handheld Computer 339
    If You've Got Problems (Of the CD Kind) 339

Index *341*

IDG Books Worldwide End-User License Agreement *354*

Installation Instructions *356*

Book Registration Information . . . . *Back of Book*

Introduction

● ●

When I get a little money I buy books; and if any is left over I buy food and clothes.

— Erasmus

This book that you hold in your hands is a "*must have*" survival kit. Whether you're a seasoned professional or a recent graduate . . . whether you work for someone or own your own business . . . whether you're technical, techless, or anywhere in between . . . *Business Professional's Kit For Dummies* is a life raft in the sea of constant change.

What's Your Business Survival Quotient?

Just how savvy are you when it comes to doing business in the world of technology and globalism? Take the following quiz to learn your business survival quotient (BSQ). Write "yes" or "no" on the line next to the question. If you don't ace this, no one is going to rap you over the knuckles. You find the answers at the end of the Introduction together with the relevant chapter that delves into the topic.

1. You're in your office talking to a salesperson when the company CEO walks in. You introduce them as follows: *Ms. Bigshot, I'd like you to meet Mr. Salesperson.* Is that the correct way to introduce these folks?

   ──────────

2. You make a toll-free call from your hotel room and find a service charge on your bill. Should you complain to the hotel manager? ──────────

3. You just finished eating dinner at a fine restaurant in Europe and left a 20 percent tip. Your dining partner said the tip was excessive. Was he correct? ──────────

4. You treat e-mail as a quick way to send messages. Someone mentioned that it's rude not to use a salutation or complimentary closing. Is the critic correct? ──────────

5. Is it politically correct to refer to someone who's disabled as *handicapped?* And does it really matter? ──────────

6. Is it tacky to put someone on hold and play a recording that gives tips of the trade or promotes your specials, instead of playing Beethoven's *Fifth Piano Concerto*? _____

7. You're visiting a company in Japan and receive a business card from a Japanese colleague that has no business title beneath his name. You notice the omission and quietly ask the person sitting next to him who he is. By the person's response, you feel that you made a blunder. Did you? _____

8. You just received a lovely gift from a colleague at the office, but it's something you really can't use. Would it be rude to exchange the gift? And if so, should you tell your colleague? (This is a two-part question.)

    _____

9. Do many foreign governments require that your passport be valid for at least six months from the date you enter their country? _____

10. When you attend a seminar or conference and are given a plastic card holder to clip on your jacket, should you always insert your business card in the plastic holder? _____

How to Use This Kit

I realize that the book portion of this kit isn't the great American novel that you read breathlessly from cover to cover. It's part of a reference kit for your professional survival. Feel free to jump to whatever topic interests you or applies to the challenge you face.

Load the CD-ROM onto your computer. At the end of each chapter, you see a list of all the elements of the chapter that are on the disk. Some of what you find are Web sites, toll-free numbers, and lists of valuable information. Beam whatever is appropriate onto your palm unit or other portable computer device, and you have the information you need at home, in the office, or on the road. (Appendix C tells you how.)

Preview of Coming Attractions

Here's a sneak preview of the seven parts of the *Business Professional's Kit For Dummies*. I include a lot of cross references, so when I write about something important in one chapter that's covered in more detail in another chapter, I tell you where to turn.

Part I: The Road to Success Is Always Under Construction

Unless you've been marooned on a deserted island for many years, you know that today's business culture has shifted from hierarchical to networked, from national to global, from manual to technological, and from the boss-secretary relationship to do it all yourself. This part teems with information on everything from fielding irate telephone calls to fixing minor glitches in your computer and other office equipment.

Part II: High Octane on the Information Superhighway

This part prepares you for your journey on the Information Superhighway. It discusses how to use e-mail effectively, cut information overload, do business on the Internet and intranets, set up a home office, and use the principles of ergonomics to keep your body in tip-top shape.

Part III: Streamlining the Paper Trail

Despite everything we hear about the paperless office, the trees continue to wince. The paperless office seems to be as real as the paperless bathroom. This part offers general guidelines to prepare letters that get priority attention. Use my powerful Six Step Process to energize all your business writing, use mail services to your advantage, and get your paperwork organized.

Part IV: Minding Your Business Manners

If you want to succeed in business (and who doesn't?) it's crucial that you make introductions with panache, know the rules of etiquette for wining and dining, understand when gift giving is appropriate (and what to give), and survive in two worlds that often collide — men and women in the workplace.

Part V: Be a Fearless Road Warrior

Business travel is part of a professional's work experience. This experience becomes a pleasure, rather than a chore, when you know the ins and outs of air travel and hotels, understand what you need for travel papers, and learn how to interact with people in other countries.

Part VI: Conducting Meetings People Relish

Meetings can be very productive or marathon sessions that leave you with an empty head and full bladder. This section discusses ways to host a productive meeting and be productive at the meetings you attend. You also learn how to get the most from a trade show and how to make a dramatic presentation so you're not just another talking head.

Part VII: The Part of Tens

The Part of Tens is a *...For Dummies* classic. It's not intended to make the book heavy so we can sell it for more money. It's intended to provide you with lots of valuable information that didn't fit anywhere else. This part shares great tips on accommodating people with disabilities and dressing for the job you want to move up to.

The Appendixes round out the *Business Professional's Kit For Dummies* with travel and technical terminology and handy-dandy charts and tables. It also has details of using the CD-ROM and uploading the information to your palm unit so it's always handy.

Icons, Icons Everywhere

Icons appear throughout this book. Their purpose isn't to break up the white space. They're to help you find the important stuff easily — somewhat like road signs. Each of the icons pinpoints something vital to your business survival.

The Sheryl Says icon helps you benefit from my experiences — the blissful, the painful, and everything in between. Sometimes I use this icon because I want to talk to you. In addition to being a writer, I'm an avid talker and sometimes get lonely sitting in front of my computer.

The Tip icon gives you nifty tips for being a savvy professional. These may be time savers, frustration savers, life savers, or just about anything else.

The Remember icon represents little tidbits to tie around your finger. It may be something like: "Every time you make a sales presentation, always leave something of value with the customer. It may be a single sheet of paper called 'Ten Tips to [something of value to the customer]' so they think of you every time they refer to your sheet."

The Caution icon calls attention to pitfalls you should avoid. If you don't heed this caution, it won't trigger a seismic event in this nation's history, but you may be sorry you didn't take the advice.

The Success Story icon plays off the adage, "Nothing succeeds like success." You may find it helpful to hear other people's success stories.

The Global Savvy icon is peppered throughout this book for dealing with people from around the world without getting pie in your face. (There's a complete discussion of Europe, Asia, Latin America, and the Middle East in Chapter 19.)

The CD-ROM icon appears at the end of each chapter (except Chapter 1) to let you know what's hot on the CD-ROM. Don't forget to transfer all this good stuff to your palm unit.

The Web icon makes references to important stuff on the Internet.

Don't Call the Gender Gendarmes

I searched for an elegant pronoun that would cover males and females. Unfortunately, I wasn't able to find one. Rather than getting into the clumsy he/she or him/her scenario, I opted to be an equal-opportunity writer. I tossed a coin and here's how it landed: I use the *male gender in the even chapters and the female gender in the odd chapters.* (If this offends anyone, please send up a smoke signal with a better suggestion.)

Answers to the BSQ Quiz

Without any further ado (the drum roll, please), here are the answers to the questions at the beginning of the Introduction:

1. **No.** While business introductions generally respect status and power, it's important to remember that the customer comes first. Therefore, the correct introduction would be, "Mr. Salesperson, I'd like you to meet our CEO, Ms. Bigshot. **(Chapter 12)**

2. **No.** Hotels reserve the right to add a service charge for using the hotel switchboard, regardless of whether you make a toll-free call or a paid call. **(Chapter 17)**

3. **Probably yes.** In many foreign countries, service is included in the total price of the check. If you see *service compris* written on your check, it means the restaurant added a service charge of 10 to 20 percent. If you don't see it, it's perfectly acceptable to ask the waitperson if service is included. If service isn't included, leave a 15 to 20 percent tip just as you would in the U.S. **(Chapter 13)**

4. **Yes** Your critic is correct. Don't you say "hello" to the caller when you answer the phone and start a letter with "Dear Reader"? And don't you say "goodbye" to the caller and "Sincerely" to your reader? With any form of communication — including e-mail messages — you should always greet and say goodbye to the person you're communicating with. People who don't do that are the same ones who come into the office and bark out orders before they remove their coats. **(Chapter 4)**

5. **No.** The politically correct term is *disabled*. More important than your words, however, are your actions. Always be respectful, and if you err in terminology, the person generally won't take offense. **(Chapter 23)**

6. **No.** If you put someone on hold, it's perfectly acceptable to use it to your business advantage; however, you must present it as a business advantage to the caller. If you use a high-quality recording with a pleasant-sounding speaker, no one should be offended. Also, make sure you change your recording regularly so callers don't feel they're listening to same-old, same-old. **(Chapter 2)**

7. **Yes.** If you receive a business card from a senior-level Japanese businessman, it may have no title beneath his name. The blank space means he's a high-level person and "everyone should know" who he is. So don't even think about asking. **(Chapter 19)**

8. **No.** It wouldn't be rude to exchange the gift, and **yes**, you should tell your colleague. Exchange the gift for something you'll enjoy and tell your colleague you've done so. Also, let the person who gave you the gift know how much pleasure you're getting from the new gift. **(Chapter 14)**

9. **Yes.** Therefore, it's wise to renew your passport if it's about to expire within the next year. **(Chapter 18)**

10. **No.** Many business cards have people's names printed in such a small font that the names can't be read without a magnifying glass. If your name isn't large enough to be read at arm's length, print your name on the back of the card with a marker and display that side. **(Chapter 22)**

Part I
The Road to Success Is Always Under Construction

The 5th Wave   **By Rich Tennant**

"FOR A MORE AGGRESIVE APPROACH, WE HAVE OUR 'OR ELSE' SERIES OF MOTIVATIONAL POSTERS."

In this part . . .

Technology is constantly changing the way we work, play, and see the world. Like every revolution or evolution, however, technology leaves victims in its wake. When factories multiplied during the industrial revolution, blacksmiths closed up shop. With the arrival of new methods of communication, scribes dried out their pens. During the sexual revolution even a few bra manufacturers went "bust."

This part talks about many of the changes that have taken place as a result of the technology revolution and how you can *make them work for you* to accelerate your career. Remember that change is the one constant!

Chapter 1

Surviving in an Ever-Changing World

In This Chapter

▶ Living in a changing world

▶ Surviving changes in the modern office

▶ Managing knowledge

▶ Recalling those who said it couldn't be done

> *It's hard for me to get used to these changing times. I can remember when air was clean and sex was dirty.*
>
> — George Burns, actor and author

*A*fter the United States survived the breakup of AT&T, it became apparent how adaptable its citizens are. If you look back over the last 30 years (which is merely a flash in time), you realize how much has changed. We went from jet-setters to cyber-surfers; from Flash Gordon to Luke Skywalker; from *The Twilight Zone* to *The X Files;* from Royal typewriters to palm units; from U. S. Steel to Microsoft; and yadda, yadda, yadda (an expression which didn't exist before Jerry Seinfeld).

In the professional arena, the mindset changed from single-skill to lifelong learning, from security to risk taking, from hierarchical to networked, from status quo to constant change, from national to global, from time-is-of-the-essence to mission critical, and from the dirt road to the Information Superhighway. You have a 9-digit ZIP code, shop on the Internet, and a see a depleting ozone layer. Today, even pickpockets no longer say "please" and "thank you."

Then there's the issue of time. Thirty years ago, overnight delivery services just hit the scene. It was so exciting to get a letter hand delivered by noon the next business day. Today, even those services aren't the fastest way to *deliver da letta*. Faxes and e-mail messages deliver text and graphics faster than a speeding bullet.

Voice of Commerce Past

Going back to the turn of Y1K, what was happening? The foot-powered sewing machine and hand-powered wringer were high tech. Major debates erupted about women riding bicycles because critics viewed this as a transgression from the pathway of motherhood and apple pie. The early 1900's ushered in the hand-cranked telephone and wireless radio as means of widespread communication. Back then, people made purchases with cash, and a Visa was something you needed to cross the border. Banking meant depositing a nickel at a time into a savings account, and the average life expectancy was mid-to-late 40's.

We can only imagine how the civilization of today will be viewed when Y3K rears its distant head. Will people, clones, robots, or ET's look back at us reminiscently?

Computers blaze at gigahertz speeds, workdays are indicated in terms of 24/7 (no more 9 to 5), virtual meetings are held via teleconferencing or on the Internet, and the World Wide Web (www) puts information at your fingertips.

One day this generation may sit in rocking chairs telling grandchildren stories of the invention of the Internet and look stodgier to their grandchildren than Grandpa Simpson — just as we heard stories from our grandparents about how they walked miles to school barefooted in snowstorms.

The One Constant Is Change

In our ever-changing world, the nature of the workforce has changed dramatically. The secretary no longer sits outside the door of her boss's office, and the "boss" is now called a *manager* or *supervisor*. Some lucky managers have or share an administrative assistant (also known as an AA or admin). These AA's, however, work at a higher level than secretaries used to. They don't take shorthand, don't make photocopies, and don't fetch coffee. And the *she's* are often *he's*.

As a result, people at all levels prepare their own letters and memos, stand in line at the copy machine, and get their own coffee. They also make their own travel arrangements, prepare meeting agendas, select gifts, and perform a host of other functions they once handed off to the gal with the steno pad glued to the palm of her hand.

Managing Knowledge

In today's office, you no longer deal with *data* and you no longer deal with *information.* You deal with *knowledge,* and knowledge is power. *Knowledge management* refers to distributing, accessing, and retrieving the experiences of people and work groups. This knowledge can be used over and over. It means sharing ideas and relevant information (such as lessons learned) to create new opportunities. The three successful components of knowledge management are people, processes, and technology.

1. **People** provide brain power, innovation, creativity, and the experiential knowledge to solve problems. Without these skills, the visionaries in the next section, "In Their Infinite Wisdom," wouldn't be household names. Perhaps the visionaries among your peers may be the next wave of names in the history books.

2. **Processes** must be in place for people to share knowledge and accelerate its flow. Companies can no longer afford to have all the history of a project, product, or company rest with just a few people. Colleagues impart knowledge every day at the water cooler, in the elevator, or at lunch — and this type of sharing needs to be formalized into a process. Building this process involves a major paradigm shift and change in culture, which is difficult. Chapter 5 expands on what it takes to change a culture.

3. **Technology** doesn't mean just having a computer or downloading information from the Internet. Technology includes human interaction, business plans, and a structure that allows knowledge to be saved, retrieved, and transferred to a new computer. Check out Chapter 5 for how to do business on the Internet and use the Internet as a vehicle to capture your corporate memory.

In Their Infinite Wisdom . . .

For the sake of progress, it's fortunate that such visionaries as Thomas Edison, the Wright Brothers, Alexander Graham Bell, Henry Ford, Johann Gutenberg, and the like existed . . . because on the other side of the fence are some naysayers. Just for yucks, here are some of the skeptics who said it couldn't be done:

> So we went to Atari and said, "Hey, we've got this amazing thing, even built with some of your parts, and what do you think about funding us? Or we'll give it to you. We just want to do it. Pay our salary, we'll come to work for you. And they said 'No.' So then we went to Hewlett-Packard, and they said, 'Hey, we don't need you. You haven't even gotten through college yet.'

> — Steven Jobs, founder of Apple Computer, in his attempt to get Atari and H-P interested in his computer idea.

This [telephone] has too many shortcomings to be seriously considered as a means of communication. The device is inherently of no value to us.

> — Western Union internal memo

The wireless music box has no imaginable commercial value. Who would pay for a message sent to nobody in particular.

> — David Sarnoff's associates in response
> to his urgings for investment in the radio.

Heavier-than-air flying machines are impossible.

> — Lord Kelvin, President of the Royal Society,
> 1890–1895

Everything that can be invented has been invented.

> — Charles H. Duell, Commissioner of U.S. Patent
> Office, suggesting that the Patent Office be
> closed.

New and exciting things appear when you provide an environment to let them in. Everyone must be able to let go of old ideas, opinions, and ways of doing things. Change and letting go are difficult, but we must embrace new concepts to move forward in life.

Chapter 2

Telephone Talk

· ·

In This Chapter

▶ Animating your voice

▶ Dealing with unusual situations and abrasive people

▶ Giving telemarketers the boot

▶ Using voice mail without getting tongue tied

▶ Calling around the world

▶ Choosing a cell phone that doesn't crimp your neck

· ·

An irate banker demanded that Alexander Graham Bell remove 'that toy' from his office. The toy was his telephone.

— United Technologies Corporation advertisement

*W*hen Alexander Graham Bell summoned his assistant with the words, "Watson, come here, I want you," spoken through his new invention, little did he know that it was an inaugural moment that would transform the way people communicate.

In your work life, the telephone can be one of your biggest assets or the bane of your existence. It's a wonderful tool in that it can serve as a mask — no one on the other end can see your body language or what you look like. On the flip side, some people use the phone as a license to be more abusive than they would be in person. This chapter focuses on using the telephone with style and a smile.

Putting a Smile in Your Voice

Before you place an important call, stand up and stretch. This puts animation and enthusiasm into your body which reflects in your voice. (You don't want the person you phone to think you need a defibrillator.) You never get a second chance to make a first impression, and very often a telephone call is a caller's first impression of you or your company. Here are some ways to say *hello* with a smile in your voice:

Appropriate: *Hello, this is Jim Rogers speaking.*

Hello, this is Jim Rogers.

Casual: *Jim speaking.* (Okay in some offices.)

Abrupt: *Rogers speaking.*

Rogers here.

Handling Sticky Wickets

The more time you spend on the telephone, the more situations you encounter and interesting people you come across. Here are a few techniques that may make take the edge off "interesting" callers.

Dealing with a grumpy caller

Everybody has to deal with irate callers. People who are upset tend to take their frustrations out on the person who answers the phone. Remember that the caller isn't angry at you personally; he's angry about a situation or problem. Following are a few ways to soothe the savage caller:

- ✔ **Don't yell back or be rude.** Continue to be polite — it's difficult to continue yelling at a polite person. Try to defuse the anger by saying, *I understand how you feel.* (Your nose may grow, but that's okay.)

- ✔ **Transfer the call.** Suggest that the caller talk to someone who may be more appropriate than you. Offer to transfer the call or give the name and number.

- ✔ **Put the caller on hold (briefly).** Take a few moments to explain the situation to the person to whom you're forwarding the call.

- ✔ **Stall for time.** Ask the caller to slowly repeat his complaint so that you can write it down. This may defuse some of the anger. If you can provide the caller a chance to let off steam, often he may wear himself out.

Don't be an irate caller yourself. Remember that the person you speak to isn't necessarily the person who caused the problem, but he may be the person who can solve it for you.

Putting someone on hold

It's impolite to leave a caller on hold for more than 30 seconds. Check back every 30 seconds or so to see whether the caller can continue to hold or would like a call back.

When you do put a caller on hold, be sure there's something for him to listen to.

- **Music.** If you're piping music into someone's ear, make sure that it's easy-listening music. Remember, music isn't a license to keep someone on hold indefinitely. The caller didn't place the call to hear *Beethoven's Fifth Piano Concerto* in its entirety. Also be certain the volume isn't too loud.

- **Tips or promotions.** While your caller is in holding mode, it's perfectly acceptable to use the listening time to your business advantage. Offer tips of the trade, talk about a special promotion, or give driving directions. Change your recording regularly so that callers don't feel they're listening to the same-old, same-old.

I recently called my accountant's office and was put on hold. Instead of music, his message talked about an investment seminar he was offering. The message gave a preview of some of the tips he would share. I got some wonderful information from listening to his message and it whet my appetite: I made reservations to attend his seminar.

Cutting a caller short

Some people get chatty and are hard to get off the phone. Use these tactful ways to get rid of motor-mouths:

- Explain that someone just handed you a note for an urgent call or that you need to be in a meeting.

- Politely say, *Jack, before I hang up . . .* or *I know we have a lot to talk about, why don't we. . . .*

Once I was desperate to get rid of a chatty caller. I started shouting, "Hello!, Hello!, Hello!" into the receiver as if we had lost the connection. I'm not suggesting you do that, but there are times you may resort to a desperate measure.

Getting rid of telemarketers

You can always pick out a telemarketer. He asks for you by name and then poses the give-away question: *How are you today?* After he inquires about your health, he tries to sell you storm windows, insurance, or widgets.

If you're plagued by unsolicited phone calls (Sorry telemarketers!), you can get off these lists by writing to the following address. Include your name, address, and phone number. They don't take phone calls!

Telephone Preference Service
Direct Marketing Association
P.O. Box 9014
Farmingdale, NY 11735-9014

In the meantime, don't just hang up on these pesky people or put them on hold for all eternity. Instead, tell them that you want your name taken off their calling list. They're obliged by law to remove your name. If they continue to plague you, notify your phone company. You may be entitled to monetary remuneration.

Whenever you order something by phone, be sure to tell the person taking the order that you don't want your name sold for telemarketing purposes. The order taker can check off a special box on the form to exclude you from the lists. If you don't make it clear that you don't want your name shared, you'll be back on everyone's calling list.

Dialing the wrong number

If you misdial, it's rude to just hang up. Following is a pleasant telephone exchange:

Caller: *May I please speak to John Doe.*

Callee: *I think you have the wrong number.*

Caller: *I'm sorry to have bothered you.*

Callee: *No bother. Have a nice day.*

If the caller dials you again:

Caller: *May I please speak to John Doe.*

Callee: *This is the same number you just called. I think you're calling the wrong number.*

Caller: *What number is this?*

Callee: *I'd rather not give out my number. What number are you trying to reach?* (In this era of unsolicited and unwanted phone calls, it's often better not to give out your phone number.)

Caller: [number]

Callee: *This isn't the number you're trying to reach. Please recheck it.*

Caller: *I'll do that. I'm very sorry to have bothered you.*

Callee: *No bother. Have a nice day.*

Selecting a long-distance carrier

In days of old, the most difficult choice you had was whether to get a wall-mounted phone or a desk-top model. It's no longer that simple. Along with all the other decisions you make regarding telephone selection and service, you need to decide on a long-distance carrier. Following are questions to ask prospective carriers so you can make an intelligent decision:

✔ Do you provide ancillary services such as conferencing, prepaid debit cards, calling cards, and Internet access?

✔ Does your company bill in 6-second or 1-minute increments? (The smaller the incremental billing, the smaller your bill.)

✔ Do you own your switches or will my calls go through multiple routings?

✔ Are you a private or publicly held company? (Public companies are bound by strict rules that ensure greater reliability.)

✔ Are you licensed by the Public Service Commission in all 50 states? (This gives you a sense of whether you're talking to a well-established company.)

✔ Are you a member of the Telecommunications Resellers Association? (Membership indicates that the company abides by good business practices.)

Answering the Phone for Someone Else

Here are some ways to answer the phone for someone else:

Appropriate: *Good morning, this is Mr. Roger's office.*

Good morning, Marketing Department.

Long, but okay: *Good morning. This is the Marketing Department, Mr. Roger's office.*

Good morning, this is Mr. Roger's office. Kathy speaking.

Inappropriate: *Hi, this is Kathy.*

If you're a manager and suspect that incoming calls aren't being handled appropriately, you can try this devious tactic: Call your company (or get someone else to call) posing as a job candidate or a prospective client. See what impression you get of the company from the person who answers the phone.

Screening calls

Busy executives often ask their administrative assistants or others to screen calls. When you screen calls, you must exercise great tact to hide the fact that you're doing that, otherwise the caller will feel unloved.

Appropriate: *Ms. Smith isn't able to take calls at the moment. May I ask who's calling?*

Inappropriate: *May I ask who's calling?* (This may make the caller feel shunned.)

Dealing with telephone emergencies

Understand what constitutes an emergency. An emergency, for example, may be a crisis in someone's home or business that needs immediate attention. If you or someone else can't handle the emergency, you may have to interrupt an important meeting. Use good judgment. *When in doubt, pull him out.* When you must interrupt a meeting, knock on the door and ask to speak to the person you need or ask that he be handed a note.

Placing a Call

Before you pick up the phone, always know why you're calling, what information you want to convey, and what to say if you get the person's voice mail. Following are some tips to prepare for your phone call:

- ✔ Make a list of the items you want to talk about in order of priority.
- ✔ Have all the files and papers you need close at hand.
- ✔ If your call is a difficult or complicated one, write out what you want to say.

Identify yourself

When you place a call, always identify yourself. Unless the caller knows you intimately, it's egotistical and rude to expect someone to recognize your voice. Something as simple as, *Hello, this is Mary Jones from [company],* will suffice.

A penny saved is a penny earned

Following are several ways to save money on your telephone bill:

- ✔ **Call during off-peak hours.** For example, at 6:01 you can call the West Coast from the East Coast at a reduced rate. It's only 3:01 on the West Coast. Remember that most of Indiana and Arizona don't use Daylight Savings Time, so folks in those states don't spring forward and fall back. Check out Example 2-1 for a map of time zones across the United States.

- ✔ **Dial direct.** You pay dearly for operator-assisted calls.

- ✔ **Ask for credit.** When you dial the wrong number, get a poor connection, or lose service for even one day, dial "0" and get credit.

- ✔ **Let your fingers do the walking.** Use your telephone directory or the Internet to look up telephone numbers. You also pay dearly for operator assistance.

- ✔ **Use toll-free numbers.** They are 800, 888, and 877.

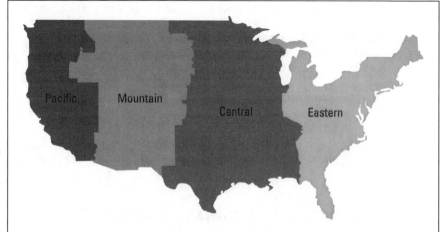

Example 2-1:
Times zones
across the
U.S.

Always return your calls in a timely manner or you may be thought of as rude, uncaring, or unprofessional.

Voice Mail Mania

No chapter on telephoning would be complete without addressing the dreaded answering machine. Many people are intimidated by answering machines and feel foolish talking into the mechanical devices. However, the answering machine is a fact of life. The following guidelines are guaranteed to improve your productivity and reduce frustration.

Superb outgoing messages

Following are tips for recording a brief, professional message that won't make the caller feel like hanging up:

✔ **Mention your name, company name, and current date.** Show your callers that you're on top of things. You may say, *Good morning. This is Jim in HR. Today is Monday, April 2, and I'll be in the office all day.*

✔ **Keep your message up-to-date.** If you're going to be away, even for a day or two, mention that on the message so that callers won't expect you to get back to them immediately. (When it's appropriate, leave the name of someone the caller may contact for urgent matters.)

SHERYL SAYS

A business associate referred me to a financial planner. I called the financial planner on March 29 and heard the following outgoing voice message: "I will be out of the office until March 22. . . ." (That was a week before I made the call.) Her message unwittingly told me that she doesn't pay attention to details. That's not the person I want assisting with my finances, so I took my business elsewhere. If I find out that she was abducted by aliens and was unable to return for a few weeks, I may reconsider.

✔ **Practice, practice, practice.** Before you record the message, practice what you want to say. After you record it, play it back. If it isn't something you'd want to listen to, re-record it.

✔ **Check the timing.** Don't let too much time elapse between the time the machine picks up and the time the caller can start leaving the message.

Refreshing incoming messages

When you leave a message, be certain that the information is clear, including your name and phone number. Some people say their names and numbers so quickly that it sounds like a foreign language. Use these few hints:

✔ **State your name clearly.** If your name isn't as straightforward as Jane Smith or Joe Adams, spell it out — letter for letter. For example, when I don't spell my name, it's often heard as Sherylyn Zell Roberts. Also, I have a friend named Dave Farrison. If he doesn't spell his last name, people think it's Dave Harrison.

✔ **Articulate all numbers carefully.** For example, instead of saying *sixteen,* (which may be heard as *sixty*) say, *one, six.* In fact, all the teens can be confusing, so state them clearly.

✔ **Identify the purpose of your call succinctly.** If your call is in response to someone's question, repeat the question, then give the answer: *Hello, this is Matt Smith with Ace Company. You asked about the availability of. . . .*

✔ **Give a time when can you be reached.** Always include a good time to reach you or when you'll call again.

✔ **Repeat your name and phone number slowly and clearly at the end of the message.** If the caller didn't get your name and number the first time, you save him from having to replay your message.

SHERYL SAYS

Update that message

When I moved into my new home, I was looking for a chiropractor and had two recommendations. I called Doctor A, whose message said that he was on vacation and would be back the following Monday. "That's fine," I thought, "Perhaps I'll call back then." I then called Doctor B. His message said: "Hello, this is Doctor B. I'm not able to take your call right now. Please leave your name. . . ." I expected him or his assistant to return my call. I called a few days later and got the same message. "The heck with him I thought."

The following Monday I called Doctor A and made an appointment (and have continued to see him). A few days later Doctor B returned my call. He told me he'd just gotten back from vacation. Because he didn't update his message, he lost me as a patient.

Spanning the Globe

Before you place a call to a foreign country, be aware of the time differences. When it's noon at your location, it may be the middle of the night at the other end.

Table 2-1 shows you how to figure out what time it is in key locations around the world. The hours are based on Greenwich Mean Time (GMT). You can calculate GMT from your time zone within the 48 contiguous states as follows: Eastern is –5 hours; Central is –6 hours; Mountain is –7 hours; and Pacific is –8 hours. Some of the times in Table 2-1 may vary by an hour because not all places change clocks for Daylight Savings Time.

Table 2-1	International Time Zones
GMT	*Location*
0	Great Britain, Scotland, Ireland
+1	Most of Europe (from Spain through Hungary), Southern Africa, Most of the Middle East
+2	Finland, Romania, Greece, Turkey, Some of the Middle East
+3	Moscow, St. Petersburg
+4	Iran
+5	India

(continued)

Table 2-1 *(continued)*

GMT	Location
+8	Philippines
+9	Japan, Korea, Indonesia
-3	Brazil
-4	Argentina
-6	Most of Mexico and Central America

Table 2-2 lists international country codes to dial before the telephone number.

Table 2-2   International Telephone Codes

Country	Code	Country	Code
Argentina	54	Guatemala	502
Australia	61	Honduras	504
Austria	43	Hong Kong	852
Belgium	32	Hungary	36
Brazil	55	Iceland	354
Chile	56	India	91
China	86	Indonesia	62
Columbia	57	Iran	98
Czech Republic	420	Iraq	964
Denmark	45	Ireland	353
Ecuador	593	Israel	972
Egypt	20	Italy	39
El Salvador	503	Japan	81
Finland	358	Jordan	962
France	33	Korea, Republic of	82
Germany	49	Kuwait	965
Greece	30	Libya	218

Country	Code	Country	Code
Liechtenstein	41	Romania	40
Luxembourg	352	Russia	7
Malaysia	60	Saudi Arabia	966
Mexico	52	Singapore	65
Morocco	212	Slovakia	421
Netherlands	31	South Africa	27
New Zealand	64	Spain	34
Nicaragua	505	Sweden	46
Norway	47	Switzerland	41
Oman	968	Taiwan	886
Pakistan	92	Thailand	66
Panama	507	Turkey	90
Paraguay	595	United Arab Emirates	971
Peru	51	United Kingdom	44
Philippines	63	United States	01
Poland	48	Uruguay	598
Portugal	351	Venezuela	58
Qatar	974	Yemen Arab Republic	967

Just For the Cell Of It

People all over the world have cell phones. In today's on-the-go society, cell phones keep you in constant touch with the world. There are cell phones that can read your e-mail, check the weather, look up a stock, respond to voice mail commands, access the Web, and let you know when the Yankees win the World Series. These phones, however, rudely ring in restaurants, theaters, museums, elevators, and everywhere else.

Selecting a cell phone that's right for you

Following are a number of things to think about so you pick a cell phone that's right for you:

- **Are the size and weight for you?** Cell phones come in different weights and sizes. If you plan to keep the phone in your shirt pocket or a belt holster, consider one of the smaller and lighter units. If you plan to keep it in your purse or briefcase, size and weight may be less important.

- **Does it feel right ergonomically?** Is the phone comfortable against your ear and in your hand? Some cell phones are the traditional concave units; others are flat or convex.

- **Can you control the volume?** It's important to be able to control the volume. Side-mounted controls can be adjusted during a conversation. Front-mounted controls require you to move the unit away from your head.

- **How easy is the phone to use?** You certainly don't want to walk around with the user manual, so look for a phone that's menu-driven and make sure that the menus are intuitive.

- **What's your battery preference?** When your battery dies, so does your phone. Lithium ion (Li-ion) batteries hold the longest charge and are the most expensive option. Nickel Metal Hydride (NiMH) are the second best choice and are moderately priced. Nickel Cadmium (NiCd) don't hold a charge as long as the others but are the least expensive.

- **Do you need to connect to other equipment?** If you need to connect your cell phone with your fax machine or computer, you need a cell phone that's data-capable.

Paying at the pay phone

One day the pay phone will be as obsolete as the typewriter, but those who don't yet walk around with cell phones attached to their ears do place calls from pay phones every now and then. Following are some things to check out:

- **The owner of the phone.** Check the name on the phone. There may be a big difference in price when calling from a phone owned by one of the big names (such as Bell Atlantic) and one of the independently owned carriers. Many independent carriers claim they charge less for a local call and have lower rates for coin-drop calls.

- **The rates.** Pay phones are required to post the rates somewhere on the face of the phone. You may need a magnifying glass to read them, but they're there.

- **Which carrier to dial.** Most pay phones instruct you to dial zero plus the area code plus the seven-digit number you're calling. Even with a calling card, you're charged the rate set by the phone carrier, not your calling-card carrier. It's wise, therefore, to dial your own carrier.

Avoiding cell phone perils

More and more car accidents are attributed to using cell phones while driving — and some states have made it illegal to do so. Instead of cradling your cell phone on your shoulder and drifting across the road because your attention isn't on your driving, turn your cell phone into a speaker phone that attaches to your dashboard, not your ear.

Here's another reason to attach your cell phone to your dashboard: Mounting scientific studies show that the microwave radiation of the phone's antenna may contribute to brain cancer and long-term memory loss. Therefore, you should keep the antenna as far from your head as possible so you don't fry your brain.

Take the sting from the ring

Finding the company that offers the best rates can be a daunting ordeal. Rates vary widely, and they aren't always what they seem to be. For example, a company may advertise that it charges 8 cents a minute for the first 100 minutes. What they may neglect to tell you that if you use less than or more than 100 minutes, the rates are a lot higher. There's one company that tells you they charge "no monthly fee," but if you read the fine print you find they charge a daily fee.

Help is at hand. Check out www.point.com. Fill out the questionnaire, and you'll be advised of the best rates based on your cell phone usage.

Honing your cell phone etiquette

Cell phones are so new that there's little etiquette surrounding them. However, some rules have surfaced. Unless you're in a profession where lives depend on your being reached instantly, turn off your cell phone when you're in a restaurant, theater, or any other place where ringing and conversations will annoy people.

If you insist on keeping your cell phone with you at all times, be considerate of those around you. I was in a restaurant recently and there were three people seated at the next table. All three of them were on their cell phones having three separate conversations. (These were not doctors who were making life-and-death decisions on the phone.) One woman was describing what she ordered for her meal, another was making a date for the following evening, and the other was involved in some other idle chatter.

Some restaurants are prohibiting cell phones in the dining area and offer cell phone lounges for the self-important people who must be reachable at all times.

A word about beeper bloopers: It's inconsiderate to beep someone's pager unless it's of dire importance or you've been invited to do so.

What's Hot on the CD-ROM

Here's what you'll find on the CD-ROM:

- ✔ 2-1: Dealing with a Grumpy Caller
- ✔ 2-2: Putting Someone on Hold
- ✔ 2-3: Cutting a Caller Short
- ✔ 2-4: Getting Rid of Telemarketers
- ✔ 2-5: When You Dial the Wrong Number
- ✔ 2-6: Screening Calls
- ✔ 2-7: Placing a Call
- ✔ 2-8: Saving Money on Calls
- ✔ 2-9: Selecting A Long-Distance Carrier
- ✔ 2-10: Superb Outgoing Voice-Mail Messages
- ✔ 2-11: Refreshing Incoming Voice-Mail Message
- ✔ 2-12: International Calling Codes

Chapter 3

Learning to Love Your Office Equipment

In This Chapter

▶ Keeping your computer running like a charm

▶ Keeping your laptop secure

▶ Coping with your photocopier

▶ Avoiding white knuckles when using your fax machine

▶ Computing in the palm of your hand

Any sufficient advanced technology is indistinguishable from magic.

— Arthur C. Clarke, *The Lost Worlds of 2001*

HAL, my computer, sat on my desk ailing. I gently wrapped HAL in a blanket (like a pet) to cushion it for a trip to Dr. Rob, my computer repairman (a.k.a. my computer vet). Dr. Rob suggested that I leave HAL with him for a few days. As I pulled away, I started to feel disconnected from the world. No e-mails from family, friends, and business associates. No chat rooms. No Internet.

I felt as though I had stepped into an episode of *The Waltons,* suddenly realizing how dependent I had become on technology — which was sci-fi fodder when John-Boy was a tot. Eventually, I learned some home remedies — something akin to "Take two aspirins and call me in the morning."

Technology is wonderful when it's working properly. Have you ever gone into a bank when the computers were down? You can't make a deposit or a withdrawal let alone discover your account balance. The bank becomes immobilized — and so does your money. This chapter guides you through ways to be your own technology doctor and minimize persnickety problems so that you don't immobilze your business.

Learning to Love Your Crabby Computer

You're in the middle of a very important proposal when all of a sudden you see the dreaded Blue Screen of Death or the infamous Macintosh bomb. The keyboard is frozen and the mouse is dead. You see the message: "A fatal error has occurred." And worst of all, you didn't back up any of your precious files. The best you can do at this point is reboot and hope autosave captured most of your hard work. Why do things like this happen and how can you prevent them?

Understanding what lurks inside the computer is essential to knowing why crashes occur. Two of the things working in your computer are *applications* and an *operating system*. Applications are Lotus Notes, Microsoft Word, and others. You also have an operating system, such as Windows, DOS, Mac OS, Linux, and the like. The operating system controls how and when applications run. Its job is to prevent applications from bumping into each other. When information becomes garbled, the operating system can get confused and freeze (crash).

Avoiding the crash site

When your computer freezes, you're in for some guaranteed frustration. Here are some suggestions for de-icing after a freeze and preventing crashes from happening in the first place:

- **Buy stable and tested software.** Using the latest version of previously released software is always better than using an older version. With newly released software, however, you risk struggling with bugs that haven't been worked out. So make sure your software is stable.

- **Open only one or two applications at a time.** The large amounts of memory computers have today make it possible to perform many operations simultaneously. But when you have too many applications running, your computer's brain may have trouble absorbing it all — something like an overload.

- **Leave tinkering to the experts.** Unless you're a computer ace, don't add a faster processor or fiddle with the operating system's control panel. When you add hardware, bring your computer to a dealer or call your Information Technology (IT) department at work.

- **Have patience.** When you rush an application, you may create too many overlapping commands that confuse the computer. For example, if you print a long document and start to reformat the paragraphs, the computer may get confused. Don't give your computer more than it can handle. After all . . . it's only human.

With all these precautions, you may still experience a crash. This may help: Press Ctrl+Alt+Del simultaneously to see a list of which programs are not responding. If you press Ctrl+Alt+Del twice, your computer should reboot (restart), so don't do it twice unless you're sure you want to reboot.

When you reboot, you'll be asked to run ScanDisk to prevent possible problems. If your computer isn't configured for this to happen automatically, you can find ScanDisk under Start⇨Programs⇨Accessories⇨System Tools.

If you're a Mac user, try Option+Command+Esc to abort a stuck program or Shift+Option+On/Off to restart a frozen computer. With Macs, the general rule is this: The newer the operating system, the fewer the freezes and crashes. If you're using Mac OS 8.6 or newer, your Mac will automatically scan and repair your computer on startup. If it doesn't, check out Norton Utility (Symantec) for some first aid.

If you try these quick fixes and still can't revive your drive, contact your local computer guru. If your guru shakes her head in wonder, call one of the companies that salvages data from crashed hard drives. You can be triaged to an *e-chiropractor* who fixes disks. One company to consider is DriveSavers, 800-440-1904, `www.drivesavers.com`. The company claims a 90 percent success rate.

Waking up a sluggish computer

Your computer may operate at a snail's pace for several reasons:

- ✔ **Dirty Windows.** The Windows operating system gobbles up memory faster than a college student guzzles down beer. When you load lots of applications, Windows may run low on memory and require more time to load files.

- ✔ **Inconsiderate applications.** Some applications don't release space after you close them. That means you have less memory (RAM) available for other applications; your computer becomes something akin to a data landfill. When this happens, you see a message telling you there isn't enough memory. Actually, your computer *does* have enough memory; it just can't access it. The remedy is to close out all the applications and return to the desktop. Then start again.

  If you find yourself staring at the spinning beach ball on a Mac or the hourglass on Windows, chances are your hard drive needs cleaning up or defragging (see the following bullet).

✔ **Too much fragmentation.** Data sometimes becomes fragmented, which means you need to defrag the hard drive. Defragging is painless and isn't as scary as it sounds. Here's why it's important to defrag your hard drive: When you create or save a new file, your computer places the file somewhere on your hard drive. As you edit the document and add more information, the file may become too large for where it's stored. So the computer splits the document and stores it in two different places. You don't even know this is happening, except for the fact that it takes the computer longer to retrieve the document. When too many documents are fragmented, your computer's performance is slow. The defrag program tidies up and organizes your files.

Norton to the rescue

Norton Utilities is an integrated suite of programs that fixes problems and enhances performance — somewhat like the Viagra of the computer world. Norton Utilities can defrag your hard drive. For more information about all the neat things Norton Utilities can do to make your computer run more efficiently, check out `www.symantec.com`. You can download a trial version.

Spring cleaning

If defragging doesn't speed up your computer, go through your hard drive and clean house. This is the electronic equivalent of cleaning up the infobog — you know, the paper piles on your desk that are higher than your head.

✔ **Memory:** If you use Windows, look at the Explorer screen and click C: so you see the C: drive. At the bottom of the screen, you see how much available memory you have. If you're running low, you may need to add more memory. "Low" is relative to your computer and how much you have on it, so check with a computer guru for what's appropriate for your needs and your computer's.

If you use a Mac, you can set the amount of memory each application sets aside with the click of a mouse. Just click once to select a program icon, then choose Get Info from the File menu. Bumping up the numbers will often result in a happier Mac. Be careful not to go too crazy, though; you may start freezing more often.

✔ **Files:** Delete large files you no longer need. Files that contain a large amount of graphics tend to take up a lot of disk space. If there's a chance that you may need the files in the future, save them to a floppy disk or backup system.

✔ **Software:** Uninstall software you'll never use. When you bought your computer or inherited it from someone else, it probably came loaded with stuff you've never looked at and will never use. For example, preinstalled games, applications, or online services. (To avoid conflicts down the road, it's better to uninstall a program rather than delete it because uninstall cleans out everything associated with that program.)

✔ **Temp folder:** Purge the files in the Temp (short for "Temporary") folder of your Windows directory. Temp files are documents or Internet files that are created for your protection when you surf the Web. If your computer crashes, the Temp file "remembers" what you were working on and stores it in the Temp directory.

✔ **Recycled folder:** Clean out the Recycled folder of your PC Windows directory. It fills up each time you delete a file. Mac users just "empty the trash." This may be the equivalent of saving three months' worth of newspapers and piling them up on your kitchen chairs. Imagine all the seating space you have once you recycle those "yellowing" newspapers.

Do a good spring cleaning because a clean machine is a happy machine. At least once a month, take a dry cloth and wipe down your equipment. Use cotton swabs to tickle the little ball under the mouse to get rid of dust or other small particles that interfere with performance.

Searching for a missing file

Perhaps you're searching for a document you created last week or last month and don't remember what you called it or where you filed it. All is not lost.

If you have Word 97, try this:

1. **Select File➪Open.**

2. **In the Open dialog box, select the drive you want to search.**

3. **Select Word Documents and type the phrase you know is in the document.**

If you have Word 2000, try this:

1. **Select File➪Open.**

2. **In the Open dialog box, select All Word Documents.**

3. **Select Tools➪Find.**

4. **Type the phrase you know is in the document.**

If you have Word 98 for Mac, try this:

1. **Select File➪Open.**

2. **In the Open dialog box, select Find File.**

3. **Choose the filename, type, and/or drive or other search criteria.**

For the love of Linux

Linux is a new, reliable operating system. It has been compared to the Energizer Bunny because it keeps going and going — and it doesn't crash like its major competitor, Windows. Linux is built on several decades of Unix development, which businesses have used for years. Following are some advantages to Linux:

✔ Linux is an open source operating system, which means the code is available and can be modified.

✔ Linux is versatile, reduces your total cost of ownership, and supports multilingual extensions.

To learn more about the Linux operating system, search the Internet for the term "Linux" and you'll find all the information you need.

Protecting against outages: More power to you

In many parts of the country, blackouts and brownouts are the norm because of weather conditions. Blackouts also occur because of lightning strikes or accidents that knock down poles. Brownouts are commonplace in warm-weather areas when overuse of air conditioners prompts power companies to reduce the standard 120 volts sent to the outlet. These situations can destroy sensitive components in your computer, which can result in lost data or permanent hardware damage.

A surge protector can protect against these disasters because it acts as a protective piece of hardware between your computer and your power source. It's like a bodyguard that jumps in and commits suicide for your computer in case there's a sudden power surge or outage.

Don't buy one of those cheap under-$10 power strips. Purchase an uninterruptable power supply (UPS) that can nip surges in the bud. A few reliable ones are TrippLite and APC. If you plan to use the Internet, buy a power strip with telephone connections. If lightning strikes your telephone line, your computer won't fry.

Avoiding viruses

When your computer starts to do weird things, it may have contracted a virus. There are demented people who stay up at night inventing viruses that can be transmitted by floppy disks or downloaded from e-mail or the

Internet. Some of these viruses are just plain annoying that may result in odd characters in strange places on your screen. Some viruses, however, have the potential to erase your hard drive.

There are two virus checkers available for Mac or Windows operating systems that detect viruses: Norton AntiVirus and McAfee Virus Checker. If you use either of these virus checkers, you'll be able to disinfect files you download from the Internet. After you purchase anti-virus software, you can download updated editions from the Internet at no charge. Be sure to do that regularly because new viruses are always a threat. Look these virus checkers up at www.symantec.com and www.mcafee.com

Speeding up Internet access

If your hair turns gray while you're waiting to access the Internet, here are several options:

- **Buy a high-speed modem.** Make sure you use a modem that will transmit at the highest speed. Check with a technical guru or computer store to find out what the latest speeds are.

- **Check out a digital subscriber line (DSL).** DSL is provided by your long-distance telephone carrier and Internet Service Provider (ISP). It's a great option for high speed Internet access if you're within 18,000 feet of a main switch office and your office is properly wired. A great advantage to DSL is that you're always connected, so there's no dial-up connection. And, unlike cable access, download time doesn't decrease as the subscriber base increases.

   If you have a DSL, consider using a firewall that makes your data secure. (A firewall is like an e-customs agent at an airport who determines what can move through.) Without a firewall, your files are more vulnerable to hackers because they're easy to find. In simple terms, if someone targets you for a burglary, it would be easier to focus on your house (which is always in the same place) than your car (which comes and goes).

- **Get cable access.** Cable companies provide access for computers as well as televisions. Cable access is very fast when you receive data, but slow when you send data. The reason for these differing speeds is that cable access was originally designed for one-way transmission to bring television into your home. (As of this writing, cable access isn't available everywhere.)

Protecting your data

Have you ever deleted a file accidentally or hosed your hard drive without a backup? Such calamities do happen. If you have a backup, you can always restore your data. If you don't have a backup, you may still find your missing files in the Recycled folder. Open the Recycled folder and drag the files you want to restore to the place they belong.

Getting Help Online

Although a good online Help program is better than an ill-mannered humanoid, it's not a panacea. Here are some ways to find solutions to your problems:

- **Jot down the details of what went wrong.** Whenever you experience a problem that requires help, always jot down as much information as you can, including the following:

    - When you first noticed the problem.

    - The details of the problem.

    - The steps you took to correct the problem.

- **Go to frequently asked questions (FAQs).** You can find FAQs and answers on most software Help screens. If you don't find the exact topic, look for related topics. For example, if you have a problem with the system clock, you may try CMOS or BIOS. Also check out the readme.txt files that you may have ignored when you installed your software.

- **Search the vendor's Web site.** Vendors have Web sites with Help information. Know which version of software you use and have information on the specifics of your computer. Both Microsoft (Windows) and Apple (MacOS) have great sites for technical support.

Save, save, save!

Get into the habit of saving your work regularly.

- **Autosave:** Set your Autosave feature so it automatically saves to your hard drive every 10 to 15 minutes. This way, you never lose more than the last 10 to 15 minutes' worth of work. Check your user manual for directions.

- **Manual save to hard drive:** If you don't set Autosave, click on the Save icon on your toolbar every 10 to 15 minutes. For critical work, this gives constant backup.

- **Manual save to a floppy disk:** If you want even more assurance that you've captured your gems, save to a floppy disk in addition to the hard drive.

- **Tape or zip disk.** Install a tape or zip disk as a backup system and save all your data each week, month, or quarter. You determine how often that should be by how critical the work is and how often you make major changes to the data. Keep the tape or zip disk at a site other than where you have your computer. For example, keep it in a safe deposit box. If something happens to your hard drive or your computer, you'll be able to restore lost or damaged files and software applications.

✔ **Send e-mail.** Send an e-mail message to the vendor. You find the e-mail address on the vendor's Web page. When you create your message, give as much information you can about the nature of your problem, your software, and your hardware. This isn't like a telephone call, however, where you get a response to questions on the spot.

As a last resort, call the software vendor. If you hear, "Your call will be answered in 3 days, 1 hour, 15 minutes," you know you're in trouble. Some vendors list a toll-free number; others don't. If yours doesn't, be prepared to run up a hefty bill.

You Come from Alabama with Your Laptop on Your Knee

Many travelers schlep around laptops and have concerns about keeping them safe. Here are some tips:

✔ **At the airport:** Keep your laptop in a case that doesn't identify it as a computer. (This holds true for other electronic devices such as cameras, VCRs, and the like.) Pass the case to the security guard and ask for the case to be searched manually, rather than put it on the conveyer belt to be X-rayed.

To boot up your laptop quickly after going through airport security, put the computer in suspend mode instead of shutting it down completely. Mac users simply put the PowerBook to sleep.

✔ **On the plane:** Don't store your laptop in the overhead compartment because it may get banged around during the flight. Keep it underneath the seat in front of you. If you don't have work to do, you may get the urge to play solitaire or update your resume.

✔ **At the hotel:** Travel with extra batteries in case the hotel doesn't have modem and data ports in your room. Keep an extension cord for plugging into difficult-to-reach spots. Outside the U.S., you may find that phone jacks aren't compatible with your modem. Be sure to check out the sort of adapters you may need.

Loving Your Copy Machine When It Eats Your Original

What do you do when you put a valuable, irreplaceable document into the copier and it eats your original? Some people stand and yell at the copier as if

---

A snake bite kit for your PC or Mac

Chances are you'll never be bitten by a poisonous snake. But if you hike in the woods and mountains, you'd be remiss if you didn't carry a snake bite kit. Similarly, you'll probably never experience the loss of all your computer data, but if you do business on your computer, you'd be remiss if you didn't have a computer "snake-bite" kit.

If you back up all your data, this may not be necessary. If you don't, you risk losing everything. Here are some things you should have in your snake-bite kit. It may be wise to keep the kit off site in the event of a fire or other disaster.

Operating system startup disk: This is the disk that installed your operating system (OS) onto your PC. Following are just a few of the many occasions when you may need the operating system startup CD.

✔ If a deadly virus contaminates your hard drive you may need to reinstall the OS.

✔ If you somehow lose a file, you can find it on the OS CD. (Just recently I tried to open a greeting card and got the message that I was missing a .dll file. I popped the OS CD in my D: drive and moved the .dll file to my Windows/Systems file. It was that simple.)

✔ If you install a new peripheral, such as a printer or external hard drive, you may need to load drivers from your OS CD. If you're a Mac user, the drivers are usually preloaded on your computer, or you can automatically update them on the Internet.

Application disks: Keep copies of all your application disks for the reason just mentioned.

File disks: Keep floppy disks of all your critical data — the data your business can't live without. Be sure to label each disk carefully.

Box of tissues: In case of a major loss, you may cry a lot.

---

insulting it will spew the original out as good as new. Others kick the copier like a vending machine, hoping the merchandise will shake free. And others stand back, scratch their heads, wrinkle their brows, and figure out what to do next.

The good news is that most copy machines tell you what's wrong. For example, if there's a paper jam, you see a message telling you where the jam is. Open the copier and look for the number inside that corresponds to the number in the message. Then free the offending paper. Some companies prefer that everyone doesn't monkey around with the copiers, so they post a number or special person to call.

Finding a photocopier you can live with

Copiers come in a variety of flavors — from black and white to color — from multi-purpose (desktop models that serve as a fax, printer, copier, and scanner) to dedicated (large, corporate size). Following are some options you may find in dedicated copiers. (You find these options on the top of the copier as icons or words).

- ✔ **Number of copies.** Regardless of the number of copies you make, try to limit the quantity of paper you run through to 50 sheets. Some copiers get jammed if you stuff too much through in one pass. Therefore, if you need to copy a 100-page document, run 50 pages through in two batches.

- ✔ **Sort or unsort (collate).** If you need multiple copies, decide if you want them collated (page 1-2-3, 1-2-3) or uncollated (page 1-1, 2-2, 3-3).

- ✔ **Staple.** With collated copies you may opt to have the copier place a staple in the upper left corner.

- ✔ **Paper tray.** Trays often accommodate paper in assorted sizes: 8½ x 11 inches, 8½ x 14 inches, or 11 x 17 inches.

- ✔ **1- or 2-sided copies.** You can often copy from a 1- or 2-sided document to a 1- or 2-sided document.

- ✔ **Lightness and darkness.** You have the option of adjusting the lightness and darkness of the documents.

After you finish copying, reset the copier to the default so the person who uses the copier after you doesn't mistakenly use your settings. Always close the cover. Also, before you use a copier, make sure the settings are what you need; the person who used it before you may not be as courteous as you are.

Know if you should place your copies face up or face down. This differs from one copier to another. A guy I worked with fed a 20-page document upside down in the copier. He pushed the button for 15 collated, stapled copies and returned to his desk. He returned to the copier shortly thereafter and found out that he had 15 blank, collated, stapled copies. I walked by as he was kicking and yelling at the "stupid" machine.

When you prepare a presentation, use your copier to print viewgraphs (also called overhead transparencies). There's a right and wrong side on which to print the viewgraphs, so check the directions on the box and put the viewgraphs in the copier correctly.

Preventing chewing

Here are a number of ways you can help prevent the copier from eating your papers:

- ✔ **Remove all staples.** It's handy to keep a staple remover on or near the copier.

- ✔ **Unfold dog ears.** Those are the little folds in corners that tend to jam.

- ✔ **Smooth out crinkled documents and raveled edges.** If you can't, place the page flat on the glass rather than feed it through the automatic feeder.

Just the Fax, Ma'am

Unlike personal computers and photocopiers, there's not much that can go wrong with a fax machine. When problems do occur, they're generally related to human errors, not machine errors. The following sections give you a few ways to avoid common human errors.

Oops! Wrong number

When you misdial a telephone number, you merely excuse yourself and try again. When you misdial a fax number, your message goes to the wrong person — and you often don't know it. For sensitive material, that can be a disaster. Here are a few ways to safeguard yourself:

- ✔ **Use speed dial.** Just as you do with telephone numbers, you can program the numbers of people to whom you generally send faxes. Check your user manual for instructions.

- ✔ **Check the window.** Always check the window on the fax *before* you send to confirm that you punched in the right fax number.

- ✔ **Get a confirmation.** With many fax machines you can get confirmation of the date and phone number – another way to check for the accuracy of the number, albeit after the fact.

The case of disappearing ink

If you use a desktop fax that prints on rolls of thermal paper, it's like using invisible ink. The message will be here today and gone tomorrow. Perhaps not quite tomorrow, but messages on thermal paper last only a year or two. When the fax is one you need to keep for longer than a year, recopy it on a copy machine. (There's no warning on the box of thermal paper to tell you that it's not permanent — I learned the hard way.)

Save our forests

Rather than waste paper on a cover sheet, affix a Post-it fax transmittal memo to the first page of your transmission. This speeds up transmission, thereby reducing long-distance charges. Example 3-1 shows a large size pad; 3M also makes smaller ones.

Example 3-1:
Keep the
trees from
wincing
when
you fax.

Post-it® Fax Note **7672**			No. of Pages	Today's Date	Time
To			From		
Company			Company		
Location			Location		Dept. Charge
Fax #		Telephone #	Fax #		Telephone #
Comments			Original Disposition: ☐ Destroy ☐ Return ☐ Call for pickup		

Courtesy of 3M

You Have the Whole (Computer) World in Your Hands

One of the frustrations of today's office workers is too many options. Can you recall the last time you frantically searched for someone's card in your Rolodex and realized (several days later) that you misfiled it? Can you recall placing a sticky note on your calendar only to find that it was nowhere to be seen when you needed it? Can you remember when you needed a computer file and didn't have your computer with you? Everyone can probably answer "yes" to at least one of these questions. The reason is that, in addition to being overloaded with information, we're overloaded with "stuff."

An early attempt to consolidate all this information was with a daily planner, which many people use today. A planner may have a card file for a limited number of business cards, a yearly calendar broken into weeks or months for noting appointments, and blank paper for writing notes. However, when you schlep around the day planner, laptop, briefcase, pocketbook (for women), and who knows what else, you need a chiropractor as a traveling companion.

Why not marshal this menagerie into a palm unit, which is so small you can put it in your pocket? With a palm unit you can carry around your address list, to-do-list, appointment book, expense reports, computer files, and more. You can read your e-mail, surf the Web, check voice mail, and take copious notes. The features causing quite a buzz with newer models are modules for wireless paging and cellular modems, audio file players, global positioning system (GPS) receivers, and digital books. Here are some of the nifty capabilities you get with many of the new palm units:

- ✔ **Carry your business cards:** Store about 6,000 names that show addresses, phone and fax numbers, e-mail addresses, and more. You can sort the names into categories and attach notes.

- ✔ **Make appointments in the date book:** Make appointments, gain instant access to your appointments, and attach notes.

- ✔ **Start a to-do list:** Set priorities, check off completed items, and carry forward the things you don't complete.

- ✔ **Keep track of expenses:** Keep track of all your expenses while you're on the road. The great thing is that you can sync the palm unit with your computer and transfer the expenses without having to re-key all the information.

- ✔ **Take copious notes:** Use a memo pad to store more than a thousand notes. You can use a keyboard-like facility or learn a shorthand method, which is quite simple after you use it once or twice.

- ✔ **Send and receive e-mail:** Synchronize your palm unit and you can view, read, and send e-mail; look up an address; attach a signature; set priorities; and do almost anything else you do at your computer.

- ✔ **Exchange moolah:** Beam cash from your credit card account to someone else's Palm unit. The recipient gets a "You've Got Cash" e-mail message. Check out www.paypal.com to learn how PayPal will receive the money as a direct deposit into a bank account or as a check.

- ✔ **Get a wake-up call:** Use the alarm feature to remind you of events or get you out of a boring meeting. The palm unit even has a "snooze" button to dismiss the reminder temporarily.

- ✔ **Use the calculator:** Perform basic calculations, store and retrieve values, and more.

- ✔ **Play a game:** Install a host of games, check for high scores, and set game preferences.

- ✔ **Find directions:** Get the benefits of a global positioning system (GPS) for directions.

- ✔ **Design forms:** Design forms and spreadsheets and fill them out in the palm of your hand.

- ✔ **Use as a digital camera:** Buy an adapter and turn your palm unit into a digital camera.

Can you imagine this scenario? An insurance adjuster is out in the field and keeps track of her appointments on her palm unit. She uses her palm unit to get driving directions to each appointment. When she reaches a client, she pops an adapter on her palm unit and takes digital photographs of the damaged automobile. She takes lots of notes and fills out the accident report. When she returns to the office, she's ready to sync her palm unit with her computer. It's that easy.

One of the neat things about having a palm unit is that you can line up your infrared port with someone else's palm unit and beam information back and forth. I recently joined Business Network International (BNI), an international networking group. A fellow member who has a palm unit beamed me his address list of all 40 chapter members. I didn't have to key in all the names and information myself. Captain Kirk would have been proud.

What's Hot on the CD-ROM

Here's what's on the CD-ROM:

- ✔ 3-1: What to Do When Your Computer Crashes
- ✔ 3-2: Waking up a Sluggish Computer
- ✔ 3-3: Searching for a Missing File
- ✔ 3-4: Protecting Against Power Surges
- ✔ 3-5: Avoiding Viruses
- ✔ 3-6: Speeding Up Internet Access
- ✔ 3-7: A Survival Kit for Your PC or Mac
- ✔ 3-8: Getting Help Online
- ✔ 3-9: Protecting Your Laptop
- ✔ 3-10: Dealing with Photocopiers
- ✔ 3-11: Solving Fax Problems
- ✔ 3-12: Using a Palm Computer

Part II

High Octane on the Information Superhighway

The 5th Wave — By Rich Tennant

"The new technology has really helped me get organized. I keep my project reports under the PC, budgets under my laptop, and memos under my pager."

In this part . . .

*I*n the world of "e" everything, this part is the plop, plop, fizz, fizz for anyone who wonders what the "**e-ing**" is all about. Here are some of the *e*'s it demystifies:

- ✔ **e**-mail
- ✔ **e**-commerce
- ✔ **e**-business
- ✔ **e**-auctions

This part also includes how to select *ergonomically* sound furniture, how the *electronic* office plays into home offices, and how *exercising* during the workday relieves tension.

Chapter 4

It's a Bird! It's a Plane! It's E-M@il!

In This Chapter

▶ Improving the way you do business

▶ Learning the parts of an e-mail message

▶ Understanding safety and security issues

▶ Getting rid of electronic junk mail

▶ Knowing your responsibilities as a reader and writer

▶ Filing electronically

I picked up a pay phone, called a toll-free number, and checked my e-mail. That's right. I listened to an electronic voice read me the text of my message. The voice sounded like Joshua, the devilish mainframe that [talked to] Matthew Broderick in the 1983 movie WarGames.

— Maryann Murray Buechner, writer

*I*n the world of business communications, electronic mail (e-mail) is like the un-cola. It's something like mail, but not quite. E-mail adheres to the guidelines of business communications, but has a unique flavor. If you're armed with a computer, a modem, and e-mail software (such as AT&T WorldNet, AOL, or others), you can send e-mail messages to one person at a time or to gazillions simultaneously — whether they're across the room or across the world.

E-Mail Gives You the Business Edge

Occasionally, e-mail is used for informal chats; otherwise, it's a serious business tool that's changing the way people do business and communicate with each other. The following sections show you some unique ways businesses are extending their reach with e-mail messaging.

Breaking down barriers

Time and distance are no longer barriers to communicating. Because e-mail messages can be delivered in a matter of minutes, or even seconds, people can send and receive messages 24/7 — no matter where they are. Even road warriors can reach the "mothership" through remote access from anyplace, anywhere. E-mail eliminates telephone tag and the charges associated with phone calls. People typically respond more quickly to e-mail messages than to traditional media.

Accelerating teamwork

Keep colleagues in different departments, states, or countries constantly in the loop. You can send files with text and graphics, or even send video and sound. For example, an engineer may be dedicating his time to solving a specific problem on a piece of machinery. He can get constant updates on the progress people at other locations are making that may shed light on his problem.

Holding virtual meetings

If you have an issue to discuss or a problem to solve, is it really necessary to schedule a face-to-face meeting? It's disruptive to people's schedules and can take days or weeks to gather people from the far reaches of the earth. You can "gather" these people by e-mail. They can respond in real time and stay focused.

Sending corporate communications

E-mail is relatively inexpensive. For example, companies use this exciting medium to send electronic newsletters. This eliminates the expense of postage and printing. It's a wonderful way to keep in touch with customers.

What good is having an e-mail address if people don't know what it is? Put your e-mail address on your business cards, stationery, fax cover sheets, and everything else that has your name, address, and phone number.

Anatomy of a Message

This section isn't intended to teach you how to use e-mail; it's to help you understand its anatomy. Remember that e-mail screens differ from one program to another. Therefore, what you see on your screen may be slightly different from what you see in Example 4-1. An explanation of each part follows the example.

Following is an explanation of the callouts in Example 4-1.

✔ **Attachment:** Click the Attach button at the top of the screen and select the file you want to send. The attachment you choose appears in the Attach field below the subject line.

✔ **To:** Enter the e-mail address of the person, people, or group to whom you want to send the message. The following list breaks down the components of an e-mail address.

- "myname" is the name of the local part — the e-name the sender uses. The name can be real or fictitious.

- @ (the at sign) appears in every address. It separates the local part (the left) from the domain address (the right).

File is attached

Subject

Courtesy copy   Attachment

Addressee   Electronic signature

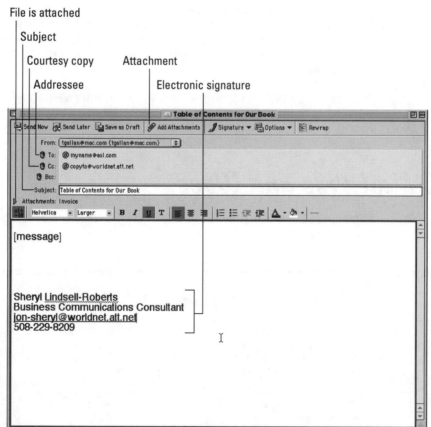

Example 4-1:
The key
parts of an
e-mail
screen.

- "aol" is the domain name — the service provider. In the above example, it's America Online.

- The last part (after the period) is the community. (That's not what .com stands for.) The commonly used communities are: .com for commercial, .org for organization, .gov for government agency, and .edu for educational facility.

✔ **Cc:** Stands for *courtesy copy*. This indicates that you're sending the message as a courtesy to someone in addition to the recipient. Copy only those people who need to see the message. Otherwise you contribute to overload.

Some software has a blind copy (bc) notation. Use bc prudently because it's a clear indication that you're sending something behind the recipient's back. And there's always the slight chance it may get into the hands of the wrong person.

✔ **Subject:** Write a compelling subject line that entices the reader to open your message.

Although the screen in Example 4-1 doesn't have a priority option, many do. If you want to designate a priority, select *high* or *low*. Use the high priority designation only when your message is truly urgent. Otherwise you become the "little boy who cried wolf." When you send an urgent message, no one will pay attention.

Don't confuse a URL (uniform resource locator) with an e-mail address. URLs are used on the Web for finding people on the Internet. URLs have nothing to do with e-mail.

E-Mail Pros and Woes

Although e-mail is probably the greatest thing since sliced bread, there are pros and woes:

Your "John Hancock" Please

At the end of 1999, Congress passed a bill that gives electronic signatures the same validity as handwritten signatures. Most e-mail software lets you set up a signature file that automatically adds your signature to the end of each message you send. You may also include in the signature block your telephone number, fax number, and any other information you want the reader to know.

If you can't figure out how to set up a signature file, check with a guru at your company or check out the Help screen.

Pros

Here's what makes e-mail the hottest stop on the Internet:

- ✔ Fast delivery.
- ✔ Inexpensive as compared to other forms of mail.
- ✔ Nonintrusive — send and receive when you're ready.
- ✔ Reach people who might not take your phone call.
- ✔ Attach files with text, graphics, sound, and video.
- ✔ Recipients can print the message, forward it to someone else, or save it to a file.
- ✔ Reach multiple readers at one time.

Woes

As wonderful as e-mail is, it has its disadvantages — as everything does.

- ✔ Recipient needs a computer, a modem, and e-mail software. Not everyone is connected.
- ✔ Not secure or confidential.
- ✔ Formatting may be lost at recipient's end.
- ✔ Some e-mail service providers don't have the equipment to handle demand during peak hours.
- ✔ Occasionally unreliable. (Computer glitches may cause problems.)
- ✔ Junk mail prevails.

E-Mail Security: Not Exactly Snug as a Bug in a Rug

Your e-mail communications are about as private and secure as postcard. First of all, you don't know what system your message is passing through or what system other people's messages are passing through. Second of all, there's nothing to stop a system administrator from snooping through your mail.

E-mail raises a lot of issues about privacy, and many cases have been brought before the courts. The Electronic Communication Privacy Act (ECPA) upheld a company's right to monitor its e-mail. The premise is: The company provides it and pays for it. Therefore, the company owns it! So, it's prudent not to send anything that you wouldn't want posted on the company's bulletin board.

Keeping your system safe

After teenage hackers have broken into the Pentagon system several times, you really have to wonder just how safe any system is. However, there are a few things you can *try* (the key word here) to safeguard your system:

- Configure your system to remember your user name and password so you don't have to type them in each time.

- Never ever give your password out to anyone — not even if you're tortured and deprived of your morning coffee.

- If you're in a high-security position, get a program to encrypt e-mail when it's sent and decrypt it when it's read. (*Encryption* means messages are coded so that only the intended reader can read them.)

Looking at a more secure future

Help is on the way. Several companies are working to make e-mail private and secure — somewhat the equivalent of a virtual shredder where the sender can order the message to self-destruct. Search the Web for companies such as QVTech and Disappearing Inc., who are movers and shakers in this arena. You'll be seeing a lot more of these types of companies in the years to come.

Spam, Spam, No Thank You Ma'am

Unsolicited e-junk mail is known as *spam*. It accounts for nearly 30 percent of all e-mail messages. Spam can be anything from annoying get-rich-quick schemes to pornography or worse. Many companies report having their computer systems brought to a standstill when thousands of spams are generated within a period of several hours.

Here's how spam works: There are little "robots" that crawl around the Internet looking for unsuspecting victims to spam. Often the spammers use false return addresses to avoid being traced.

Unlike snail mail, however, the person receiving the message pays the delivery cost. If you're barraged with spam, here are a few things to try:

- **Never open a message from someone you don't recognize.** Electronic lists are sold just as they are in the paper world. (Just look at the junk mail and catalogs you get to realize how prolific this practice is.) Once you open the message, the spammer recognizes your address as a live one and continues to pester you.

- **Contact your e-mail provider.** Give the sender's address to your e-mail provider with the strong message that you don't want unsolicited mail from that sender. In many cases, the spamming stops.

- **Consider using two addresses.** Give one to your friends, relatives, and business associates. Save the other for public messaging such as chat rooms, registering software, and e-commerce.

- **Check out the web.** Take a look at www.spamrecycle.com or www.junkbusters.com for some helpful hints.

Cutting Information Overload

Information overload is a term that's bandied about a lot. The writer is usually blamed for the overload, but the reader must share some of this responsibility. Following are ways to cut the overload and return some of the humanity back to this relatively new communications medium:

E-mail horror stories

Hit the wrong button, and any Machiavellian scheming behind your back may throw your e-mail in your face. There are thousands of stories that demonstrate this. Here are just a few:

- Jennifer was the new office manager of a large company. Her first day on the job, James sent an e-mail message to Sam saying that he thought Jennifer was "pretty hot." Over the next several weeks James and Sam exchanged messages about Jennifer. The messages got more and more descriptive. The gents in question weren't aware that "big brother was watching." Both were called in for disciplinary action under the company's sexual harassment policy. Even though neither James nor Sam ever said a word directly to Jennifer, both were reprimanded and their employment records blemished.

- In a small New Jersey town, the police seized the e-mail of a murder suspect in order to further the investigation of the homicide case.

On the strength of the evidence — which included incriminating e-mail messages — the man was charged with the murder.

- Then there's the story of the hapless e-mail user who inadvertently sent 100 copies of a romantic letter to 100 shocked co-workers. Romeo immediately realized what he'd done and called his provider to retrieve the letter. No dice. It was like dropping a letter in a mailbox. Once you've done it, it's on its way. (Some providers do have an "unsend" button. This guy's didn't.)

On a final note of privacy: If you receive an e-mail message that isn't intended for you, be polite and forward it to the intended recipient (if you know who he is) without reading any more than you have to. Also notify the sender that the message was sent to the wrong address. The error may have been because of an incorrect address that was in the server's directory.

As a writer of e-mail messages . . .

You can do a lot to cut information overload in the e-world. Here are a few tips:

- ✔ **Ask yourself whether e-mail is the best means of communication.** Perhaps a phone call is more appropriate? For example, if you'll be late to a meeting, call the person who's expecting you. People typically listen to voice messages more often than they read e-mail messages.

- ✔ **Don't use e-mail as a shotgun.** People have a tendency to prepare e-mail messages on the fly and fire them off to everyone in the universe. Send your messages only to people who need to see them.

- ✔ **Write a compelling subject line.** Write a subject line that entices the reader to look at the message. And if you can deliver the message in the subject line, do it. For example, write *Sales soar 15%,* rather than *Sales status.*

- ✔ **Change the subject line when replying or forwarding a message, if appropriate.** When you reply to someone's message, change the subject line if you change the theme of the message. Don't keep the same subject line floating around for several generations.

- ✔ **Delete those unsightly > marks.** When you forward a message someone sent you, be considerate enough to delete the ">" marks that begin each line.

- ✔ **Don't be the little boy who cried wolf.** There are people who designate "urgent" as the priority to all their messages. Unless a message *is* urgent, don't tag it as such. If something is truly urgent and you must get the message through as quickly as possible, consider phoning rather than risking that the recipient won't see the message in time. People are more likely to listen to phone messages than read e-mail messages.

- ✔ **Use a conversational tone for easy reading.** In every form of business writing, your tone is your personality on paper. E-mail messages often go to masses of people you haven't met, so it's critical that those people "hear" the tone of your voice. Following are suggestions at a glance for getting your tone across. (For details, check out Chapter 9 for honing the tone domestically and internationally.)

    - KISS the message; keep it short and simple.

    - Use the active voice.

    - Select positive words.

    - Be courteous and direct.

    - Use upper and lower case letters, not ALL CAPS.

✔ **Break the chain.** Chain letters and scams are rampant in the electronic world; they contribute dramatically to information overload. Bill Gates isn't experimenting with an e-mail tracing program and asking for your help; National Public Radio and the Public Broadcasting Service aren't gathering support to defend funding; Mrs. Fields isn't selling her cookie recipe; and the sky isn't falling. Even if there were a rocket disaster that contained plutonium and it spread over the entire Northern hemisphere, do you really think this information would reach the public in an e-mail chain letter?

As the reader of e-mail messages . . .

You can also do your part to make e-mail use efficient for all concerned:

✔ **Check your mailbox at least once a day.** Don't let mail sit in your inbox longer than necessary. If you're overloaded with e-mail messages, as most of us are, you may not reply to all your messages. You must discriminate between what is and isn't important and reply to what is in a timely manner.

If you'll be out of the office for an extended period of time and won't be checking your e-mail, you can often set your program to answer your e-mail automatically with a message much like a voice mail message. Check your Help screen for advice on how to do it.

✔ **Delete unwanted messages.** They just take up disk space.

✔ **Download files you want to keep.** Save them to a file. Print only when you need to.

✔ **Routinely scan for viruses.** When you download files, your computer is vulnerable; therefore, you should have a virus checker on at all times. Check out Chapter 3 for information about virus checkers.

Showing a Little Emotion

When you're engaged in conversation with someone, it's easy to understand the speaker's emotions through his tone of voice, inflections, and body language. It isn't easy to understand these emotions via the written word.

Consider conveying your emotions using emoticons — little cyber-symbols that you see in Table 4-1. Avoid using them in formal business e-mail correspondence; they're more for people you know. In order to read or understand any of these emoticons, turn your head counterclockwise.

Example: Bill, you did a great job. :-)

Outsource and leave the headaches to someone else

When you outsource your e-mail service, you leave the headaches about storage requirements and increased traffic to someone else. Here are a few features you may check out with the outsourcing vendors listed in this sidebar: filtering tools, autofiling, calendars and address books, custom signatures, automatic responders, vacation replies, spam blocking, virus protection, and secure sockets layer (SSL) to encrypt your messages. Popular outsourcing services include the following:

- ✔ **Electric WebMail**, (800) 490-3615, www. electricmail.com
- ✔ **USA.net Professional**, (719) 265-2930, www. usa.net
- ✔ **CommTouch bMessaging**, (408) 653-4330, www.commtouch.com
- ✔ **Critical Path**, (877) 441-7284, http:// criticalpath.net

Table 4-1	E-Mail Emotions
Emoticon	*Emotion conveyed*
:-||	Anger
:-|	Apathy
X-(	Brain dead
%-|	Confusion
;-(	Sadness
:-}	Happiness
:-o	Shocked
:-/	Skeptical
:-D*	Laughing so hard you don't notice a 5-legged spider hanging from your lip

Minding Your E-Manners

It's strange how people send e-mail messages they'd never send as paper messages. **Always remember that e-mail is a serious business document.** Treat it with the same respect as any other business document you write. Following are tips for e-mail etiquette — known as *netiquette*:

Douse the flame

I'm sure you've received e-mail messages that are rude, lewd, or crude. In the e-mail world, these Rambograms are known as *flames*. It's easy to forget that real people read your e-message. Follow these suggestions if you must let off steam so that you don't burn yourself and your reader with a flame:

1. **Compose the message in your word processor.** Include all the juicy insults you need to get off your chest.

2. **Don't send the message.** Instead, save it to a file.

3. **Give yourself a cooling-off period.** The longer the better.

4. **Defuse the anger.** Then look at the message again and ask yourself this question: *Would I say this to the person's face?* If you answer *No,* don't send the message.

Identify yourself

Always identify yourself and your affiliation. When you send e-mail to people outside your company, there's no letterhead to make the identification. You can use the electronic signature function to tag this information at the end of each message.

Be aware of libel and copyright issues

E-mail communications *are* subject to the same libel and copyright laws as paper-based documents. E-mail is the electronic version of a paper trail. You don't want the trail leading you to a courtroom.

Look Ma, no screen

What follows is a series of e-mail messages I exchanged with a colleague after she had taken my workshop "Energize Your Business Writing." We scheduled a meeting using the subject line. Neither one of us ever had to open a message screen.

Subject: Mon. doesn't work. How's Tues? – SLR

Subject: Tues. is NG. How's Wed? – MN

Subject: Wed.'s fine – LR

Subject: CU Wed. at 3:00 – MN

Delivering long messages

When your message is longer than two screens, prepare the document in your word processor, spreadsheet, or graphics software. Following are a few suggestions for delivering it:

✔ **Attach the file to an e-mail message.** Most e-mail software lets you attach multiple files to one message. Be sure your reader can receive the file, let the reader know what file format you're sending, and zip the file if it's long or has lots of graphics. (Check your manual or Help screen for zipping a file.)

✔ **Post the message to your intranet.** If a message is static (not likely to change) and is of interest to a wide range of people within your company, post it to your company's intranet. Then send an e-mail message with a hyperlink (the URL) to let readers know it's there. This is a great way to share the details of the company picnic and other issues of interest to your colleagues.

✔ **Point to it on your Web site.** If the message is appropriate for a large number of people outside your company, post it on your Web site and send the e-mail message with a hyperlink. Examples may be newsletters, price changes, or updated catalogs.

Say "hello" and "goodbye"

Do you say "hello" when you answer the telephone and "goodbye" when you end a conversation? Of course you do. You use salutations and complimentary closings in business letters and should use them in e-mail messages.

Salutations and closings are generally less formal in e-mail messages than in other business correspondence. Instead of *Dear Karen*, you may substitute *Karen* or *Hi Karen*. Instead of *Very truly yours* or *Sincerely yours* you may substitute *Regards*.

Avoid mud in your face

Never send a message you wouldn't want your mother or grandmother to see. Remember Murphy's Law: Assume that the message will go to the worst possible recipient.

Here's a case in point: Chris attended a meeting recently where everyone was criticizing a manager who was out for the day. E-mail messages about the meeting — with negative comments about the manager — were sent from one person to another. Eventually they were distributed around the region. And, as you may have guessed, that message wound up in that manager's mailbox.

Use international dating

It's good business practice to write out the month, date, and year because
you never know who may read your message. For example, assume you send
an e-mail message to someone in Europe to let him know about an urgent
deadline of April 5, XXXX. You write 4/5/XX. He would miss an important
deadline because Europeans format dates differently. Instead of
month/date/year, they use date/month/year. So, 4/5/XX to a European means
May 4, XXXX. People in Japan put the year first: year/month/date. So a
Japanese colleague talking about April 5 may write it as XX/4/5.

Create an Electronic Filing Cabinet

It's prudent to save copies of the important e-messages you send and receive.
However, it's not advisable to keep streams of messages in your inbox or
outbox any more than it's advisable to keep hundreds of papers piled on your
desk. And it's also not advisable to print everything out.

Create an electronic filing system so that you can find documents when you
need them. Your diligent record keeping may also come in handy for business, legal, or historical reasons. Many people print out messages of value,
but the following tips may keep the forests from wincing:

- Create a file structure in your e-mail system, much like you would with a
  paper-based filing system. Example 4-2 shows the electronic version of
  files as they correspond to paper folders.

- Save important messages to appropriate folders in your word processing files.

- If the message is something to share with your colleagues, post it on
  your company's intranet and send an e-mail message with a hyperlink to
  let everyone know where it is.

What's Hot on the CD-ROM

Here's what you'll find on the CD-ROM:

- 4-1: Keeping Your E-Mail System Safe
- 4-2: Eliminating Spam

✔ 4-3: Using Emotion

✔ 4-4: Minding Your E-Manners

✔ 4-5: Creating an Electronic Filing Cabinet

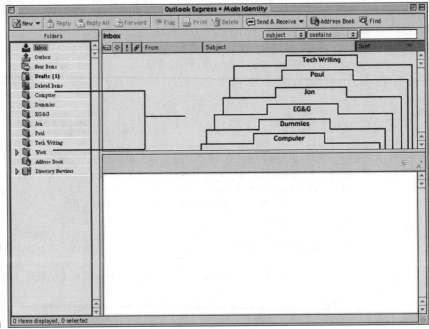

Example 4-2:
Electronic
file
cabinets.

Chapter 5

Doing Business on the Net

● ●

In This Chapter

▶ Surfing the Web

▶ Using an intranet to do your business

▶ Changing a business culture

▶ Shopping 'til dropping on the Internet

▶ Going up on the auction block

● ●

It's not a store, but it moves merchandise. It's not a TV network, but it broadcasts to millions of people. It's not a magazine, but it publishes plenty of material. [It's the Internet.]

— Aaron Zitner, staff writer for *The Boston Globe*

Although the Internet is still in its infancy, it's weaving itself into the fabric of the economy at a remarkable pace. The Internet isn't the latest techno-fad; it's here to stay. It has become a key ingredient in every sector across the globe. The Internet is reshaping the way we speak, the way we think about communications, the way we do business, and the way we conduct research. Following are just a few of the neat things that make the Internet the way to do business:

✔ Check out what the competition is doing.

✔ Get the latest scoop on research.

✔ Book a trip.

✔ Click and shop.

✔ Attend an auction.

✔ Send and receive e-mail.

If geek-like terms such as the Web, hypertext, and JPEG make you feel like a dinosaur, you're not alone. The advent of computers — and more specifically the Internet — ushered in an entirely new vocabulary. For example, in days of old, surfing was something to do in Hawaii. You'd hear, "surf's up," you'd grab your surfboard, and off you'd go into the mighty Pacific. "Surf's up" is still a familiar cry in coastal areas, but new technology has brought another meaning to the expression. In geek-speak, *surfing* means searching the Internet for knowledge.

The purpose of this chapter is to demystify the mysteries of the Internet and show you how you can use it to do your business. If there are words you don't understand, check out Appendix A. It's chock full of words, acronyms, and initialisms you may bandy about at a cocktail party.

Internet Surfing 101

Just to set the record straight, even though *algorithms* are associated with the Internet, Al Gore didn't invent them. The Internet — the network of all networks — was launched in 1969 when the Advanced Research Projects Agency (funded by the U.S. Department of Defense) designed a network where different types of networks could freely move knowledge in a common language among users without regard for differences in computer workstations, operating systems, or networks. Example 5-1 shows the Internet as a worldwide knowledge link between research laboratories, universities, government agencies, businesses, and homes across the world.

The Internet is becoming ingrained in the public consciousness as a communications medium much like the telephone. Companies around the globe rely on the Internet as a way to do business to . . .

✔ Lower their costs dramatically up and down the supply and demand chains.

✔ Improve customer service.

✔ Conduct business activities collaboratively with suppliers, customers, and business partners.

✔ Enter new markets and add new revenue streams.

Plain and simple

If you haven't used the Internet because you think it's complicated, think back to when you first drove a car. All those gadgets. All those mirrors. All those choices. What's a person to do? So you start the engine, press down on the gas pedal (and clutch if you learned on a stick shift), and the car shakes and jerks until it stalls. But, eventually you get the hang of it and driving becomes second nature. Even though the Internet isn't something you can wrap your arms around, learning to travel around it is much the same thing. Like driving, it's a matter of just sitting down and doing it.

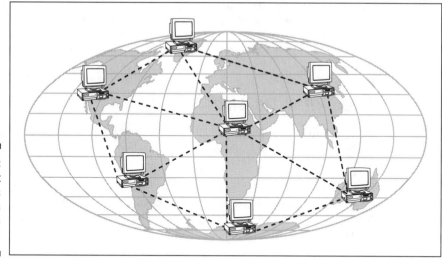

Just one big global library

Think of the Internet as a colossal card catalog for a global library complete with unlimited knowledge on almost every subject you can imagine. With just a click of the mouse, you can make airline reservations; visit a UFO site; order books, CDs, or videos from an electronic bookstore; take a whirl through the Louvre in Paris; or buy a Pez dispenser. It's all there.

Through the Internet, you have access not only to e-mail, chat groups, news-groups, and the World Wide Web (the Web or www) — but also to free software. The Internet abounds with the latest freeware, trialware, and shareware for most any computer platform. You can find free software through a search engine (more about that in a moment) by typing the search word **freeware**. In addition to free software, you can also download free upgrades to current software.

When you download anything from the Internet you do run the risk of catching a computer virus. Always make sure you have a virus checker on your computer to alert you to any potential problems. Two popular virus checkers are Norton and McAfee. (Check out Chapter 3 to learn more about them.) Once you install a virus checker and register, you can download upgrades from the Internet to guard against the constantly mutating, harmful invaders.

The Web

There's a spider that crawls through our offices and homes. It's so seductive that it ensnares us. Perhaps that's why it's called the Web. The Web is the star attraction of the Internet because it gives you access to computers all over the world.

The Web is growing like topsy. It consists of billions of connections called *hyperlinks* (a pointer from text or a graphic on which you click your mouse) that let you jump from one page or site to another. All you do is choose a hyperlink and you open a page or file with the information you want.

Seek and ye shall find

There are two ways to find things on the Web: using a URL and using a search engine.

You are el

A Web address is called a URL. It stands for Universal Resource Locator and is pronounced "you are el." Example 5-2 shows the URL on a home page with the parts called out:

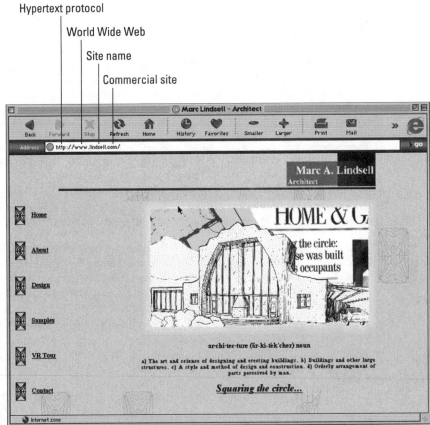

Hypertext protocol
World Wide Web
Site name
Commercial site

Example 5-2: Sample Web page with the parts of the URL identified.

Dot what?

Perhaps you're confused by all the "dot whats" at the end of a Web address. Although .com is the de facto Web extension, there are many others. Following are extensions you commonly see and the type of sites they represent: **.com** is a commercial site, **.org** is a nonprofit site, **.edu** is an educational site, **.gov** is a government site, and **.net** is a general site. Adding to the confusion, here are country-specific extensions:

.ar	Argentina		.it	Italy
.at	Austria		.jp	Japan
.au	Australia		.kr	Korea
.be	Belgium		.lu	Luxenbourg
.br	Brazil		.mx	Mexico
.ca	Canada		.nl	Netherlands
.ch	Switzerland		.no	Norway
.cn	China		.nz	New Zealand
.de	Germany		.pl	Poland
.dk	Denmark		.pt	Portugal
.es	Spain		.se	Sweden
.fi	Finland		.tw	Taiwan
.fr	France		.uk	United Kingdom
.ie	Ireland		.za	South Africa
.is	Iceland			

Search engines

If you don't know the URL, you can get to the site by using a search engine such as Yahoo (www.yahoo.com), AltaVista (www.altavista.com), Excite (www.excite.com), and others. All you do is type in a key word or phrase, and the search engine looks for documents that have your key word(s). The search engine then ranks the sites based on how many times your key word appears in the document, whether the key word appears in the title, how early the key word appears in the text, and so on.

Try to make your search as narrow as possible, otherwise you may get thousands of hits. For example, if you search for **dog**, you get Web sites for more dogs than you want barking at you. If you search for **poodle**, you get all types of poodles. If you search for **toy poodle**, you narrow the search to the toy variety only.

Getting to know the home page

A company's home page is the first page you see when you type in the URL, as you just saw with Marc's. It's the starting point on your journey through the company's site. You can expect to see any or all of the following:

- ✔ General knowledge about the company and its offerings.

- ✔ Buttons you can click to get to other pages, such as directions to headquarters, a catalog or list of products, company officers, and more.

- ✔ E-mail links to people in the organization.

- ✔ Links to related Web home pages.

If you have difficulty getting onto a site that you know is active, try again in a few days because the company may be having technical difficulties.

Intranets with Emphasis on "Intra"

You may remember the days when an employee got to the office early on a Friday morning to run 100 copies of directions to the company picnic being held the following day. After she ran all 100 copies, she realized she left off a critical piece of information. So, she tossed all 100 copies in the trash and went back to the computer to make the correction. As she busily retyped and reprinted the correct version, other people have arrived and there was a line waiting to use the photocopy machine.

By the time this harried employee got her turn at the photocopier, she saw the message "replace toner." So, she searched for the toner and replaced it. Finally, she printed 100 copies of the correct version. Then she single-handedly placed 75 copies in the mailboxes of the people on-site and faxed copies to the 25 people who would be coming from remote locations.

Does this sound like a lot of wasted effort? It is! And *there is a better way – it's called an intranet.* Intranets are different from the Internet. The prefix *intra* means "within." Therefore, intranets are Web sites for communications within a company. Companies use intranets to post many of the documents they once distributed on paper (such as memos).

Intranets typically run behind firewalls. A firewall is an electronic security measure that stops all people who aren't authorized from entering. Employees behind the firewall don't typically need a password because they're already part of the intranet family. There are many reasons to post on an intranet. For example, the directions to the company picnic could be posted on the company's intranet, and the person responsible for posting could send one e-mail message to the group's distribution list with a hyperlink to the intranet site. It's quick, easy, and efficient!

A curve in the road

Sometimes you get weird messages that really don't mean anything when you see them on the screen. Here are a few you may see and what they're trying to tell you in cybertalk:

404 not found. This means one of two things:

✔ The link is no longer available, in which case you may search for the information through your browser. If you don't find the site through the browser, the site may have vanished into cyberspace.

✔ The URL isn't correct. Try typing it in again.

The server does not have a DNS entry. It's likely that you typed the URL incorrectly.

The server may be down or unreachable. The site may be overloaded, which means too many people are trying to get to the site at the same time. Or the site may be off-line for maintenance, in which case you may try again at another time.

An intranet strengthens a company's culture by providing a forum for sharing all sorts of knowledge, such as:

✔ Stock quotes

✔ Company happenings (picnics, meetings, benefits changes, and so forth)

✔ Reminders to submit forms

✔ Sounding board for people's opinions

✔ Internal job postings

✔ Employee referral programs

✔ Inventory at remote distribution centers

✔ Lessons learned from projects

Finance departments may use the intranet to list delinquent accounts so sales groups can help in the collection efforts. Marketing departments can keep people abreast of new products, trends, competition, and pricing. Engineering departments can post new features and enhancements to products. Sales departments can post customer success stories to motivate other sales people. And that's just the tip of the iceberg. We're at the cusp of an explosion and are just beginning to understand the powers of this new technology.

Don't let your intranet become a repository for musty knowledge. Intranet documents are living, breathing, and have a life span. Update them as appropriate and remove them after they outlive their usefulness. For example, after the company picnic, the person responsible for posting should remove the invitation and directions.

Attending Cyber U.

Whether you covet a bachelor's degree, a master's degree, or just a few courses, they're available on the Net. You can earn a degree at home, at your own pace, without ever getting into your car or entering a physical classroom. Going to virtual college lets you interact with professors and other students. And, yes, the degrees you earn are valid.

Like anything else, however, there are scams. To find an accredited school that meets your needs, call the Council on Higher Education Accreditation at 202-955-6126 or the U.S.

Department of Education at 800-872-5327. You can learn about the student/teacher ratio; the credentials of the faculty; access to tutoring, guidance counseling, or technical support; and more.

Here are a few Web sites to learn more about cyberlearning:

✔ www.lifelonglearning.com

✔ www.degree.net/distance-learning/home.html

✔ www.nucea.edu

If your company is still handing out paper memos, newsletters, bulletins, and the like, hold on to them. They're about to become collectors' items. Even though the prospect of the totally paperless office is about as likely as the prospect of a paperless bathroom, the trend is moving from paper documents to electronic documents. So, pack up your paper memos, newsletters, and bulletins, and send them to the Smithsonian Museum. They'll be placed alongside the old Smith Corona typewriters.

Spread the word and let the cookie crumble

I attended a seminar where Jim Brantley did one of the most clever demonstrations I've seen in a long time. He was showing the attendees how his group is doing business on the intranet. At the outset of the demo, Jim passed around a tin of cookies his wife baked. (Everyone enjoyed the cookies and thought it was a yummy way to start the morning.) Jim then did his intranet demo. At the conclusion of the demo, Jim asked, "How many of you enjoyed my wife's cookies?" All hands went up. Then he asked, "How many of you would like the recipe?" Most hands went

up. Jim quickly surfed to the intranet — and there was the cookie recipe. To those who had never used the intranet, it was akin to magic.

After the demo, many people went to the intranet to download Mrs. B's delicious cookie recipe. (Watch out Mrs. Fields.) For many, it was the first time they had accessed the intranet. I spoke to some of the attendees a few weeks later, and many have started to use the intranet to find all sorts of valuable company information. That's the way the cookie crumbles!

Going Paperless

Although there will always be a place in the office for paper, you can keep the trees from wincing. The Internet is more than an online brochure. It's a way to do business. Going paperless and doing business on the Internet embrace several key principles:

✔ Access to knowledge replaces paper reporting.

✔ Knowledge is available to people authorized to have it.

✔ The owner/creator of the knowledge is its keeper.

✔ Essential evidence is preserved for the future.

Access to knowledge replaces paper reporting

I was on an assignment at a military base and a guy I know was toting around a box filled with 24 inches of paper documents. When I asked him what all that paper was, he told me it was a report someone requested. In order for him to generate this report, he spent almost a week tracking down who had what and where it was. Most of the information was on someone's computer — somewhere. After he found who had what, he had the laborious task of getting floppy disks from the keepers of the information and printing it all out. That took several days.

If all the components of the report were on the Internet or an intranet, this guy could have spared his back and merely sent an e-mail with hyperlinks to the person requesting the report. Access to the knowledge would have replaced the two-foot-high paper report.

Make knowledge available to people authorized to have it

Security is hardly an issue anymore. Firewalls and passwords allow certain people access to certain information, keeping others from accessing information they shouldn't have.

Here's a way to make your password more difficult to be invaded by a hacker. Think of a word that's easy to remember and construct it using alphanumerics. (Hackers have an easier time breaking codes for alphas only.) For example, if you enjoy golfing, construct the word golfing as your password in the following way: g0lfing. The numeral *0* replaces the letter *O*, and the numeral *1* replaces the letter *l*.

Make the owner/creator of the information its keeper

Think of the printed telephone lists you used over the years and how often you called a number only to find that the person left the company or transferred to another division. That doesn't happen with an electronic phone list if the owner/creator of the list is the keeper. Every time a number changes, the owner/keeper changes the number on the electronic file. This keep the list current.

There are many documents you produce that aren't carved in granite, and a phone list is just one of them. When you do business electronically, you can change documents as information changes. It's quick and easy and the information is never out of date.

Preserve lessons learned for the future

History has a way of repeating itself and so do issues. If you have problems with a project, it's more than likely that people down the road will deal with the same problems. It's vital that you capture the lessons learned so you preserve them for the future.

Doing business electronically preserves your historic knowledge so it can be used again and again. Knowledge has value only to the extent it's used and in the way it's used. For each project you undertake, there are lessons learned that you can pass long after the people involved are no longer there. And moreover, your historic documents aren't at the mercy of software, and they're not trashed when you turn in your old computer for a new one.

No more wincing trees

As Bill Gates points out in his book *Business @ The Speed of Thought* (published by Warner Books), "The U.S. government alone spends $1 billion annually printing documents that are already available on the Web." Gates points out many advantages of going digital: Digital technology can transform your production processes and your business processes. . . . No more stacks of paper in which you can't find what you need. No more pawing through piles of books and reports to find sales numbers.

Changing the Culture

When you try to change a culture — whether you're instituting a paperless office, creating an e-mail environment, or encouraging employees to come to work in purple underwear — people are going to find all sorts of excuses why the new culture won't work. Most people resist change and would rather hang on to the status quo.

Who's who

Table 5-1 illustrates the four groups of people who typically emerge when a cultural change is in the air.

Table 5-1	Groups Emerging in a Culture Change
Group	*Characteristics*
Leading edgers	This group (usually the techies) is anxious to latch onto anything new. These early adopters are the folks at the leading edge of societal evolution who jump on the train just because it arrives at the station.
Middle of the roaders	This "wannabee" group consists of most of us — the group that's hesitant but can be convinced to board the train when it clearly sees the benefits.
Tag alongs	The other extreme is the group that kicks and screams any time it must make a change. This group jumps aboard in the final moments because it realizes the train really is leaving.
Dinosaurs	There's always a group that won't change, no matter what. This group fades into the sunset and misses the train completely.

A commitment from the top down

People at the top have the power to change how their employees interact and behave. The top-ranking folks must be aligned in their commitment to work in new ways, and they must *walk the talk*. Alignment is an ongoing process, not a one-time event. Following are some things people at the top can do to facilitate a change in culture:

  ✔ Create a plan with clear-cut objectives and finite time frames.

  ✔ Review the plan periodically via working sessions, coaching sessions, and ongoing feedback.

  ✔ Establish an open relationship between themselves and the team.

  ✔ Become role models for the new behavior.

Stumbling blocks become stepping stones

People respond to outcomes to which they're committed. When they have a stake in the outcome and see the real *benefit* (rather than being told they must do something because someone said so), energy and enthusiasm replace stress and burnout. When this occurs, people often achieve the "unachievable."

New ways of thinking and doing business are a function of changing how people solve problems, couch opportunities, and communicate with each other. New ways of thinking aren't a function of new knowledge or new technology. Teams form. When teams are inspired, what were once stumbling blocks can be stepping stones. Following are some concepts teams must embrace:

  ✔ The benefit(s) of the culture change. How it will make their jobs easier and/or better.

  ✔ The vision.

  ✔ The processes that exist at each step.

  ✔ The importance of taking risks. (Some things will work, others won't. That's okay. The key thing is to try.)

Keep the momentum going

Changing a culture is an ongoing process. The leading edgers are inspired early and often take leadership roles. The middle of the roaders need a little tugging. They must be exposed to ongoing public relations campaigns where benefits and accomplishments are shouted from the rooftops. They must be *trained* so they don't feel alienated. Once people understand the new culture, they take ownership of its success and feel a sense of fulfillment and accomplishment.

Remember the early e-mail days

When e-mail first hit the scene, "what if's" were rampant. What if the reader isn't on an e-mail system? What if the message gets lost? What if the computer isn't working? What if big brother is watching? What if the world comes to an end? There were as many excuses as there were people resisting the change to the new technology.

Like any other culture change, however, the *leading edgers* jumped aboard and used e-mail as their way of communicating. There was support from those at the top-levels who walked the talk. Managers started using e-mail to communicate with their direct reports, and those who didn't read the messages either missed out on key happenings or heard of them through the grapevine. With massive public relations campaigns, ongoing training programs, and a focus on a new way of doing business (not on technology), the *middle of the roaders* eventually boarded the train.

That was enough to change the culture. The *tag alongs* knew they'd sink or swim, so they joined the new culture. The *dinosaurs* who sat and waited for interoffice memos are on exhibit at the Smithsonian; they're still waiting and still oblivious. Stop by and visit them the next time you're in Washington, DC. They're easy to recognize — the ones on the shelves still pondering the "what if's."

You can tell when the culture HAS changed

To know that a culture has changed, ask yourself this question: How would you react if the person in charge mandated that you forfeit your computer and replace it with a (manual) Royal typewriter, a case of carbon paper, a dozen pencil erasers, and a gallon of white out? You'd probably "shoot the messenger" because of the love/hate relationship you now have with your computer. With all the its inherent problems, your computer opens doors to unlimited access to knowledge and provides innumerable jobs in a multitude of industries. The culture *has* changed and computers *are* the way you do business.

Click and Shop

Electronic commerce (e-commerce) is a virtual marketplace – somewhat like a bazaar on the Internet. You can buy everything from books, to wine, to cars, to travel services, to the egg of a supermodel so you can spawn great-looking kids. E-commerce is putting an end to the Lomanesque brand of selling and is ushering in the death of the salesman. Instead of a salesperson shaking your hand and saying, "Use it in good health," you strike a key to finalize the deal.

Although e-commerce is still in its embryonic stages, it's the biggest thing to hit the Internet since e-mail. E-commerce combines the shop-at-home convenience of catalog buying with real-time experiences of viewing the goods. Example 5-3 shows my page in amazon.com that lists just a few of my books.

Shop 'til you bot

Early science fiction writers imagined that by the turn of the millennium robots would be everywhere. They were right. However, it's doubtful that they imagined that robots (known as *bots*) would be bits and bytes instead of nuts and bolts. These newfangled bots on the Internet are invisible shopping agents. Their purpose is to do your comparison shopping so you become a bargain hunter with the click of your mouse. Here are some of the bots that shop so you don't drop:

- www.bottomdollar.com to compare prices of books, music, sporting goods, software, and hardware.

- www.buyingguide.com for software, computers, and other peripherals.

- www.comparenet.com for automobiles, appliances, home-office products, electronics, and sports equipment.

- www.consumerworld.org to link to individual retailers and other sites that offer price comparisons. (These are independent bots who aren't owned by sites that want to sell you something.)

- http://mySimon.com is starting a service that will send you an e-mail whenever any online merchandise you showed an interest in lowers its online price to what you're willing to pay.

Not all bots are created equal. The following sections shows a few do's and taboos to find the bots that are just right for you:

Do's

- Look for bots that give you the most flexibility to refine your search. You learn that through trial and error.

- Check out http://bots.internet.com to keep abreast of the latest bots. New ones pop up regularly.

Taboos

- Never register as a "member" or you'll find your name on every ad list in cyberspace. E-junk mail will abound.

- Don't expect too much from the bots. They're still young but will improve over time.

Safety and security

Every reputable e-tailer who sells on the Web has some elaborate encryption scheme to protect your credit card number. It's safer than giving your card number to an unknown operator when you call a catalog company.

Example 5-3:
My page on
amazon.com.

If you're still squeamish, remember that under Federal law your liability for bogus charges is only $50. Therefore, if you get a bogus statement for $1,000 and can prove the charges are false, you pay only $50. Consider getting one credit card that you use only for Web purchases and check your bill thoroughly. Here are some sites you may contact that deal with security issues:

✔ The National Consumer League at www.fraud.org/internet/intset.htm on how to avoid fraud.

✔ The American Bar Association at www.safeshopping.org for tips on online shopping security.

✔ The Federal Trade Commission at www.ftc.gov/bcp/menu-internet.htm. This site posts the latest Internet rip-offs and tips on how to avoid them.

There are snake-oil salespeople on the Internet who are ready to sell you the latest scam. If something doesn't seem right, it probably isn't. Trust your instinct.

Become a cybermerchant

The Internet has transformed entrepreneurs into netpreneurs. Unlike the physical world of shopping malls and highway billboards, one of the biggest challenges of being a cybermerchant is letting potential customers know you exist. Following are a few tips for spreading the word:

- ✔ Register with search engines such as those previously mentioned.

- ✔ Advertise in relevant publications.

- ✔ Put your Web address on all your mailings, literature, and business cards.

- ✔ Mention the site on your outgoing voice mail message.

- ✔ Use newsgroups or mailing lists to promote your company and products.

In this electronic world where you don't meet people face to face, savvy companies keep the customers coming back for more by conscientiously monitoring e-mail feedback and listening carefully to what customers are saying. They also update their online offerings so what you see is always current (unlike a paper catalog that may be outdated).

Spiffy up the storefront

To keep customers coming back to your site, make sure you have a spiffy storefront with attractive visual displays. Turn your cyberstore into a hot destination for the Net-surfing masses with digitized photos, animation, and video. If appropriate, promote your store with free samples, e-mail discussion groups, frequently asked questions (FAQs), and anything else your customers may find useful.

Provide excessive customer service

When you sell to customers on the Internet, customer service is just as important as when you sell in a store or from a catalog. Customer service is so key to the success of a Web site that electronic support services are sprouting up, increasing at the rate of 50 percent each year. To keep up with the demand and to offer quality service, many companies are outsourcing customer support. These outsourcing services have evolved into a niche industry. After all, customers don't care whom the support comes from, they just want it.

With a lot of competition vying for the same market share, you must be a savvy seller:

- ✔ Anticipate the questions potential purchasers may have.

- ✔ Answer questions promptly and completely.

- ✔ Make your product descriptions as clear and detailed as possible. (Use hyperlinks to reveal increasing levels of details.)

- ✔ Insist that buyers pay by credit card or money orders. Don't accept personal checks or you may be up the proverbial creek without a paddle.

Look Ma, No Taxes

E-commerce is expanding at such an exponential rate that state and local governments are looking for ways to get a piece of the action. The issue isn't whether they should apply taxes to their sales, but how to apply taxes.

Although every catalog company applies local taxes when they sell to customers in the same state, it's unclear whether these laws apply to e-commerce. Therefore, our legislators on Capitol Hill flounder for ways to get a bite of Internet tax dollars. As of this writing, the political winds have shifted away from taxing Internet sales because no one wants to take responsibility for smothering this emerging cyberindustry by taxing it to death. But our politicians, in their infinite wisdom, may ultimately find a way.

Personalize your site

Customers are more concerned with service than with price. Therefore, do everything you can to accommodate your e-shoppers. Get creative. For example, take a look at www.landsend.com (Land's End e-tailers) and see how creative they are. You provide your measurements (that's frightening), and Land's End shows you a virtual model with your measurements who will try on the clothes you like. The model will turn around so you can get a bird's-eye view from all sides.

Become a cybershopper

An added benefit of e-commerce is often attractive discounts or rewards. Many companies reward you for freeing up their phone lines and eliminating paper processing. For example, many of the airlines give additional frequent flyer points when you book online.

Get an e-wallet

(As with anything else, you put an "e" before a word and do business in cyberspace.) One of the frustrations of online shopping is the forms you must fill out each time you place an order with an e-merchant for the first time. Many shoppers abandon the sites because of the hassle. The solution may be an electronic wallet. You fill out a form once for all participating sites. For more information on e-wallets, visit www.passport.com, www.instabuy.com, www.brodia.com, or www.qpass.com.

E-caveat emptor

As with any other form of shopping, however, let the buyer beware! As e-commerce continues to explode, so does the potential for fraud and abuse. Because Ralph Nader can't monitor everything, a cadre of online consumer protection groups is emerging. A recognizable name is the online version of the Better Business Bureau — BBBO. For a fee, member firms may display the BBBO seal of approval. Any company who disregards BBBO policies forfeits the right to display the seal.

If you contact a site and don't find the BBBO seal of approval, that doesn't mean the company has a bad track record. It may mean the company didn't join the brotherhood. To check out a cybercompany or register a complaint, contact the Better Business Bureau online at www.bbb.com.

Another place to turn is the Federal Trade Commission (FTC). Register a complaint with the FTC at www.ftc.gov, but don't expect any action right away. The FTC waits to see if there's a pattern of fraud before taking action against a merchant.

As an e-shopper, here are a few ways to protect yourself:

- **Deal with reputable companies.** If you want to conduct e-commerce with a company you aren't familiar with, ask the company to mail you a catalog or brochure.

- **Be wary of an e-company that doesn't post its address or telephone number.** That may be a signal that the company isn't legit.

- **Don't give personal information.** This includes your social security number or your mother's maiden name.

- **Never send a check.** The money is transferred from your bank immediately. The Electronic Fund Transfer Act protects your losses up to $500 (*gulp*) if you report a cybercrook within 60 days. After 60 days, your loss has no limits.

Read the fine print

Always read the fine print. Not all sites are alike and you must be a savvy consumer.

Refunds: Just because a site tells you it offers refunds, know what it refunds. For example, if you order something from amazon.com, you can return the merchandise for a full refund if you include the original packaging and everything that came with the shipment. Other e-vendors may charge a 15 percent restocking fee, and they don't refund the handling fee. They may also expect you to pay for the return postage.

Shipping costs: Shipping costs also vary from one site to another. One site may charge $3.95 to ship an item and another may charge $19.99 to ship the same item. Here's a way to see what you should pay: Make a note of the weight, dimensions, and ZIP code of the origin and destination. Then visit http://iship.com to get the rates for the major carriers. You can then weed out the vendors that are ripping you off.

Going, Going, Gone: Online Auctions

On-line auctions are hot on the Internet. After all, would you rather advertise the sale of your original Barbie Doll or GI Joe in the local newspaper that reaches a limited number of people in a limited geographical area or on eBay, one of the online auction sites that reaches an unlimited number of people worldwide? It's a no-brainer.

Online auctions, however, aren't always a utopia. Before you bid online, read the policy of the site for bidding and selling. If you can't abide by the policies, you can simply surf to another site or choose not to take part in any transactions.

Because online auctions lack the control of face-to-face transactions, you must be a savvy bidder. One thing you may do is check into fraud insurance that some sites offer. For example, as of this writing eBay offers free fraud protection up to $200. The site at http://auctionuniverse.com offers protection up to $3,000 for a small fee. Following are ways to keep from getting burned:

- ✔ Be assertive and ask questions.

- ✔ Determine the value of the merchandise you want.

- ✔ Know the maximum you're willing to spend.

- ✔ Clarify warranty knowledge and return policies.

- ✔ Understand the shipping and handling charges.

- ✔ If the site doesn't post a return policy, call the vendor and ask for one in writing.

- ✔ Consider paying a little more and have your check held in escrow until you're satisfied with your purchase.

- ✔ Print out and save any e-mail correspondence, purchase forms, and the like until the transaction is complete.

What's Hot on the CD-ROM

Here's what's available on the CD-ROM:

- ✔ 5-1: Country-Specific Internet Extensions

- ✔ 5-2: Using Search Engines

- ✔ 5-3: Web Sites for Cyberlearning

- ✔ 5-4: Web Sites for Shopping

- ✔ 5-5: Web Sites for Safe and Secure Surfing

Chapter 6

Be It Ever So Humble, You're Working at Home

● ●

In This Chapter

▶ Knowing when to hold it and when to fold it

▶ Getting your business into high gear

▶ Knowing if you need a Web site

▶ Selecting an appropriate name

▶ Dealing with tax issues, insurance, and retirement planning

▶ Creating a business network

● ●

It's often been said that working from home isn't for everyone. That's good, of course, for the rest of us. If everyone worked from home, the neighborhood would be too noisy and too crowded — with overweight joggers and express-mail trucks and elbow-to-elbow lunch counters.

— Nick Sullivan, writer

*T*he hottest amenity to anyone's dream house is no longer the Jacuzzi, the wine cellar, or the exercise room — it's the home office. According to International Data Corporation, a research firm in Framingham, MA, "Each year, 2 million more households of the 101 million total U.S. households add home offices." Some of these folks run businesses from home, while others work at home for a company part of the time.

Once upon a time, the home office represented women who took in laundry or stuffed envelopes. That image changed when Blondie Bumstead (of the famous comic strip) surprised the world by opening up her own catering business. She reaffirmed that the home office had become a viable segment of the business culture.

Climbing the corporate ladder in your bedroom slippers

People who work at home may not always be business owners; they may be telecommuters. Companies find that telecommuters are very productive. When you work at home, you have fewer interruptions, you don't spend time commuting, and you can use your hours flexibly. Here are some advantages of telecommuting, as revealed in a study prepared by the International Telework Association & Council:

✔ **Creates a powerful perk.** Telecommuting is a great perk for luring and keeping employees. In an age in which companies are cutting back on benefits, telecommuting is a great benefit companies can offer their employees while saving money. Plus, it helps companies retain their employees longer. When you think of the large amounts of money spent on recruiting new employees, companies can save an average of $7,920 a year per employee when they don't have to place ads and work with recruiters.

✔ **Reduces absenteeism.** Because people can flex their time and work around errands and other activities, they don't need to take as many days off from work. The study found that employers save an average of $2,086 for each employee who telecommutes.

✔ **Improves quality of life.** More than 57 percent of the people surveyed mentioned the increased job satisfaction of telecommuting. Telecommuters have more control over their working hours and can balance home and office. They suffer from less stress and have a better attitude toward their jobs.

✔ **Increases productivity.** Employers found that productivity increases by 50 percent among telecommuters. Companies can quantify productivity by monitoring workloads before a person telecommutes and after.

✔ **Impacts the environment positively.** With fewer people commuting to work, the study found a significant decrease in noise and air pollution.

The streamlined corporation coupled with today's technology paved the way for the entrepreneurial spirit. If you look at the newspaper, you see start up companies and home-based businesses springing up all over. Some of these folks often do it all. When my son Dr. Eric Lindsell opened his chiropractic office, *The Baltimore Sun* quoted him as saying, "I do it all . . . everything from the bookings and the books to the bathrooms."

Don't Just Get Up and Go

You don't have to hate your boss to want more from your professional life. What do I mean by *more?* You may want to shape your own workday, take vacations when you want them, and take credit for successful projects. If you determine that working for yourself is the best way for you to have what you want professionally, keep in mind that being a prosperous entrepreneur requires calculated risks and the ability to learn from mistakes. And you should have a fire in your belly — a burning passion for what you've set out to do. If you're unstoppable, here are some points to ponder:

- ✔ **Unless you hate what you're doing, don't change fields.** Starting from scratch in a profession in which you have little or no expertise can be frustrating. Stick with what you know and do well.

- ✔ **Research your home arrangements.** Know if your home business violates any zoning or government regulations. Know what your neighbors' reaction may be to cars coming and going.

- ✔ **Accumulate a backlog of money.** If you're the sole provider for your household, you need to have living expenses for as much time as you anticipate it will take for your business to become profitable. Some entrepreneurs say it takes at least one to two years, depending on the business.

- ✔ **Have your family's support.** Having the support of your spouse or the people you live with is critical. Otherwise, your experience may be a living hell.

- ✔ **Never burn bridges.** Leave your current job on good terms and be sure to honor any nondisclosure or non-compete arrangements you made. If your business doesn't work out, you may want your former employer to welcome you back with open arms.

Look Before You Leap

To do what you love and love what you do is a key ingredient in a successful business. You also have to be a risk taker and be willing to give up the security of a regular paycheck. Here's some advice from those who've made it:

- ✔ **Perform a market survey.** Make sure there's a niche for your product or service. Keep up with the latest trends, visit trade shows, read all you can about the target industry, and talk to people in the field — those who would be your competitors and customers (or clients).

- ✔ **Write an extensive business plan.** A business plan includes a mission statement, long- and short-term objectives, and more. Surf the Internet using the search words *business plan,* and you'll find scads of information to help you formulate a business plan that's right for you.

- ✔ **Network, network, network.** Meet with everyone you can and let them know who you are and what you offer. Later in this chapter, I show you lots of networking avenues.

✔ **Know what the competition is doing.** Strive to be better than the competition and play up the uniqueness of what you offer.

 ✔ **Contact the Small Business Administration (SBA).** You can get a treasure trove of information on starting and running a business by writing to the Small Business Administration, 409 Third Street SW, Washington, DC 20416; by calling them at 800-827-5722; or by visiting them online at `www.sbaonline.sba.gov`.

What's in a Name?

Everything! A name gives you the identity by which the world knows you. Some names carry status: Rockefeller, Kennedy, Onassis, IBM, Lucent, General Motors. Some names carry terror: Stalin, Jack the Ripper, Saddam Hussein. Some names carry glamour: Elvis, Liberace, Cher.

Select a name that's clear and reflects the nature of your business, such as Ameritrust Real Estate, Inc., Nature's Florals & Gifts, Inc., Essential Family Chiropractic, All Phase Publishing. When a name is unclear or misleading, you lose business. Here are a few things to consider before you carve your company name in granite:

 ✔ **Be wary of using initials as your company name.** Although the initials may have meaning to you, they may be confusing to others. For example, BNR may be the initials of your kids (Brian, Nicole, and Robert). When people think of your company, however, they may have trouble remembering if it's BNR, B&R, RNB, or any other combination. Plus, initials on their own don't tell people what your business offers.

 ✔ **Think of a term that adds spice.** For example, many housing developers include the word *estates* in the name of the development. The word connotes large tracts of land with elaborate homes. Even if the "estates" are postage-stamp size pieces of land with small homes, the word itself sounds classy.

 ✔ **Consider foreign terms.** You expand your options by finding words in a language other than English. For example, Häagen Dazs ice cream sounds alluring because of its foreign flavor. (Yes, the pun is intended.) But did you know that Häagen Dazs is an American company that got creative with its name?

Check the translation of foreign terms to be certain the name you pick translates well. A big brouhaha erupted at Reebok a few years ago when the company selected the name "Incubus" for a new line of athletic shoes. According to a dictionary definition, Incubus is an evil spirit that descends upon women while they're sleeping. The spirit is thought to have sexual intercourse with these women. Now there's a term you'd want to check before using it to name your new company.

Check out `www.facstaff.bucknell.edu/rbeard/diction/html` to search for definitions in hundreds of languages.

✓ **Test a few choices**. After you narrow the list down to a precious few, ask people in the industry, whom you trust, which name works best.

Be careful of names that people may take literally. For example, when Kodak launched a new camera called the "Weekender," the customer service department received calls asking if it was okay to use the camera during the week. (Amazing, huh?)

To Incorporate or Not to Incorporate: That is the Question

There are legal or financial reasons why you may want to incorporate — liability and tax issues being two of them. You don't have to be a mega-giant such as IBM or AT&T to be a corporation. A close corporation or Subchapter S corporation may be just right for you.

✓ **Close corporation:** Designed for small businesses where outstanding shares are held by as many as fifty people or as few as one. Close corporations often have family members as officers and shareholders.

✓ **Subchapter S corporation:** Offers small businesses special tax advantages. If you start a Subchapter S corporation with ten or fewer shareholders, you derive income from the sale of goods and services and may avoid corporate taxes on your net income. Shareholders may opt to be directly taxed as individuals on their share of corporate profits (or losses) and avoid double taxation.

Find an attorney to shepherd you through the legal details. He will advise you if forming a close corporation, S corporation, or other type of corporation is right for you. He'll also help you deal with any other legal issues.

What You Need To Get Started

Unless your living quarters are so small that when you leave your briefcase in the middle of the room it seems like furniture, you can run a business from home. It's best to have a separate room that's your own private work space, but that's not always possible. Your work area is your nerve center — the place where you spend most of your workday. It should be a place you regret leaving and enjoying returning to — even if it's the corner of a room.

The basics

A poorly set up work space can destroy your home-based work effort. Following are some things to consider when planning your work haven:

- ✔ **Buy comfortable and practical office furniture.** Check out Chapter 7, which is chock full of ways to make intelligent decisions on selecting chairs, desks, and other items of furniture.

- ✔ **Know your filing needs.** For starters, you may consider a small filing cabinet on rollers that's small enough to fit under a table or desk. If your office is in the corner of a room, a dresser drawer for files may suffice. Or install wall shelving for papers, manuals, and the like.

- ✔ **Have good lighting.** The best ambient light for your office is natural light, so try to find a space that provides the greatest amount of daylight. Lighting must be bright enough to read without eyestrain and indirect enough to work at your computer without glare or reflections. If you have a problem with fluorescent lights, replace cool white light with a warm white fluorescent light. Adjustable blinds help block or filter sunlight.

- ✔ **Order stationery and business cards.** All your stationery products should make a statement about you and your business. Check out my other book *Writing Business Letters For Dummies* (IDG Books Worldwide, Inc.) for a great discussion on stationery and business cards that make your personal statement.

- ✔ **Set up a separate checking account.** Having a separate account for your business will be helpful at tax time. You may also consider getting a credit card to use solely for business expenses.

- ✔ **Apply for the proper licenses and tax number.** Check with the city or town hall to see if you need a license to do business at home. Ask your accountant if you need a federal tax number. Perhaps your social security number will suffice.

- ✔ **Create a brochure and generate a press release.** These are vital to looking and feeling like a professional. If you're not a marketing guru, hire a professional to write and design your marketing collateral.

It always pays to advertise, but think about ways to get your name in the face of the public without spending money. For example, if you're in a service industry, write an article that offers useful industry tips and get it published in a trade magazine or local newspaper. Even if you don't get paid for the article, the free publicity is worth a mint. Jeff Davidson, author of *Marketing on a Shoestring,* says, "An article is far more influential than an ad . . . it's as good as a third-party testimonial."

Computer issues

No office today is complete without a computer. If you're computer savvy, consider buying your computer equipment over the Internet or from a catalog. However, if you need help, deal with a local store that prides itself on customer service. Check out Chapter 7 for ergonomic issues related to computer equipment so you'll be able to ask the right questions.

As a home-based business, you don't have an information technology (IT) department to call for troubleshooting computer problems. Check out Chapter 3 for do-it-yourself tips on learning to love your computers, faxes, copiers, and palm units.

Perhaps you recall the old adage about buying a car: Don't buy the first version of any model car. Wait a year until the company gets rid of all the kinks and bugs. The same holds true when you buy a computer. Wait until a computer has been on the market for a year so the company gets rid of all its kinks and bugs. That holds true for software as well.

Telephone issues

When selecting a phone, understand how you'll use it. Not all phones are created equal. (Chapter 2 offers a wealth of information on telephone issues.) Here are some options:

- **Standard corded phone.** This works well if you plan to use your phone while sitting in front of your computer and everything is within easy reach.

- **Speaker phones.** If you'll be involved in conference calls, consider getting a speaker phone.

- **Cordless phone.** If you need to walk around your office, there's no need to be tethered. A cordless phone gives you the freedom to pace the floor.

- **Headset.** If you need to take copious notes on paper or your computer, a headset guards against those awful neck cramps.

Make sure you have sufficient telephone lines. When you run a business from home, treat it as a business. Have a phone line dedicated exclusively to your computer, business phone, and fax. If you'll spend a lot of time online, consider having your computer and fax on separate lines. You definitely don't want to share your computer and phone line with your chatty teenagers.

Check with your local telephone company about sharing fax and voice lines. These services discriminate between fax and voice calls and appropriately route each call to the proper machine. Some of the new fax machines have built in voice mail capabilities.

You can take it with you

The increasing popularity of the home office is driven by the fact that with cell phones, pagers, laptops, and other electronic tethers, people can ply their crafts when, where, and how they like — 24/7. Add to that the efficiency of faxes, e-mail, the Web, and overnight delivery, and your office can be anything from a seldom-visited corner of a basement to a sun-drenched beach to a lofty mountaintop (provided the FedEx driver has four-wheel drive).

Multifunction devices

When you run a business from home, you often have limited desktop space. Consider a multifunction devise (MFD) that's a copier, printer, fax, and scanner all in one. In addition to saving space, it's easier to learn and maintain one piece of equipment than it is to learn and maintain four.

Be Good to Yourself

You now have the greatest boss in the world! Reward yourself. Celebrate with your spouse, friends, colleagues, and family members. And don't become a workaholic. Even though you have 24/7 access to everyone on this side of Mars, remember the adage about all work and no play. Following are some hints for leading a balanced life:

- ✔ **Don't wear too many hats.** When you first open your business, you're probably everything from the president to the janitor. You can't do it all. Farm out things that will make your life easier. For example, get an accountant, marketing professional, graphics designer, or anyone else that makes sense. *Do what you do well, and leave the rest to the experts!*

- ✔ **Decorate your office space.** Surround yourself with whatever makes your office a pleasant place to spend your time. Hang pictures, buy a plant or two, get goldfish, include relics from a trip, and so forth.

- ✔ **Get an advance from clients.** Ask clients for a goodwill payment before you start work and progress payments as you go along. *Get all agreements in writing* so you don't get stiffed. It does happen.

- ✔ **Gather kudos.** Ask satisfied clients for referrals and written testimonials. And don't be shy about telling prospective clients whom else you've satisfied.

- ✔ **Dress for work.** Although you can work in front of your computer in a bathrobe like a sequestered monk, you won't feel very professional. Even a sweatsuit is a step up from a bathrobe.

Weaving a Web

The Web is a high-profile marketing and sales tool for most small and large businesses. People from all walks of life have Web sites — from the novice who's selling baskets from home to the technoid who develops sophisticated computer software. The Web has become an information smorgasbord that welcomes everyone to cook up a treat and dig in. (Check out Chapter 5 for a full discussion of using the Web for electronic commerce.)

A Web site isn't like a paper document that flows from one page to the next. Example 6-1 shows how a paper document is read in linear fashion.

Example 6-1:
Reading a paper document is as easy as 1-2-3.

A Web site is used by people to jump from one page to another in random order, as you see in Example 6-2.

Deciding whether you need a Web site

Although a Web presence isn't for everyone, it is helpful to most types of businesses. Following are questions to ask yourself to determine whether you should have a presence in cyberspace:

- ✔ **Are your competitors online?** If they are and you aren't, guess who gets the business?

- ✔ **Are your prospects and customers online?** It won't do you any good to build a Web site if your customers and prospects won't see it. If you're unsure, talk to your customers. Ask them whether they use the Web and, if they do, for what purposes.

- ✔ **Does your product or service have appeal beyond your local area?** If so, the Web is a great way to reach beyond your community.

- ✔ **Are your products and services dynamic or static?** You must offer fresh information on a regular basis to encourage people to visit often. For example, an accountant can offer a monthly tax tip, a cook can offer a weekly recipe, and so on.

> ✔ **Does your company need to be perceived as one that keeps current with technology?** If you're in a high-tech business and deal with engineers, scientists, and other technical folks, you can bet your bottom dollar that people expect you to have a Web site. Otherwise, you may inadvertently give the impression that you're a dinosaur.

> ✔ **Are you willing to devote time or money to your Web site?** Maintaining a Web site is time-consuming, and you must be willing to maintain it or pay someone to do it for you.

Putting your site together

"Build it and they will come" became a popular phrase after the release of the movie *Field of Dreams.* However, this is only true in the movies. Building a Web site is much like building anything else. It takes planning, the right mix of people, and follow-through. A poorly designed Web site is akin to a poorly designed storefront. People aren't interested.

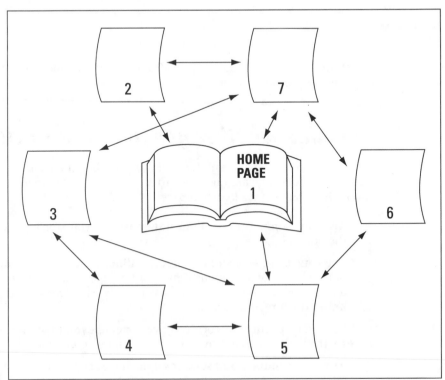

Example 6-2:
How the Web is woven.

Before you build your site

Web technology is in its infancy and people are discovering the ins and outs. So be sure to follow these suggestions:

- ✔ **Do your homework.** Visit lots of Web sites and take note of what you do and don't like about each.

- ✔ **Hire a professional.** Few people have the wherewithal to write and design a masterful Web site. Once again, do what you do well and leave the rest to the experts! This professional can help you find a Web host (a place for your site to live).

Building the site

As you observe different Web sites, you'll notice a lot of things you will and won't like. Even though you'll be working with Web professionals – and I strongly recommend that you do – you should be aware of certain key issues:

- ✔ **Downloading time.** Consider keeping your images to128KB so that people can download your Web site in a timely fashion regardless of the speed of their connections. If your site takes too long to download, people won't bother.

- ✔ **Consistency.** Provide a consistent look and feel from one screen to the next. For example, maintain consistency with color schemes, fonts, and placement of buttons.

- ✔ **Navigation support.** Good navigation lets users know where they are and where they can go. Popular buttons are Home, Next Screen, About the Company, About our Products, and others. Check out your favorite Web sites. Chances are they have great navigation tools, and you may be able to implement some of their ideas in your own site.

- ✔ **Visual impact.** You don't want your Web site to look like Times Square on New Year's Eve. Avoid elements that move incessantly such as marquees, running animations, and dancing babies.

- ✔ **Items of interest.** No surfer goes into the ocean when there's no action. And no Web surfer goes to a site where there's no action. One way to generate action is to offer links to other sites of interest (articles, events, and more).

After the site is complete

After your site is ready to go, you're still not out of the woods:

- ✔ **Have a novice computer user test your Web site.** Have a novice go through your site to make sure it's intuitive, even to an inexperienced user.

- ✔ **Try your Web site out using a variety of browsers.** Test your Web site on all the popular browsers. What displays well on one browser may not display well on another.

✔ **Keep your site current.** Keep your Web site current with timely information such as weekly or monthly tips. And, remove any obsolete information.

Get the word out! Make sure everyone knows about your Web site. Put it on your letterhead and business cards. And don't forget to mention the URL on the outbound message of your answering machine.

It's risky to put all your eggs in one basket. Think of the Web as just one tool in your marketing and sales arsenal. A Web site doesn't replace other forms of advertising or marketing – it enhances them.

Keeping the IRS at Bay

Uncle Sam is quite strict about what you can and can't deduct, so it's important to consult an accountant. Following is what it takes to qualify for a home-office deduction:

✔ **You use the space exclusively and regularly for doing business.** Regularly doesn't mean having a photo lab in your basement and using it occasionally to develop photos you place in your brochures. But it may relate to a seasonal business, such as selling plant seeds from home in the spring and summer.

✔ **The space must be your principal place of business and/or place to meet clients.** If the space isn't your principal place of business but is a place to meet clients, you may still quality. For example, a management consultant or psychotherapist may have an office outside the home, yet see clients in the home.

✔ **The space can be part of your house or a separate structure.** Your home office doesn't need to be a separate room, but it must be a clearly definable space where only business-related activities takes place. (The corner of your kitchen table doesn't count.) If you have an office or studio over a detached garage, that portion of your living space may qualify for your home-office deduction.

You can't deduct your home-based business if you show a loss or if the home office creates a loss. You can, however, carry these figures over to the next calendar year. Also, if you telecommute and your employer provides you with an office, you can't deduct your home office.

If you meet the qualifications for a home office, tally the percentage of space it takes up. For example, if your home is 2,500 square feet and your home office is 250 square feet, you're entitled to deduct 10 percent of your rent or mortgage interest, utilities, maintenance, real estate taxes, and insurance. On the down side of these deductions, your home-office deduction reduces your capital gain when you sell your house. Here are other expenses you may deduct:

✔ **Business-related car expenses.** Keep accurate records of your odometer reading when you leave home for business and return home. You can take a mileage deduction which varies from year to year. Also, keep all receipts for tolls and parking.

✔ **All purchases for your office.** You can deduct hardware, software, furniture, file cabinets, stationery products, postage, and more.

✔ **Miscellaneous expenses.** Dues for professional associations, professional magazines and newsletters, tax preparation, legal counsel, job-related educational courses, and more fall into this category of deductions.

Keep in mind that your home office may have tax ramifications when you sell your residence. Also, a home office raises a red flag with the IRS, so be careful with your claims. Keep all receipts.

To find out about tax laws for home businesses, check with your accountant. Or call 800-TAXFORM and request the most recent publication of tax changes. You may also visit the IRS Web site at `www.irs.ustreas.gov`.

When you're self-employed, you pay to the state and federal governments quarterly estimated taxes based on the previous year's earnings. Your accountant can help you figure the amount to pay each quarter.

A Little Insurance Goes a Long Way

Look into several types of insurance for your business. Check with an insurance agent, someone in an industry-related organization, or a colleague to find out what you need and how much to carry. Following are some insurance policies to consider:

✔ **Professional liability (malpractice).** If there's the slightest chance that a professional error may ignite a lawsuit, carry professional liability insurance. For example, if you work on a client's computer and accidentally crash the system, he may sue the pants off you. Insurance will protect you against losing your pants.

✔ **Equipment and property.** Be certain your office equipment is insured for full replacement value. For example, if your office catches fire, you want to collect enough money to buy new equipment. Check out Chapter 3 for ways to protect your valuable data.

✔ **Health.** If your spouse has health insurance, you can save lots of money. If you're not in the position to take advantage of a spouse's insurance, you still need to have health insurance. Look into group policies through professional organizations for reasonable rates.

✔ **Disability.** No one knows when an accident may strike, rendering you unable to earn a living. If you can't support yourself and your family for a prolonged period of time, consider long-term disability insurance.

✔ **Life.** When you have a family that depends on your income, it's wise to carry some sort of life insurance.

✔ **Workers' Compensation**. This compensates you for work-related injuries. Workers' Compensation may be mandated by your state if you hire people to work for you.

✔ **Small business.** This provides coverage for your inventory and equipment. Check with your insurance agent about adding a rider to your homeowner's policy or taking out a separate policy.

Planning for the Golden Years

No matter how much you enjoy working at home, there comes a time when you want to pack it in. You don't have a 401(k) plan that you and your employer contribute to, so it's up to you to ensure that your golden years aren't tarnished. Two popular options available to self-employed people are Simplified Employee Pensions (SEPs) and Keogh plans.

Setting up a SEP

A SEP (also called SEP-IRA) is a plan designed to provide employers with a simplified means of making retirement contributions for themselves and their employees. SEPs are a great option for self-employed people because they allow you to put away 13.5 percent of untaxed money. (That percentage may be subject to change.)

You can open a SEP or contribute to an existing one by April 15 of the calendar year following the one for which you file. For example, when you file your 2001 return, you have until April 15, 2002 to make your contribution.

Crafting a Keogh

A Keogh plan is also for the self-employed or people who work for unincorporated companies. A Keogh can be a profit-sharing plan, a money purchase plan, or a combination of both. With a money purchase plan, the employer can generally contribute as much as 25 percent of each employee's salary annually (up to a maximum of $30,000) — but the employer must set aside a constant percentage each year. With a profit-sharing plan, the employer can generally put away 15 percent of its employees' salaries annually (up to a maximum of $30,000) with the option of varying contributions each year.

You must open a Keogh by December 31 of the current calendar year. Also, Keogh plans are more complex than SEPs and have more reporting requirements. Discuss with your accountant what's appropriate for you.

Expand Your Sphere of Contacts

One of the downsides to working at home can be isolation. You listen to the drip, drip, drip of the faucet rather than the gossip, gossip, gossip at the watercooler. You often wait breathlessly for the doorbell to ring so you can drum up a conversation with the FedEx or UPS driver.

Although there's no one-size-fits-all way to stay connected to the outside world any more than there's a one-size-fits-all swimsuit to fit you and your best friend, following are several ways to work in the comfort of your own home and not suffer from loneliness. (Check out Chapter 12 for ways to network effectively.)

Join a Professional Association

Just about every profession has an association. For example, there's the American Medical Association (AMA), American Independent Architects (AIA), American Bar Association (ABA), American Society for Personnel Administrators (ASPA), and so forth. Although you often compete with these folks for the same market share, it's an opportunity to exchange ideas and share opportunities. Colleagues offer positive reinforcement by reacting to your ideas and questioning your judgment. When you defend your ideas, it brings a synergy into your decision-making process.

If you don't know of an association for your profession, go to your local library and check out the *National Trade and Professional Associations* or *Gale's Encyclopedia of Associations*.

Become active in a service club

Groups such as Rotary, Kiwanis, Lions, and others serve their local communities and provide an opportunity to get to know lots of movers and shakers in your area.

Join a professional networking group

There are several major networking groups to consider joining. Some offer professional exclusivity because once you're voted in you have no competition. For example, if you're a pharmacist, you'll be the only pharmacist in the group. If you're a real estate attorney, you'll be the only real estate attorney in the group. Therefore, the entire group is your sales force helping to grow your business (and you theirs).

The strength of these groups is that word of mouth is the best way to get business. Check out *The World's Best Known Marketing Secret*, by Ivan R. Misner, Ph.D. and Virginia Devine to master the art of word-of-mouth marketing. Following are some professional networking groups worth considering:

- ✔ **Business Network International (BNI)**, 199 South Monte Vista, Suite 6, San Dimas, CA 91773, 800-489-4264, www.bni.com.

- ✔ **LeTip, International**, 4901 Morena Boulevard, Suite 703, San Diego, CA 92117, 800-255-3847, at www.letip.org.

- ✔ **LEADS**, Box 279, Carlsbad, CA, 800-783-3761, www.leadsclub.com.

The key to meeting people and networking effectively isn't merely to join a group, it's to get involved. Unless you're a mime, you must walk the walk and talk the talk.

No matter what groups you belong to, never overlook the value of your local Chamber of Commerce. It provides countless opportunities to make contacts and get involved in your professional community. Find the one nearest you in the Business Section of your telephone book.

Stay connected through technology

Although technology doesn't take the place of face-to-face contact, it does bridge the gap for many virtual workers. For people who rarely meet with clients, the fax, phone, and e-mail serve as a lifeline. Also, consider professional online chat groups where you can share ideas with other professionals.

Create your own infrastructure

One of the biggest pluses to working from home is setting your own hours. But you need a tremendous amount of discipline to avoid falling into bad habits. Remember the old adage about all work and no play. Set aside time

---

For ladies only

Women's business organizations may be the answer to the "good old boy network." They offer a place for women to share opportunities with other women. A great networking opportunity is the National Association for Women Business Owners (NAWBO). For more information, contact NAWBO at 1100 Wayne Avenue, Ste. 830, Silver Spring, MD, 301-608-2590, www.nawbo.org. For other women's networks in your community, speak with professional women.

---

each day to do something away from your office so you rejuvenate yourself for the rest of the day. You can meet a friend or colleague for lunch, take an exercise class, go for a walk, visit the library, or simply run an errand.

Although you work at home, you're not alone. Here are a few Web sites to check out:

✔ www.gohome.com (Business@Home)

✔ www.smallbusiness.yahoo.com (Yahoo's Small Business section)

✔ www.entreworld.com (*EntreWorld*)

✔ www.startupwsj.com (*The Wall Street Journal's* Startup area)

Success doesn't happen as soon as you hang out your shingle. If you make it past the thirteenth month, you'll probably make it.

Divine wisdom

If you ever get discouraged that your success rate isn't as great as you wish, take a look at Robert Fulghum's book *All I Really Need to Know I Learned in Kindergarten* (Random House). Fulghum talks about a man who failed half the time and visited his rabbi to get guidance. The wise old rabbi suggested that the man go to the library and turn to page 930 of *The New York Times Almanac* for 1970. The man found that it listed the lifetime batting averages of the great baseball players.

It was sobering for the depressed man to learn that Ty Cobb (one of the all time greats) had a lifetime average of only .367. Cobb struck out two out of every three times. Babe Ruth didn't even do that well. Doesn't that put things into perspective?

What's Hot on the CD-ROM

Here's what you can find on the CD-ROM:

- 6-1: What to Do Before You Leave Your Current Job
- 6-2: Do What You Love
- 6-3: Selecting a Name
- 6-4: Deciding Whether to Incorporate
- 6-5: What You Need to Get Your Home Business Started
- 6-6: Leading a Balanced Work and Home Life
- 6-7: The Web Site
- 6-8: Keeping the IRS at Bay
- 6-9: Buying Insurance
- 6-10: Saving for Retirement
- 6-11: Expanding Your Sphere of Contacts

Chapter 7

Oh, My Aching Back

• •

In This Chapter

▶ Looking at ergonomics and its effect on your health and well-being

▶ Selecting ergonomically sound furniture

▶ Choosing technology

▶ Exercising to relax and relieve tension

• •

Those who think they do not have time for bodily exercise will sooner or later have to find time for illness.

— Edward Stanley, Earl of Derby

The Occupational Safety and Health Administration (OSHA) estimates that musculoskeletal disorders (MSD) account for more than a third of all occupational injuries. MSD includes carpal tunnel syndrome, tendinitis, sciatica, and muscular problems in the back, neck, wrist, and shoulders. The cost to employers for these desk-bound workers is estimated to be between $15 to $20 billion annually just in worker's compensation payouts. That doesn't include the cost of lost workdays, which is estimated to be in the tens of millions.

Run the numbers and you find that it costs much less to keep employees fit than it costs to pay for absenteeism due to job-related ailments. Without healthy and productive employees, you don't have a healthy and productive business.

That's why employers spend billions of dollars each year to keep employees fit. Savvy employers have onsite activities or insurance-funded benefits that may include fitness centers, cafeterias with healthy choices, smoking cessation classes, weight loss classes, onsite massages, stress management classes, and a host of other activities to encourage fitness and reduce stress.

The Office Environment and the Running Shoe

Let's look at the effects of the office environment as though it were athletic shoes. If an athlete's shoes are the wrong size or the shoes aren't what's required for the activity, the athlete's performance is inhibited and she may suffer from injuries. Over the short term, she suffers from minor aches and pains. Ice packs and over-the-counter treatments probably suffice. Over the long term, however, she suffers from permanent foot damage.

In other words, you won't win the Boston marathon running in golf shoes that are two sizes too small, and you won't attain top performance at the office using office furniture and equipment that's poorly designed or not appropriate for you. Poorly designed or poorly fitted office furniture may cause you to suffer from the new social diseases: MSD or *repetitive action injuries* (also called cumulative trauma disorder).

Ergonomics is the science that coordinates the arrangement of office equipment, systems, and physical working conditions with the capacities and requirements of the worker. Its goal is to optimize the needs of the worker and the organization to bring about a healthy and productive workplace. When ergonomic needs aren't met, it's a lose-lose situation for the employer and employee. Here's why:

- ✔ Employees suffer from pain and discomfort.
- ✔ Productivity decreases.
- ✔ Absenteeism increases.
- ✔ Work doesn't get done.
- ✔ Insurance pay-outs and premiums skyrocket.
- ✔ Company profits decrease.

Furniture Built for Comfort

Your first line of defense is ergonomically sound furniture. Don't surrender to your first impulse and buy inexpensive furniture. Although you may suffer mental anguish from picking the wrong hardware or software, your body suffers physical anguish when you select the wrong furniture. Properly designed furniture means a healthier and more productive work force.

Ergonomics isn't a new concept; it's just a new term. Hundreds of years ago Thomas Jefferson had the vision to apply ergonomic principles to selecting his own office furniture. Jefferson ordered special chairs and tables to accommodate his lofty height of 6 feet, 2½ inches. He had a whirligig (swivel) chair equipped with candle sconces in the armrests. He also had a backless Windsor chair that he could slip under his writing table so he could stretch his long legs comfortably in front of him.

Choosing the ideal chair

When you sit — even when you sit correctly — you place pressure on your invertebral discs, which are the shock absorbers of the lumbar spine. That's because sitting puts the weight of your upper body on your lower back, increasing the pressure on the invertebral discs. (When you stand, you distribute your weight through your lower back, pelvis, legs, and feet.)

Optimum sitting angles are 90 degrees for your legs and hips, 90 degrees for your hips and torso, and 90 degrees for your arms.

Look for flexibility and adjustability

A flexible and well-adjusted chair fits 95 percent of the population. (The other 5 percent may need a custom-fitted chair.) Here are some things to check out in a chair:

- **Armrest.** Make sure you can adjust the armrests for your height or remove them if you wish to. You're better off without armrests than with armrests that aren't right for you.

- **Backrest.** Make sure the backrest is adjustable so you can secure your lower back. If you need a lumbar pillow, the backrest isn't right for you.

- **Height.** Adjust the height of the chair so your hips are slightly higher than your knees. If the height adjustment causes your feet to dangle, get a foot rest.

- **Seat cushion.** The cushion should accommodate your hips and butt without being too snug.

- **Seat pan.** The edge of the seat should be fairly flat with a slight contour. The depth of the seat pan should have an adjustment of about four inches and should tilt back and forth.

- **Support base**. The chair should have a five-point (star) base for support and balance. Casters should be interchangeable so you have mobility and stability on carpets or hard surface.

- **Tilt.** If you have a tilt function on your chair, be sure you don't tilt backward while working at your computer. Tilting your chair backward causes you to drop your head forward and puts undue strain on your neck.

Avoiding auto aches

Here are a few ways to keep fit when taking long car trips:

✔ **Get out and stretch.** Get out of the car at least every 1½ hours to stretch your legs. Do something as simple as pressing your arms against the car and stretching the back of your legs. Or just walk around at a rest stop.

✔ **Pedal with ease.** Sit close enough to the steering wheel so you don't have to extend your foot too far to reach the pedals.

✔ **Sit away from the air bag.** Sit at least 10 to 12 inches from the wheel so you give the air bag ample room to open in an emergency. If you're a passenger, keep your legs on the floor in case the bag needs to inflate. If you have your legs crossed and the airbag inflates, your knee may wind up in your teeth.

✔ **Avoid "stuffed wallet" syndrome.** Remove your wallet from your back pocket and put it in your vest pocket, briefcase, or someplace else. When you sit on your wallet, you throw your back out of alignment and induce back pain.

✔ **Use a lumbar pillow.** If you tend to suffer from back pain (regardless of where your wallet is stashed), get a lumbar pillow to support the lower portion of your back. These pillows cost about $10 to $20.

Never buy a chair from a catalog unless you try out the chair beforehand. Make your evaluation in person. Know your needs and try out several models before you make a decision. Some vendors let you bring a chair to your office to try it for a week or two.

Get a footrest

For added comfort and circulation, try using a footrest. By elevating your feet, you lessen lower back strain and improve the circulation throughout your body. When you use a footstool, your body also has added flexibility between your chair and desk.

Desktop comfort

The work surface for the average person is between 26 and 29 inches from the floor. You'll be most comfortable when the work surface is slightly above elbow height so you can rest your arms on the surface without leaning too far forward. Use an adjustable shelf for the keyboard to lessen the strain on your forearm.

Check out www.officeclick.com for a wide array of office products — everything from office furniture to paper supplies. The site also features stories and tips for succeeding in business.

Computers and More

Everyone's needs differ when it comes to selecting and using computer equipment. You can best determine how to set up your work area to suit your needs and protect against repetitive action injuries. Here are a few suggestions:

- ✔ Always be sure you have ample room to work efficiently.
- ✔ Place supplies so they don't interfere with your movements.
- ✔ Be sure to arrange your work area to face the monitor and keyboard so you don't twist your body.

Adjusting the monitor

Headaches and eyestrain result from being too near or too far from the monitor. Set your monitor directly in front of you — about 18 inches from your eyes. Position the monitor so your eyes are level with the top of the screen.

- ✔ Position the screen at right angles to bright light sources.
- ✔ Face the monitor away from a window.
- ✔ Adjust the brightness and contrast.
- ✔ Try tilting the monitor.
- ✔ Buy an anti-glare filter that attaches to the screen.

In the blink of an eye

When many of us think of CVS, we think of a pharmacy where we purchase prescription drugs, dental floss, and Reese's Peanut Butter Cups. However, CVS is also a physical malady that stands for *computer vision syndrome.* Anyone who spends as little as two to three hours a day in front of a computer screen may develop CVS. Symptoms can include headaches, eye redness, and difficulty focusing, as well as back, shoulder, and neck pain.

CVS occurs because people's eyes become fixated on the screen and they don't blink regularly.

Screens are comprised of pixels (tiny dots) that cause your eyes to continually focus and refocus in order to keep the image sharp. When you don't blink regularly, your eyes dry out. CVS is a temporary condition and is helped by short breaks and eyedrops.

Better yet, avoid CVS. Every 20 to 30 minutes rest your eyes by looking away from the computer for several minutes. And be conscious of blinking when you're looking at the screen.

If you use a copy stand, place it at the same height and distance from your eyes as the monitor so the text is about eye level.

Don't wear bifocals when you work at the computer. They cause you to look up constantly and cause eye strain. Get a regular pair of glasses for working at the computer; even those bought over the counter work well.

Mousing around

People who use a mouse may experience finger, wrist, arm, and shoulder problems. If you choose a mouse with a design that's comfortable and use it properly, it will go a long way in avoiding or reducing these problems.

Choosing a design

Visit a local computer store and notice how many mouse designs you find. Try different models and pay attention to the following:

- ✔ **Size.** Make sure the mouse fits into your hand and your fingers curl comfortably around it.

- ✔ **Shape.** Keep your wrist at the same level as your hand. Find a mouse that doesn't require you to place the heel of your hand on the desktop.

- ✔ **Buttons.** Buttons shouldn't be too cramped or too spread out. The buttons should be easy to click without much pressure.

Using the mouse properly

One way to reduce finger, wrist, arm, and shoulder problems is to place the mouse as close to the side of the keyboard as you can. Make sure you have enough surface room to vary the position of your arm.

- ✔ **Don't squeeze.** Hold the mouse loosely in your hand and relax your grip.

- ✔ **Keep your wrist straight.** Keep your forearm, wrist, and fingers in a straight line. If you wrist falls below your hand, get an ergonomic mouse pad.

- ✔ **Adjust the speed setting.** Adjust the speed of the mouse clicks so that they're comfortable for you. (Check your user manual or help screen for speed adjustments.)

Explore other options

If you follow these suggestions and still suffer from finger, wrist, arm, and shoulder problems, consider keystroke combinations as shortcuts to cut down on using your mouse. You find keystroke combinations on the drop-down menus and in your user manual. For example, in Microsoft Windows, *Save* is Control+S and *Print* is Control+P.

Another option is the trackball, which is slightly smaller than a billiard ball. Because the hardware itself is stationary and you only move the ball, this device takes up very little desk space. You control the trackball with your fingertips and get a very smooth cursor movement.

Keyboarding with safety

The proper height and position of the keyboard are essential to avoid wrist problems, such as *carpal tunnel syndrome* (the compression of a nerve leading into the wrist that results in debilitating pain and muscle weakness) and *tendinitis* (the inflammation of the ropey part of the muscles as they insert into the bones of the shoulders, arms, and wrists).

Your best defense against these injuries is a natural, relaxed position. Place your forearms at a 90-degree angle to your arms. (If your forearms aren't in the proper position, you may need to adjust the armrest on your chair or the height of your keyboard.) Curve your fingers and place them as close to the keys as possible.

For greater comfort, get a keyboard tray that tilts slightly away from you and has a place for your mouse.

If a furniture manufacturer claims that his furniture will unequivocally prevent or cure repetitive action injuries, run for the hills. If you want to pull her chain, you may ask for scientific studies that validate the claim. Then watch *her* run for the hills. Visit your local computer store to see some of the devices that help protect against these injuries. There are wrist rests, split keyboards, and a host of other gizmos.

Don't Be a Couch (Chair) Potato

The human body wasn't designed for sitting; it was designed for moving. If you sit for prolonged periods of time, you force your muscles into a fixed position, causing fatigue and stiffness. Prolonged seating reduces the blood circulation in your legs and feet, which may cause discomfort or swelling. Prolonged sitting also stresses areas such as the hips, chest, back, and neck. And studies continually show that lack of movement increases your risk of cardiovascular disease and decreases life expectancy.

When you have ergonomically sound office furniture and add a little exercise to the mix, you may end office aches, pains, and fatigue. Why suffer needlessly?

Take five

Try to get away from your desk for a few minutes every hour. Mini-breaks and short walks may be more beneficial than longer, infrequent breaks. Walking helps the body relax and decreases anxiety. Even a short walk releases beta-endorphins, the body's natural relaxants.

Try to laugh regularly — whether it's a tiny giggle or a belly-busting whoop laugh. Laughter also releases beta-endorphins and gets rid of stress.

Listen to your body talk

Whenever you feel any discomfort or fatigue while sitting, it's your body's way of telling you something. The following sections provide descriptions of exercises you can do right at your desk as often as you like.

Take deep breaths

Breathing deeply is one of the keys to good health. In addition to affecting all sorts of body functions from the nervous system to circulation to digestion, deep breathing relieves stress.

1. Concentrate on your breathing.
2. Take five to ten long breaths, inhaling through your nose and exhaling through your mouth.

Relax your eyes

At least once every hour look away from the monitor and focus on an object 15 to 20 feet away from you. Here's a wonderful exercise for relaxing your eyes:

1. Rub your hands together briskly until your palms feel warm.
2. Make shallow cups and gently place your palms over your eyes. Without pressing on your eyes, make sure no light enters.
3. Hold your palms over your eyes for at least 30 seconds.
4. For a little variety, while your eyes are covered, roll both eyeballs to the left and back to the middle. Do this five times.
5. Then do the same thing rolling both eyeballs to the right and back to the middle.

Stretch your hands and wrists

Stretch your arms out to your sides and over your head every 15 to 30 minutes. Then work on the lower extremities.

1. Massage your hands and wrists to improve circulation.

2. Massage the spaces between your fingers and the areas around your nails.

3. Flex your fingers and do wrist stretches.

Relieve neck tension

Do this exercise while breathing deeply. Hold each step for three deep breaths.

1. Tilt your head toward your left shoulder, then toward your right shoulder.

2. With your head in a forward position, drop your chin to your chest and raise it back slightly.

3. As a variation, keep your head upright. Look over your left shoulder several times, then over your right shoulder several times.

If you use the telephone a lot, you'll save your neck a great deal of stress if you use a speakerphone or headset.

Relieve tension in your back and arms

Many people hold tension in their necks, creating additional tension in their arms and backs. Here are a few exercises to avoid these tensions:

1. Hold your right elbow with your left hand.

2. Gently push the elbow forward toward your left shoulder.

3. Hold the stretch for five seconds.

4. Repeat this exercise with the left elbow.

Get a great power stretch

Here's a power stretch you can do right in your chair. You'll be amazed at how good it feels.

1. Stretch your arms up and over your head.

2. Straighten your legs and lift your feet off the ground.

3. Arch your back and feel your muscles stretch.

4. Close your eyes and take three deep, relaxing breaths.

Exercises (even simple ones) are designed for people in reasonably good condition. If you experience pain or discomfort doing any of these exercises, *stop immediately and check with your doctor.*

What's Hot on the CD-ROM

Here's what's available on the CD-ROM:

- 7-1: Ergonomics and the Human Factor
- 7-2: Choosing the Ideal Chair
- 7-3: Avoiding Aches and Pains When Spending Too Much Time in Your Car
- 7-4: Desktop Comfort
- 7-5: Adjusting Your Computer Monitor
- 7-6: Mousing Around
- 7-7: Keyboarding with Safety
- 7-8: Exercises for Keeping Limber and Relieving Tension

Part III
Streamlining the Paper Trail

In this part . . .

No matter how much we hear about the paperless office, the concept is as real as the paperless bathroom. Papers are a fact of life and will never disappear.

Papers lurk everywhere — in halls, outside cubicles, in empty cubicles, and anywhere people can find an inch of space. This part abounds with survival tips to writing letters and memos, understanding mailing options, and cleaning up your infobog.

Chapter 8

Anatomy of a Letter

· ·

In This Chapter

▶ Letter parts and where they go

▶ What's hot and what's not in letter styles

▶ Multi-page letters

▶ Magical merging

▶ Memorable memos

· ·

All things begin in order, so shall they end, and so shall they begin again.

— Sir Thomas Browne, English physician and author

There's a natural order of everything in the universe. We crawl before we walk; we learn our ABCs before we read text; we get an education before we enter the workforce. The same holds true for letters — letters have a natural order of things.

Putting the Parts Together

Just as doctors must know and understand all the parts of the body, business writers must know and understand all the parts of a letter. The following sections list and describe the letter parts from head to toe. At the end of this section, Example 8-1 shows all the parts of a letter and where they're placed. It's unlikely that you'll ever use all the parts in any one letter — this is just to show you where to put what you use.

Date

Write the date with arabic numerals with no abbreviations, such as the following:

March 15, XXXX

15 March, XXXX (military or European usage)

Mailing or in-house notations

Place the mailing notations (special delivery, certified mail, registered mail, air mail, by messenger) or in-house notations (personal, confidential) two lines below the date – in all caps, as you see below:

PERSONAL

CERTIFIED MAIL, RETURN RECEIPT REQUESTED

Inside address

Start the inside address four lines below the date. (If you use a mailing or in-house notation, place the inside address two lines below the notation.) The inside address includes any or all of the following: addressee; addressee's title; company name; street address; and city, state, and ZIP code.

Here are a couple of options:

Ms. Lynne Schwartz, President
Michael & Associates
203 Monsey Avenue
Spring Valley, NY 10977

Ms. Lynne Schwartz
President
Michael & Associates
203 Monsey Avenue
Spring Valley, NY 10977

Whether you type the addressee's title on the same line as the name or on the following line depends on the length of the line. Try to square the address as much as possible.

> ✔ If the title appears on the same line, place a comma between the name and title, as you see in the first example.
>
> ✔ If it appears on the next line, dispense with the comma, as you see in the second example.

Mail is delivered to the address element on the line above the city, state, and ZIP. If you want the letter delivered to a post office box, place the P.O. Box number underneath (or instead of) the street address, like the following:

607 Codger Lane
P. O. Box 7344
Austin, TX 78959-7344

Postal abbreviations

The post office suggests that you use the two-letter state abbreviation. For those abbreviations you use frequently, try to think of some association to jog your memory. For example, the eight "M" states may be confusing. I live in Massachusetts (MA), so it's natural for my sons to remember "Ma." One of my sons lives in Maryland (MD). He's a doctor, so "MD" jogs my memory. Following is a list of the abbreviations in the United States and its territories:

Alabama	AL		Idaho	ID
Alaska	AK		Illinois	IL
Arizona	AZ		Indiana	IN
Arkansas	AR		Iowa	IA
California	CA		Kansas	KS
Canal Zone	CZ		Kentucky	KY
Colorado	CO		Louisiana	LA
Connecticut	CT		Maine	ME
Delaware	DE		Maryland	MD
District of Columbia	DC		Massachusetts	MA
Florida	FL		Michigan	MI
Georgia	GA		Minnesota	MN
Guam	GU		Mississippi	MS
Hawaii	HI		Missouri	MO

(continued)

(continued)

Montana	MT	Rhode Island	RI
Nebraska	NE	South Carolina	SC
Nevada	NV	South Dakota	SD
New Hampshire	NH	Tennessee	TN
New Jersey	NJ	Texas	TX
New Mexico	NM	Utah	UT
New York	NY	Vermont	VT
North Carolina	NC	Virgin Islands	VI
North Dakota	ND	Virginia	VA
Ohio	OH	Washington	WA
Oklahoma	OK	West Virginia	WV
Oregon	OR	Wisconsin	WI
Pennsylvania	PA	Wyoming	WY
Puerto Rico	PR		

Attention line

Use an attention line when you write directly to a company and want the letter directed to a person and/or department. For example, you may consider using an attention line when you want the letter handled by someone other than the addressee, if he isn't available. The following are a few styles:

- ✔ ATTENTION SHERRIL MORSE
- ✔ Attention Personnel Manager
- ✔ Attention: Accounting Department

Here are two ways to deal with the attention line:

Besen Brothers
4 Marric Court
Peru, OH 44847

Attention: Laurence Alan

Besen Brothers
ATTENTION LAURENCE ALAN
4 Marric Court
Peru, OH 44847

Salutation

The salutation is a greeting — a way of saying "hello" to the reader. Place it two lines below the address. The salutation should correspond directly to the first line of the inside address, as you can see in Table 8-1. (You should also use a salutation when you write an e-mail message.)

Table 8-1	Salutations
Inside Address	*Salutation*
Mr. Elijahu Zimmerman	Dear Mr. Zimmerman: Dear Elijahu: (informal)*
Ms. Leah Zimmerman	Dear Ms. Zimmerman: Dear Leah: (informal)*
Mr. and Mrs. Elijahu Zimmerman	Dear Mr. and Mrs. Zimmerman: Dear Leah and Elijahu: (informal)*
Messrs. Robert Lajoie and Ken Levine	Dear Messrs. Lajoie and Levine: Dear Bob and Ken: (informal)*
Mmes. Sheila Franceschi and Sue Colton	Dear Mmes. Franceschi and Colton: Dear Sheila and Sue: (informal)*
The Comptroller**	Dear Sir or Madam:
A & D Corporation**	Ladies and Gentlemen:

* Use first names only if you're on a first-name basis.

** Try to find the name of the person you're writing to. You can often do it by calling the company and talking to the receptionist.

Never use "To Whom This May Concern" as a salutation; it's cold and impersonal.

Subject line

The subject line is part of the letter, not the heading. Place it two lines below the salutation — not between the inside address and salutation. Its purpose is to direct the reader to the theme of the letter. For more information about crafting a compelling subject line, check out Chapter 9. You can use the word *Subject:* or *Re:* (for reference).

Re: Special rebate if you act before 10/20/XX

Subject: Year-End Sales Results — 10 percent increase

Body (The message)

Single space the body of the letter and double space between paragraphs. Here are some suggestions for breaking down the body of a typical three-paragraph letter:

- ✔ **Make the opening paragraph relatively short.** Its purpose is to introduce the reason for the letter.

  Thank you for your letter of July 16 calling our attention to our mistake in filling your order.

  or

  Our research staff has successfully solved the problem of insulating older homes about which you inquired in your letter of May 10.

- ✔ **Support the opening paragraph with one or more supporting paragraphs.**

  In its annual report, the XYZ Fire Insurance Company stated that our community has suffered the least fire damage of any district in the state. Of course, this means that your valuables are safer than those of your distant neighbors. But more important is the fact that your family is well protected from the dangers of ravaging fire.

- ✔ **Make the *final paragraph* short. It serves as a summation, request, suggestion, or look to the future.**

  The enclosed brochure should answer your questions. If you need more information, please let us know.

  or

  If you'd like to take advantage of this order, please sign the enclosed form and return it to me in the enclosed envelope.

Complimentary closing

Place the complimentary closing two lines below the last line of the body. Capitalize only the first letter of the first word.

- ✔ **Formal:** Yours truly, Very truly yours, Yours very truly, Respectfully, Respectfully yours,

- ✔ **Informal:** Sincerely, Sincerely yours, Cordially, Cordially yours,

- ✔ **Personal:** Best wishes, As always, Regards, Kindest regards,

Signature line

You can prepare the personal signatures in any of the following ways. Don't forget to sign the letter; it's amazing how many people forget.

Very truly yours,

John Hancock

John Hancock, President

Very truly yours,

ABC Corporation

John Hancock

John Hancock, President

Reference initials

Use reference initials to identify the typist, if someone other than the writer is keyboarding the letter. Place the initials at the left margin, two lines below the signature line. You can use any of the following styles. (The typist's initials in the following examples are *lz*.)

PSmith/lz

PS/LZ

PS:lz

lz

When you type your own letter, don't use any reference initials.

Enclosure notation

When you enclose anything in the envelope, include an enclosure notation. Place the enclosure notation on the line directly below the reference initials. Consider any of the following styles:

Enclosure

1 Enc.

Enc.

Attachments: 2

Encls.

Enc. (2)

1 Attachment

Enclosure: 1. Purchase Order No. 3434; 2. Check No. 567

When you attach something rather than enclose it, you may using consider the word *Attachment* instead of *Enclosure.*

Copy notation

When you send a copy of the letter to a third person, make a notation directly below the enclosure notation (or reference initials). The cc notation is a holdover from the dark ages when people made carbon copies. Another option is *pc* for photocopy. If you don't want the addressee to know you're sending a copy to a third party, use *bc* for blind copy.

Use the bc notation sparingly because it's a clear indication you're going behind someone's back. (The stock market won't crash. Governments won't fall. And the world won't shake. But you may be pretty embarrassed.) Place the bc notation on the *office copy and third-party copy only,* otherwise it's no secret from the addressee. You can use any of these styles:

pc: Alex Stark

bc: Alex Stark

CC Alex Stark

Copy to: Alex Stark

Postscript

It's appropriate — and often advisable — to use a postscript for emphasis. This is a great way (especially in a sales letter) to call attention to an important message you want to leave with your reader. For extra emphasis, type the postscript in a different font or handwrite it. Place the postscript two lines below your last notation. You may include the initials P.S. or leave them out.

P.S. Participants of my workshop typically tell me that as a result of the workshop they cut their writing time by 30 to 50 percent!

Use postscripts sparingly and strategically because you don't want the words to appear as an afterthought that suggest a lack of organization.

SHERYL SAYS

If you want to generate letters with sizzle and style, check out my other *For Dummies* book, *Writing Business Letters For Dummies* (IDG Books Worldwide). It's chock full of letters for employment, sales, collection, and much more.

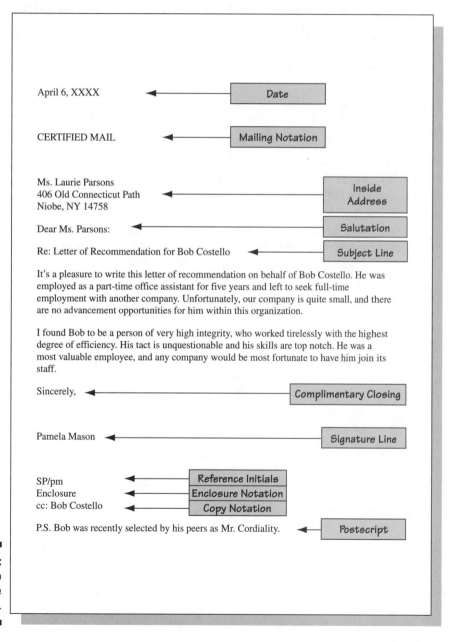

April 6, XXXX — Date

CERTIFIED MAIL — Mailing Notation

Ms. Laurie Parsons
406 Old Connecticut Path — Inside Address
Niobe, NY 14758

Dear Ms. Parsons: — Salutation

Re: Letter of Recommendation for Bob Costello — Subject Line

It's a pleasure to write this letter of recommendation on behalf of Bob Costello. He was employed as a part-time office assistant for five years and left to seek full-time employment with another company. Unfortunately, our company is quite small, and there are no advancement opportunities for him within this organization.

I found Bob to be a person of very high integrity, who worked tirelessly with the highest degree of efficiency. His tact is unquestionable and his skills are top notch. He was a most valuable employee, and any company would be most fortunate to have him join its staff.

Sincerely, — Complimentary Closing

Pamela Mason — Signature Line

SP/pm — Reference Initials
Enclosure — Enclosure Notation
cc: Bob Costello — Copy Notation

P.S. Bob was recently selected by his peers as Mr. Cordiality. — Postscript

Example 8-1:
Where to place all the letter parts.

What's Hot and What's Not in Letter Styles

Choosing a letter style is a big step in delivering your message because it may be an indication of how "fashionable" your company is. Regardless of the style you use, center the letter vertically and horizontally so the margins form an imaginary frame around the text. Table 8-2 shows you the four styles and what they represent:

Table 8-2	Four letter styles	
Letter Style	*Characteristics and Comments*	*Fashion Statement*
Full block (see Example 8-2)	Everything starts at the left margin.	Chic; right off the fashion runway. Efficient, business-like, and very popular.
Block or modified block (see Example 8-3)	The date and complimentary closing are slightly to the right of center. Everything else starts at the left margin. Involves setting one tab. Very traditional and very popular.	Sophisticated and always in good taste.
Semiblock (See Example 8-4)	Identical to block, except the first line of each paragraph is indented. Involves setting two tabs.	Slightly dated but still functional.
Simplified (See Example 8-5)	Salutation and complimentary closing are omitted. Everything else is in full block. Triple space above and below the body of the letter. Critics say it lacks warmth and is too unconventional.	Futuristic.

Letterhead

Date

Addressee
Street Address
City, State ZIP

Salutation:

Subject: Full Block Letter Style

Characteristics

The full block letter is quickly becoming the style of choice in the modern office. It's a very efficient style and is the easiest to prepare. Why? *Everything starts at the left margin.* You don't need to set tabs or wonder where to put the date and complimentary closing.

Benefits

We live in a fast-paced society and people are constantly trying to simplify their cluttered lives. This style will — over time — increase the flow of paperwork and save time.

Complimentary closing,

Name of Sender

Example 8-2:
Full block
style.

Letterhead

Date

Addressee
Street Address
City, State ZIP

Salutation:

Subject: Block or Modified Block

Characteristics

The block or modified block style is quite similar to the full block style. The key
differences are that the date and complimentary closing are slightly to the right of center.
Everything else is flush with the left margin.

Benefits

This letter style has traditionally been the most commonly used of all letter styles.
Therefore, it's the one most people are comfortable with.

Complimentary closing,

Name of Sender

Example 8-3:
Block or
modified
block.

Letterhead

Date

Addressee
Street Address
City, State ZIP

Salutation:

Subject: Semiblock Style

Characteristics

The semiblock style is quite similar to the block or modified block style. The key difference is that the paragraphs are indented one tab stop. Therefore, you need to use two tabs: one for the indented paragraphs and one for the date and complimentary closing.

Recognition

This is also a familiar-looking style and people are comfortable with it. It is, however, playing second fiddle to the block or modified block.

Complimentary closing,

Name of Sender

Example 8-4:
Semiblock
style.

Letterhead

Date

Addressee
Street Address
City, State ZIP

SUBJECT OF LETTER

Characteristics

The simplified letter is quite streamlined. Here are some characteristics to remember if you use this letter style:

- Eliminate the salutation and complimentary closing.

- Eliminate the Subject: or Re: notation. Just type the subject.

- Type the SUBJECT LINE and NAME OF SENDER in all caps.

Recognition

This letter style isn't commonly used. It is, however, expected to become more popular because it's the least time consuming of all the letter styles.

NAME OF SENDER

P.S. Please note that there are three line spaces above and below the subject line.

Example 8-5:
Simplified
style.

Multi-Page Letters

Never try to cram all your pearly words on one page if it means narrowing the margins, decreasing the font size, or compromising the visual impact in any way. There's nothing wrong with an occasional two-, three-, or four-page letter or memo when it's absolutely necessary. *Absolutely necessary* means you limit your letter to one topic and streamline the text as much as possible.

Here are some tips for multi-page letters:

- ✔ When a letter is longer than one page, use letterhead for the first page and *matching plain paper* for the rest of the pages.
- ✔ When you divide a paragraph between pages, leave at least two lines on the current page and carry at least two lines to the next page. If you can't do that, don't divide the paragraph.
- ✔ Never divide a three-line paragraph.
- ✔ Never carry a complimentary closing over to a second page without having at least two lines above it. You need the text for continuity.

The following are heading examples for the multi-page letters:

Full block second page:

> Ms. Myra Bushell
> Page 2
> October 2, XXXX

Modified block or semiblock block second page:

> Ms. Myra Bushell   Page 2   October 2, XXXX

Mail merge

Mail merge is one of the nifty things about word processing. It lets you create a letter once and send as many personalized copies as you want. Each copy will have an original name, address, salutation, and whatever else you designate. You can also create personalized envelopes.

Whether you're running a large-scale sales campaign, inviting people to a seminar, or doing a massive job search, mail merge can save you lots of time. Check the user manual of your word processing software for details.

Memorable Memos

Although e-mail messages have replaced many of the memos that were once the mainstay of the business community, memos are still alive and kicking in the business world. Memos are frequently used to transmit information, ideas, decisions, and suggestions among people in the same organization. What's the difference between letters and memos? Primarily, format.

If your company uses memos frequently, it probably has printed forms. If not, consider the styles in Example 8-6 and 8-7.

Before you send a memo, ask yourself if it's the best means of sending your message. Would it be more appropriate to send an e-mail message, post the message to your company's intranet, hold a face-to-face meeting, or make a phone call?

(Letterhead)

Date:

To:

From:

Subject:

_____

_____

Exmple 8-6:
Memo style
with
heading
aligned at
the left
margin.

(Letterhead)

Date:

To:

From:

Subject:

_____

_____

Example 8-7:
Memo style
with
heading
aligned at
the left
margin,
except the
date.

Signature or initials

In a memo, there's no designated space for your signature as there is in a letter. Anyone can send a memo and use someone else's name. Although this doesn't happen often, you may want to safeguard yourself. Write your initials or sign your name next to your name on the *From:* line or on the bottom of the memo. When people get used to seeing that, they'll know the memo is from you. If they get a memo that doesn't have your initials or signature, that will raise an eyebrow.

Proper protocol

On the *To:* line, type the names of all the people who will receive the memo. Each organization has its own protocol for the order in which to list the recipients. If you have an employee handbook, you may find protocol there. If not, here are a few tips:

- ✔ List people in order of ranking, from high to low. For example, the President's name would appear before the Vice President's.
- ✔ Who should receive a copy? Err on the side of copying everyone who may be offended if they're neglected.

Limit each memo to one subject only. If you need to cover two or more subjects, send two or more memos.

What's Hot on the CD-ROM

Here's what you can find on the CD-ROM:

- ✔ 8-1: Putting the Parts of a Letter Together
- ✔ 8-2: Letter Styles
- ✔ 8-3: Multi-Page Letters
- ✔ 8-4: Writing Memos

Chapter 9

The Great "Write" of Passage

In This Chapter

▶ Step 1: Getting started and getting rid of writer's block

▶ Step 2: Writing headlines and strategic sequencing

▶ Step 3: Writing the draft

▶ Step 4: Designing for visual impact

▶ Step 5: Honing the tone

▶ Step 6: Proofreading

Words are, of course, the most powerful drug used by mankind.

— Rudyard Kipling

*H*ave you ever considered that poor writing may be costing you big bucks in lost revenue?

- ✔ If the proposal you wrote doesn't land you the project you want, do you assume that it went to an insider or to someone with a lower bid?

- ✔ If the direct marketing letter you sent out doesn't yield the results you expect, do you blame it on a slumping market or on a list that wasn't targeted closely enough?

- ✔ If your collection letter doesn't get your bill paid, do you blame it on a deadbeat client?

- ✔ If your e-mail message doesn't get results, do you blame it on a lazy reader?

It's time to stop blaming outside influences for the revenue and opportunities you're losing. Take control of your writing so that you can affect your readers as you wish.

If William Shakespeare were alive today, do you think he'd sit in front of his computer and bang out *Hamlet, King Lear, Othello,* or any of his other classics? Of course not. No writer just sits down and writes. Every writer starts with a plan, and you should too. Following are the Six Steps to effective business writing:

1. Understand your audience, purpose, and key issues.

2. Create an outline, table of contents, headlines, or whatever makes sense.

3. Write a draft.

4. Use visuals to enhance the text.

5. Hone the tone so that it's appropriate for your readers.

6. Proofread, proofread, proofread!

Perhaps you don't consider yourself a writer because it's not your profession. However, you write letters, e-mail messages, proposals, reports, and presentations — so you are a writer! When you apply the preceding Six Step Process, you can become "The Bard" of dynamic and energized business writing. For a full discussion on how to energize your business writing, get a copy of the great Business Writing For Dummies, which I wrote. What follows are the highlights.

Step 1: Getting Started

Before you put your pencil to paper or fingers to keyboard, you must identify three critical issues: *Audience, Purpose,* and *Key Issue.* Also decide what's the best method of *Delivery.* Example 9-1 is the Start Up Sheet that walks you through these critical elements. This is a crucial part of the planning process.

Getting comfortable with the Start Up Sheet

After the first time, filling out the Start Up Sheet takes only a few minutes. You'll wonder how you ever wrote without it. Following are some tips for filling out the Start Up Sheet:

1. **Who's my primary reader? Do I have multiple readers?**

   Even if you don't know your reader personally, try to imagine her as a real person. What color eyes does she have? What is she wearing? If you're writing to multiple readers, rank them in the order of importance. Ask yourself, "Who will take action on the basis of this message?"

Start Up Sheet

Audience

1. Who's my primary reader? Do I have multiple readers?

2. What does my reader *need to know* about the topic?

3. What's in it for my reader?

4. Does my writing need a special *angle* or *point of view*? (Managerial? Technical? Other?)

5. What's my reader's attitude toward the topic?

Purpose

6. My purpose is to _____ so that my reader will
   _____.

Key Issue

7. What's the *key point* I want my reader to remember?

Delivery

8. Who should receive a copy of this message?

9. What's the best way to deliver this message? Hard copy? E-mail? Fax? Phone? Personal meeting? Other?

10. When is the best time to deliver the message? When is too early? When is too late?

Example 9-1:
Jump-start all your business writing.

2. What does my reader *need to know* about the topic?

Think of what your reader needs to know — not what she already knows — so you don't give too much or too little information. Understand whether your reader has any preconceived ideas that may be barriers to understanding your message.

3. What's in it for my reader?

When you receive a message, don't you mentally ask yourself: "What's in it for me?" Your reader will ask the same question. Perhaps your message will make your reader look good to her superiors, propel her career, or offer her a wonderful opportunity.

4. Does my writing need a special *angle* or *point of view*? (Managerial? Technical? Other?)

Determine your reader's point of view by understanding her needs. For example, managers want the big picture. Technical people want the details.

5. What's my reader's attitude toward the topic?

You may not always tell your reader what she wants to hear, but you must tell her what she needs to know. Will she be responsive? Neutral? Unresponsive? Think of how you would react to the message if you received it.

6. My purpose is to _____ so that my reader will _____ .

Whether you think your purpose is to communicate, to inform, to sell, or whatever, chances are you're trying to *persuade* your reader to do something. Do you want your reader to halt shipping, refund your money, write a new contract, wait for your call, or do nothing? Make your purpose and your reader's next step clear.

7. What's the *key point* I want my reader to remember?

If your reader forgets everything else, what's the one key point you want her to remember? Think about this very carefully; it's the most critical part of your message.

8. Who should receive a copy of this message?

Send your message only to people who need to read it. In an e-mail environment, it's too easy to send messages to groups of people when only one or two need to read the message.

9. What's the best way to deliver this message? Hard copy? E-mail? Fax? Phone? Personal meeting? Other?

There are times when you should refrain from writing and talk to someone face to face. And there are times you shouldn't hide behind an e-mail message. Think of the message you're delivering and how you'd like it presented to you.

10. **When is the best time to deliver the message? When is too early? When is too late?**

    Timing is everything. For example, if you're sending out an announcement about your great Christmas sale, you should know that the biggest shopping day is the day after Thanksgiving. Send your notices so that people have them early that week.

Getting beyond writer's block

Think like a newspaper reporter and ask these questions: Who? What? When? Where? Why? How? The answers to these questions provide the basis for what your reader needs to know and get you beyond writer's block. Following are examples that may apply to a meeting called by the Director of Human Resources regarding a company merger.

Who? Director of Human Resources

What? Meeting about company merger

When? Monday, May 5, XXXX

Where? The cafeteria

Why? Everyone needs to attend to learn details

How? (Not applicable in this example)

Make sure that you're specific. For example, if you need something by a certain date, mention the exact date. As soon as possible (ASAP) isn't a date. Deep six those four letters.

Step 2: Writing Headlines and Strategic Sequencing

Using headlines in all your documents (yes, even in letters and e-mail messages) works the same way it does in a newspaper. Headlines direct your reader's attention to what's important and gives key information at a glance. That's critical to affecting your reader as you wish. After all, most people don't read; they scan. You may prepare headlines in the form of an outline, table of contents, or stream of key issues. When you prepare headlines, you provide a framework for writing your draft, which is Step 3.

Each of the following headlines provides the reader with key information:

Subject: Production up 15% for April

Deadline: June 15

Recommendation: We need to conduct a more in-depth study

Next step: I'll call you next Monday at noon

After you write your action-packed headlines, organize them for the most impact. For instance, if you're delivering *good news*, put the key issue at the beginning — perhaps as a subject line. If you're delivering *bad news*, cushion the key issue between a positive opening and a friendly closing.

Step 3: Writing the Draft

This is where your planning really pays off. Your document is already focused and organized so you can settle down comfortably and go to work on the details. This is just like filling in the blanks.

1. **Start expanding one headline at a time.** You don't have to start at the beginning; your reader won't know where you started. Just get going on the headline that's the easiest.

2. **Keep writing.** Don't edit or correct typos. The thing here is to get the information from your head to the computer without distracting yourself. You can edit and make corrections later on.

3. **Take a break.** When you finish, go for a walk, have a cup of coffee, return a phone call. The idea is go get distance from your work.

After you get some distance, revisit your work and ask yourself these questions:

✔ Are the headlines action packed?

✔ Did I explain the problem or situation clearly?

✔ Should I change the sequencing for greater impact? (Number 5 on the Start Up Sheet.) Look at Step 2 for hints on sequencing for good news and bad news.

✔ Did I give enough or too much background information? (Number 2 on the Start Up Sheet.)

✔ Did I provide closure? (Number 6 on the Start Up Sheet.)

Step 4: Designing for Visual Impact

A document must be visually appealing to invite readership. Visual impact establishes the credibility of your message. Following is the *Readers Digest* version to let the reader see at a glance what's important:

- ✔ **Enjoy the white open spaces.** Leave 1- to 1½-inch margins on the top, bottom, and sides of all pages.

- ✔ **Keep the sentence and paragraph length readable.** Limit paragraphs to 8 printed lines. Limit sentences to no more than 25 words.

- ✔ **Use bulleted and numbered lists when appropriate.** Bullets give everything on the list equal value. Numbers show the order of importance or steps in sequence.

- ✔ **Include charts, tables, figures, and graphs.** Yes, even in letters and e-mail messages. After all, a picture is worth a thousand words wherever it appears.

Step 5: Honing the Tone

Remember that a real person will read your document. Use a natural tone so that your documents represent your words on paper. Here are some tips for talking to your reader in a conversational tone:

Leave out unnecessary words

KISS (keep it short and simple) your document so that it doesn't resemble the Tower of Babble.

> **Kissed:** We will consider your request.

> **Wordy:** We've come to an agreement to give consideration to your request.

Be positive, not negative

Presenting yourself as an optimist is a winning strategy.

> **Positive:** I appreciate your suggestions about ways to improve our order handling.

> **Negative:** I'm disappointed that you found our order handling didn't meet your expectations.

Invoke the active voice, not the passive voice

This puts life into your message by focusing on the action of the doer.

> **Strong, active voice:** Jon Berlinger will be next month's guest speaker.

> **Weak, passive voice:** The speaker at next month's meeting will be Jon Berlinger.

Select reader-focused words

When you use *you* and *your*, you focus on the reader, not the writer. Notice how often advertising folks use those words.

> **Reader-focused:** Your order will arrive next Monday.

> **Writer-focused:** We'll deliver your order next Monday.

Avoid clunky he/she and her/him constructions

When most readers see "he/she" or "him/her," they stumble a little. Those constructions tend to draw attention toward something that really isn't important – namely, your pronoun choice. When possible, try turning a singular subject into a plural subject.

> **Gender-free, plural subject:** Candidates will receive their notifications by May 15.

> **Singular subject:** Each candidate will receive his/her notification by May 15.

 Avoid euphemisms, humor, idioms, and clichés. Jargon is fine when you write to people in your industry who understand your shop talk. Otherwise, using lingo may make your tone exclusionary and insulting.

Step 6: Proofreading

Just one typo in your document can be as obvious to the reader as a tarantula on a slice of angel food cake. Despite all your wonderful work, errors make the most lasting impressions. Carefully proofread each document before you send it out. This includes e-mail messages, which people often just write, click, and send.

Following are some things to pay attention to so that your document is free from defects. After you go through this list, review the Proofreading Checklist (Example 9-2) at the end of this section. It gives you the big picture.

- ✔ **Check all names, including middle initials, titles, and company distinctions.** Did you write *Lynne* instead of *Lynn?* Did you write *Company* instead of *Co.?*

- ✔ **Double-check numbers.** Did you tell the reader she should send $4,535.00 instead of $5,435.00?

- ✔ **Keep an eye out for misused or misspelled homonyms.** Did you use *principal* instead of *principle*?

- ✔ **Look for repetitive words.** Perhaps you wrote, "I'll call her her back in a week."

- ✔ **Be on the alert for small words that you repeated or misspelled.** It's easy to type *of* instead of *if* and not notice the error.

- ✔ **Check dates against those on the calendar.** If you wrote Monday, September 16, be certain September 16 is a Monday.

- ✔ **Check for omissions.** Did you leave off an area code, parcel number, or other critical piece of information?

- ✔ **Check spelling, grammar, and punctuation.** Use your eyes as well as your computer tools. (See one of the bonus documents on the CD for more information.)

- ✔ **Print out the message and re-read the hard copy.** Why? Everyone is used to reading the printed word. Therefore, you tend to see errors on hard copy that you didn't notice on the computer. Also, with hard copy there's continuity from one page and section to the next.

- ✔ **Read the message aloud.** See whether you can you read the document just once and thoroughly understand it. If you have to scratch your head, wrinkle your brow, back up, and re-read it, then you need to rewrite the troublesome section.

- ✔ **Get a second opinion.** Ask an office buddy to take a look at your document if it's something critical.

- ✔ **Read from bottom to top and/or from right to left.** This helps you see typos and misspellings.

- ✔ **Scan the document to see that the formatting is correct.** If it doesn't look right, it probably isn't.

- ✔ **If time allows, re-read the message after you've gotten some distance.** For example, you just let off steam and are ready to send a heated e-mail message. Wait. Save the message to a file and re-read it after you've cooled off.

Proofreading Checklist

❏ I'm delivering a subject line (headlines) that will whet the reader's appetite.

❏ I've included a key word(s).

❏ I'm telling a story.

❏ The message has visual impact.

❏ The headlines are informative.

❏ There is ample white space.

❏ I used bulleted and numbered lists, and charts and tables, where appropriate.

❏ Sentences are limited to 25 words.

❏ Paragraphs are limited to 8 lines.

❏ I've reviewed the message for clarity, format, and style.

❏ The message will be clear to my reader.

❏ The message is logically organized.

❏ I've sequenced the message to keep the reader interested and moving forward.

❏ The tone reflects my personality on paper, including the active voice and *you* approach.

❏ I am clear about what action I want the reader to take.

❏ My spelling, grammar, and punctuation are correct.

❏ I used the spelling checker.

❏ I checked my grammar and punctuation.

Example 9-2:
A perfectly "poof read" proofreading checklist.

Although your spelling and grammar checkers can be invaluable, *don't turn your computer on and your brain off.* Look at the difference between these sentences. Your software wouldn't pick up an error, yet you send the opposite message.

> I will no*w* process the application.

> I will no*t* process the application.

A woman in one of my business writing workshops told this story: She's the Public Relations Director of a large international company. She sent out an e-mail message to hundreds of customers in the U.S. and overseas. If she had proofread the message carefully, she would have realized that she gave herself the title of Pubic Relations Director. Oops! She left the "l" out of "Public."

What's Hot on the CD-ROM

Here's what you'll find on the CD-ROM:

- 9-1: Six Steps to Effective Business Writing
- 9-2: Start Up Sheet
- 9-3: Proofreading Tips
- 9-4: Proofreading Checklist

For more help . . .

For an in-depth look at the Six Step Process in action and more, check out my other *For Dummies* books:

- *Business Writing For Dummies* gives you insights into applying the Six Steps to writing letters, reports, proposals, presentations, and a host of other business documents. It's a complete guide to effective business writing.

- *Writing Business Letters For Dummies* gives you ready-to-use business letters and e-mail messages for all occasions — including sales, employment, customer satisfaction, collection, and personal business letters people often shy away from. If your business letters and e-mail messages don't get the action you want, this is the book for you.

Chapter 10

Purely Postal

• •

In This Chapter

▶ Understanding domestic services

▶ Saving money on postage

▶ Sending mail abroad

▶ Using private carriers

• •

Neither snow nor rain nor heat nor gloom of night stays these carriers from the swift completion of their appointed rounds.

— Motto of the U.S. Postal Service

The United States Postal Service (USPS) has been the tried-and-tested method of delivering letters and parcels for what seems like eons. In addition to performing these functions and traipsing through all sorts of weather conditions to deliver the goods, the USPS offers a wide range of services that can be helpful to your business. Stop by your local post office and pick up some of the following brochures. Also visit the USPS Web site at www.usps.com.

✔ "Quick Service Guide" (Pub. 95). Find a plethora of information on first-class mail, periodicals, standard mail, postal terms, and more.

✔ "Design Flat Mail" (Pub. 63). Learn if you qualify for flat-mail size postal discounts.

✔ "Designing Reply Mail" (Pub. 353). Speed up response time for your mailing.

✔ "Nonprofit Standard Mail Eligibility" (Pub. 417). Learn about eligibility and authorization.

✔ "Letter-Size Mail Dimensional Standards Template" (Notice 3A). Learn about minimum and maximum size envelopes.

✔ "Business Guide to Advertising with Direct Mail" to develop a successful direct mail campaign. (This one doesn't have a Pub. #.)

Subscribe to "Memo to Mailers" for free updates on postal services and products. Write to Memo to Mailers, National Customer Support Center, 6060 Primacy Parkway, Suite 201, Memphis, TN 38188.

Understanding Domestic Mail

Domestic mail includes everything between the United States, its territories and possessions, the United Nations, Army and Air Force Area Post Offices (APOs), and Navy Fleet Post Offices (FPOs). Table 10-1 shows standards that domestic mail must adhere to:

Table 10-1	Domestic Mail Standards
Weight	Less than 70 pounds.
Length and girth	Less than 108 inches, except parcel post which maxes out at 130 inches.
Thickness	A minimum of 0.07 inches thick. Pieces that are ¼ inch thick or more, must measure at least 3½ by 5 inches.

First class all the way

Mail all business letters first class. First class applies to sealed letters, postal cards (sold by the post office), postcards (sold commercially), business reply cards, and greeting cards. A standard postage rate (stamped or metered) applies to all mailings up to 1 ounce. If you don't use the correct postage, the post office will return your mailing — eventually.

My next door neighbor had a mild heart attack and was home from the hospital in a few days. I mailed a card from our local post office to his home and stuffed it with funny clippings. Inadvertently, I didn't put enough postage on the envelope. Eighteen months later the envelope was returned to me. So, I walked the card over to his home — a year and a half later. At least he knew I thought of him.

Don't use bulk mail postage for important letters — even for mass mailings — because it shrieks "junk mail." After you put in the effort of writing, sealing, and stamping, you at least want the addressee to open the envelope.

Special sending methods

The post office offers many special delivery services. The following sections highlight some of the popular ones.

Certificate of mailing

Many people don't know that a certificate of mailing exists. Instead they use certified mail, which is three to four times more expensive. If you merely want proof that you sent a letter to the addressee on a certain date, get a certificate of mailing. This is great when you mail your tax return at the stroke of midnight on April 15 and you want proof that you made it under the wire. Example 10-1 is a sample certificate of mailing.

```
U.S. POSTAL SERVICE       CERTIFICATE OF MAILING          Affix fee here in stamps
MAY BE USED FOR DOMESTIC AND INTERNATIONAL MAIL, DOES NOT  or meter postage and
PROVIDE FOR INSURANCE — POSTMASTER                         post mark. Inquire of
                                                           Postmaster for current
   Received From:                                          fees.

   _____

   _____


   One piece of ordinary mail addressed to:

   _____

   _____

   _____

PS Form 3817, Mar. 1989
```

Example 10-1:
A certificate of mailing.

Certified mail

Send a letter certified mail when you need proof that the letter reached its destination. You can indicate restricted delivery so that no one other than the addressee can sign for it, or you can indicate that anyone at the address can sign for it. The receipt for certified mail card is returned to you for your records. Example 10-2 shows one of the certified mailing forms.

Certified letters can't be insured, so don't use certified mail when anything of monetary value is in the envelope, such as bearer bonds. Use registered mail instead.

Registered mail

Registered mail gives you maximum protection and security when you mail anything of monetary value. Registered mail may be combined with restricted delivery, return receipt, or cash on delivery (COD) mailings. If the registered item gets lost, you can receive compensation for the declared (and paid for) value up to $25,000.

Example 10-2:
A certified
mailing
form.

Z 194 113 510

US Postal Service
Receipt for Certified Mail
No Insurance Coverage Provided.
Do not use for International Mail *(See reverse)*

Sent to

Street & Number

Post Office, State, & ZIP Code

Postage	$
Certified Fee	
Special Delivery Fee	
Restricted Delivery Fee	
Return Receipt Showing to Whom & Date Delivered	
Return Receipt Showing to Whom, Date, & Addressee's Address	
TOTAL Postage & Fees	$
Postmark or Date	

PS Form 3800, April 1995

Fold at line over top of envelope to the right of the return address

CERTIFIED

Z 194 113 510

MAIL

Priority Mail

Priority mail is defined as first class mail that's supposed to reach its destination within 2 to 3 days. The delivery time isn't, however, a guarantee. The benefit of Priority Mail over regular first class is that it looks important because of its attractive red, white, and blue packaging. Also, a priority mail package is more difficult to lose than a plain envelope. The USPS will pick up Priority Mail at your home or office for a fee.

Express Mail

Express Mail is a premium service that's guaranteed for next-day or second-day delivery — whichever you choose. Insurance of up to $500 is included in the fee, and you can purchase additional insurance of up to $5,000. The USPS will pick up Express Mail at your home or office for a fee.

Bar codes

The bar code is a series of vertical black lines on the lower portion of an envelope. Keep the bar code area on your envelope free of printing and symbols so the USPS optical character reader (OCR) can read it. OCRs and bar codes helped to automate the sorting of mail. For more information on bar coding, visit your local USPS for a copy of "Designing Letter Mail" (Pub. 25).

Keeping Costs Down

Here are a few ways to keep postal costs down:

- ✔ Keep your mailing lists up to date.
- ✔ Don't use special services unless you need to.
- ✔ Have current postal rates on hand.
- ✔ Have postal scales checked regularly for accuracy.
- ✔ Don't use airmail postage for domestic mail because air is automatic.

Mailing Abroad

When you send mail or packages abroad, you may need to be familiar with a few common terms. You can find the regulations for the following categories in "Global Delivery Services" (Pub. 51), listed under LC mail, AO mail, and CP mail:

- ✔ **LC mail:** Abbreviated from the French term *lettres et cartes,* meaning "letters and cards."
- ✔ **AO mail:** Abbreviated from the French term *autres objets,* meaning "other articles."
- ✔ **CP mail:** Abbreviated from the French term *colis poataux,* meaning "parcel post."

Postage meters

Following are a few things to keep in mind when you use a postage meter instead of stamps:

✔ Change the date each day.

✔ Be certain the amount of postage is correct. If the envelope is borderline, err on the side of additional postage.

✔ Check to see that the imprint is clear.

✔ Make sure all the envelopes face in the same direction when you run them through the meter. If you don't, your postage imprint may be on the back of the envelope or on top of your return address.

Special services

The USPS offers a variety of services for mailing packages abroad. Here are a few of the frequently used services:

✔ **Registered mail:** This is available to all countries except Cambodia and the Democratic People's Republic of Korea (North Korea). Return receipts for registered mail and insured parcels are also available. (Certified mail and COD aren't available for international mail.)

✔ **Express Mail International Service (EMS):** This is a high-speed service for mailing sensitive items that may be mailed to recipients in most countries in the world.

✔ **Global Priority Mail (GPM):** This is an expedited mail service for pieces up to 4 pounds going to Canada, Mexico, some South American countries, Western Europe, the Middle East, and the Pacific Rim.

Special treatment

When you send a letter abroad, it may need special treatment. Always ask your post office about delivery because issues vary from one country to another based on politics and other local or national events. Here are a few situations you may encounter:

✔ When you send a letter or package to certain countries, the political situation may dictate that mailings are opened and read by security personnel.

✔ If your document must be translated by an interpreter, make sure the contents aren't highly sensitive.

✔ Consider buying a reply coupon from the post office that can be used for return postage. This is useful when you send something to people of limited means.

If you know the recipient's special interests, consider buying one of the decorative stamps to reflect that interest. The person may find the stamp to be a real treasure and remember you for sending it.

Standard regulations for mailing abroad

Anytime you send a letter internationally, mark *AIRMAIL* or *PAR AVION* on the envelope. It's not necessary to use air mail rates because the letter isn't sent on a slow boat to China or in a bottle; it automatically goes via air. Here are some vital statistics to keep in mind:

- ✔ Minimum length and height = 5½ by 3½ inches
- ✔ Maximum thickness = 0.07 inches
- ✔ Maximum length = 24 inches
- ✔ Maximum length + height + thickness = 36 inches

Addressing the envelope

When you send a letter to an international address, always type the address in English. (Of course, you don't translate into English the name of the street or town.) Type the name of the country in all capital letters on the last line of the address block.

The post office requests that envelopes be typed in all upper case (domestic and international) with no punctuation. However, the public fish haven't taken the bait. In other words, people don't use the all caps and no punctuation format too often. Here's what may appear on an envelope to England if it were in all upper case.

MS KATHY BLYTHE
4563 PALACE ROAD
LONDON WIP 6HQ
ENGLAND

Non-USPS Carriers

Carriers other than the USPS can be a great help in getting your packages where you need them to go. When you use any of the following services, you can access their Web sites to track anything you mail:

- ✔ Federal Express (FedEx) at www.fedex.com
- ✔ United Parcel Service (UPS) at www.ups.com
- ✔ DHL Worldwide Express at www.dhl.com

You can also send mail from Mail Boxes, Etc., Kinko's, or drop boxes outside professional buildings or shopping centers. Also, Check the Yellow Pages of your phone directory under "Delivery Service," "Messenger Service," or "Courier Service" to find out about local carrier services and the applicable rates. (My local directory intersperses limousine and taxi services with mail delivery services. Many of them provide messenger services.)

What's Hot on the CD-ROM

Here's what's on the CD-ROM:

- ✔ 10-1: Web Sites for Carriers
- ✔ 10-2: Keeping Costs Down

Chapter 11

Cleaning Up the Infobog

In This Chapter

▶ Being a filer, not a piler

▶ Preventing more growth

▶ Knowing what to keep and for how long

▶ Recycling what you don't need

The volume of paper expands to fill the available briefcase [or office space].

— Jerry Brown, erstwhile governor of California

Why is it that you may yell at your kids to clean up their rooms and fail to notice that your office is overrun by papers, magazines, and anything else that didn't crawl away? If you need a machete to carve out a path to your desk, it's time to get a grip.

Time is money, and time is one of the few things you can't replace. Every time you search for papers on your messy desk, you cause bottlenecks in your productivity and waste time and money. This mess adds to your level of stress and frustration. Get out from under the infobog!

There's no single right or wrong way to get yourself organized. How you do it depends on your personality type, work habits, environmental constraints, and what works best for you. This chapter is chock full of tips that will prove helpful.

Cleaning Up the Burial Ground

The burial ground exists in all shapes, sizes, and colors: loose, stapled, white, ivory, embossed, matte, textured, and gloss, to name a few. Papers pile high on our desks. They teeter on top of file cabinets. They bulge from in-boxes, out-boxes, cardboard boxes, and trash baskets. They lurk everywhere — in the halls, outside cubicles, in empty cubicles, and anywhere people can find an inch of space.

If you're overrun by paper, this section offers great tips for getting out from under. No matter how hopelessly you're buried, don't go through the piles with a machete. Once you throw something out, it's gone forever. There's undoubtedly valuable information buried in those piles. Your aim isn't to have the neatest desk around; it's to get organized so that you know where to find the information you need when you need it.

Phase 1: It's as easy as 1-2-3-4

What follows is one way to clean up the 3 X 5 foot workspace you call your desk. Divide your papers into four piles. If you're buried so deeply that the piles will fall over, start with a few empty boxes.

- ✔ **Pile 1: Needs quick attention.** Activate everything in this pile. Answer the letter, file the report, get rid of the old sales literature that turned yellow. Or put the papers in a file folder with other papers that are in the same category. Don't just re-pile the stuff on your desk!

- ✔ **Pile 2: Saving just in case.** This is the hardest pile to deal with because we all need just-in-case assurance. If in doubt; don't throw it out. Put this stuff in a special file and revisit it regularly.

- ✔ **Pile 3: The paper turned yellow.** Immediately get rid of everything in this pile. If you haven't missed the stuff by now, chances are you never will. Even if the yellowed letter is a once-in-a-lifetime opportunity to win a million dollars, your chance to collect has probably passed.

- ✔ **Pile 4: Give the paper to someone who cares.** Divvy this pile up between colleagues who can act on what needs to be done.

Once you straighten out your desk, go through the rest of the infobog. Apply the "pile approach" to clean out what's on top of and inside your file cabinets, in boxes in the corner of your office, and wherever else papers are lurking.

What impression do you create?

What would you think if you walked into a bank and each teller's station was strewn with loose bills and coins? Would you have confidence in that bank? Or if you walked into a surgeon's office and her desk was cluttered with body parts? Wouldn't it gross you out? Even if she were tops in her field, you'd take your kidney problem elsewhere. Neatness sends a message. It says, "I'm organized and in control."

Phase II: Divide and Conquer

You now have piles 1 and 2 to deal with; they need to be organized by how frequently you need to use them. Divide them into three groups, and you'll conquer the clutter.

Group 1: Working files

Working files are for routine functions and current projects. You'll find the 80/20 principle applies. Approximately 80 percent of your work involves 20 percent of your files. Keep these working files within reach and divide them into these suggested categories:

- **Needed on the spot:** Keep phone numbers, address lists, or other information you need at your fingertips. (One tip is to store all this information on a palm unit so it's with you at all times. Check out Chapter 3 to learn more about the wonders of palm units.)

- **Timely papers:** Have a nearby file for hot files such as ones you need for meetings with colleagues. You can place these files in a drawer in your desk.

- **Routine functions:** Use a nearby file cabinet for papers you need weekly, monthly, or occasionally.

- **Tickler file:** This may be either a small box for 3 X 5 cards divided into days or months, an electronic tickler file that you refer to each morning, or a palm unit.

Group 2: Reference files

Reference files are those you may need for future reference but not on an ongoing basis. This may include past projects, research for future projects, resource information, client account information, and the like. You need access to these files, but they don't have to be on top of you.

Group 3: Archive files

Archive those papers you may need for statutory or other reasons down the road. Archives may be stored off the premises. They must be indexed properly so that people who need the information can find it.

Also, clean out archives regularly so they don't take on a life of their own. For example, you may want to destroy records that detail a manual process done back in the early 1900's that's now computerized.

Retaining Valuable Records

Records, like everything else, have a life cycle. You should keep some records forever; others, for a limited period of time. The following guidelines offer suggestions on retaining records:

Keep for all eternity

Some records are so vital that you should keep them in your safe deposit box so they're protected from fire, theft, or other disasters. These records include the following:

- Articles of incorporation
- Contracts for major business transactions
- Corporate charter
- Deeds, mortgages, and bills of sale
- End-of-year-financial statements
- General ledgers
- Minutes of meetings of the board of directors and stockholders
- Stocks and bonds
- Tax returns and related documents
- Trademark or logo registration

Keep for seven years

Following is a list of important records you should keep for seven years. That's the length of time the Internal Revenue Service can backtrack. If the IRS suspects fraud, however, the clock never stops ticking.

- Accounts payable and receivable ledgers
- Bank statements
- Canceled checks
- Commission records
- Creditor and customer invoices
- Employee personnel records

✔ Inventory records

✔ Payroll records

✔ Purchase orders

Keep for three years

Following are useful records that may come in handy. You know Murphy's Law, however: As soon as you throw it away, you'll need it.

✔ Bank statements

✔ Employment letters and applications

✔ Expired insurance policies and warranties

✔ General correspondence and reports

Keep for one year

These are the just-in-case records:

✔ Employment applications

✔ Routine correspondence

Be sure to shred (or rip into small pieces) sensitive documents that you wouldn't want your competitor retrieving from the dumpster.

Preventing Molehills from Turning into Mountains

Cleaning up your clutter is only half the battle. The other half is to keep it from building up again. This is akin to people who put a lot of effort into losing weight, only to gain it all (or more) back again. The next few sections offer tips that may help to keep clutter down permanently.

Identify the sources of your clutter

Once you understand where your clutter comes from, you can start to reduce it. For example, if a coworker copies you on things you don't need, talk to her and let her know what is and isn't important to you.

✔ If you accumulate mail, open mail near your wastebasket and recycle anything you don't need. Act immediately on what you do need.

✔ Bundle all papers that relate to a specific project. The bundle may be a file folder, rubber band, or anything else that creates a single unit.

✔ If you're inundated with junk mail, here are several ways to ebb the flow:

- Write "no" or "not interested" on return cards and ask to be taken off the mailing list.

- Write to the Mail Preference Service of the Direct Marketing Association, P.O. Box 9008, Farmingdale, New York 11735-9008 and ask for its free "mail preference" form. You can reduce your junk mail by as much as 40 percent over the next five years.

- Send e-mail messages instead of paper messages, and people will follow your lead. (Check out Chapter 4 for ways to clean up the electronic infobog.)

Ditch magazines

Look through all the magazines you've been piling up. Clip the articles you want to save, then recycle the magazines. When you get new magazines, look through them as soon as you can so that they don't pile up.

Put the articles you save into a folder and keep the folder in your briefcase. You have the articles on hand during the train commute home or on your next business trip.

Empty your in-box and out-box

These boxes tend to become a dumping ground for everything you consider miscellaneous. To avoid letting them get out of hand, set deadlines for emptying them and stick to your deadlines. This deadline may be daily, weekly (not weakly), or monthly. The longer you let the papers accumulate, the bigger the cleaning job is.

Toss out old drafts

Even though your rough drafts represent your blood, sweat, and tears, once the document is done, do you really need each paper version? You probably don't. If you did get a sign-off on the last copy, you may keep that for CYA (you know — cover your anatomy) purposes.

Use electronic media

Instead of sending interoffice memos, think about sending e-mail messages or posting to an intranet. For example, if you're notifying a few colleagues about a meeting, e-mail is a great way to do that. If you're giving information about a new corporate policy, post it on the intranet. Check out Part II for more information on electronic media because that may become an e-infobog.

Save the Forests

It's estimated that 70 to 80 percent of all the paper used in offices is waste. Therefore, it's economically and environmentally prudent to recycle. If your office doesn't have a recycling program, shame on them! Consider starting a program to recycle bond paper, computer paper, envelopes (without windows and self-sticking labels), uncoated fax paper, newsletters, laser/copy paper, and other paper products. To learn more about recycling, contact the American Paper Institute:

American Paper Institute
260 Madison Avenue
New York, NY 10016
212-340-0600

What's Hot on the CD-ROM

Here's what's you can find on the CD-ROM:

- 11-1: Retaining Valuable Records
- 11-2: Recycling Info

Part IV
Minding Your Business Manners

The 5th Wave   By Rich Tennant

"I ADVISE TO COMPANIES WHERE THE USE OF HURTFUL LANGUAGE APPEARS EPIDEMIC. THAT'S RIGHT, YOUR HONOR — I'M AN INSULTANT CONSULTANT."

In this part . . .

Peter Drucker, American business philosopher and author once said: *Start with what is right rather than what is acceptable.* His words are at the heart of good business manners because too many people are misguided by stereotypes, generalizations, and trends. Impeccable manners are key to your success in the business world.

To shine as a professional, you must know how to make proper introductions, exercise good table manners, give tasteful gifts, and interact in the workplace. Otherwise, you may wind up like Douglas "Wrong-Way" Corrigan — the Patron Saint of Faux Pas.

Chapter 12

Getting to Know You

In This Chapter

▶ Introducing yourself and others
▶ Glowing with the golden handshake
▶ Determining the art of conversation
▶ Reading body language
▶ Working a room

Man doesn't live by words alone, despite the fact that sometimes he has to eat them.

— Adlai E. Stevenson, American lawyer and diplomat

Making introductions and mingling with strangers doesn't have to be an angst-provoking experience. After all, what is a *stranger*? Merely a person you haven't yet gotten to know. Think of these experiences as opportunities to meet new and interesting people and expand your network of social and business contacts. Who knows where these experiences may lead. Opportunities often come from the most unsuspecting sources!

Introducing Others

Many people avoid making introductions because they don't know the right way or can't remember someone's name. Don't be a slave to rules and don't lose your warmth or sense of humor. Just do it!

The pecking order

Here's the basic pecking order: Introduce a younger person *to* an older person and a junior person *to* a senior person. Don't get hung up on this stuff, however. The critical thing is to put people at ease, make them feel comfortable, and get them talking.

Men and women

Present a man *to* a woman. Many feminists may disagree with this statement and feel that the guidelines in the next section should supersede gender. The jury's still out, so do what's comfortable for you.

Younger person to older person

Present a younger person *to* an older person, mentioning the older person's name first.

> *Mr. Leary, I'd like you to meet my son, Marc, who just graduated from Georgia Tech. Marc, this is Mr. Leary, my supervisor.*

Peers from different companies

Present a peer in your own company *to* a peer in another company, mentioning the peer in the other company first.

> *Ellen Matthews, I'd like you to meet Barbara Jameson from our Communications Department. Ellen is Communications Manager at Ace & Jones.*

Non-official and official

Present a non-official *to* an official, mentioning the official first.

> *Congressman Jones, I'd like you to meet my mother, Mrs. Lorenz. Mom, I'd like you to meet Congressman Jones, from my district.*

Junior and senior executives

Present a junior executive *to* a senior executive, mentioning the senior executive first.

> *Mr. Jones, I'd like you to meet Jim Stanton, who joined our group last week. Jim, this is Mr. Jones, the Vice President of Marketing.*

Fellow executive to client or customer

Present a fellow executive *to* a client or customer, mentioning the client or customer first.

> *Stan, I'd like you to meet Grace Petry from our Purchasing Department. Grace, this is Stan Gregory, a salesman from ABC Chemical Company.*

Newcomer

When someone you know joins your company or group, introduce that person immediately. Nothing makes a person feel more left out than standing with a group of strangers. Here are a few suggestions:

- ✔ **It's appropriate to interrupt a group's conversation to introduce a newcomer.** Excuse yourself for interrupting, and you're covered.

  > *Excuse me for a moment. I'd like you all to meet. . . .*

- ✔ **Provide some background about the person you're introducing.**

  > *Beverly, I'd like to introduce you to some of our guests. This is Jim, who's also a sailor. This is Gloria, our HR director. Jim and Gloria, this is Beverly, my long-time friend and business associate.*

 Avoid using the term *old* friend or business associate. Substitute *long-time*. Some people are sensitive about the word *old*.

What's in a name?

Everything! You flatter people when you remember their names – and flattery can get you everywhere. Check out these tips for remembering names:

- ✔ **When you're introduced to someone, concentrate on that person's name and repeat it.**

  > *I'm glad to meet you, Tim.*

- ✔ **Try to form an association with the person's name.** For example, perhaps Mr. White has white hair or is wearing a white shirt.

- ✔ **If you don't understand the person's name when you're introduced, don't be shy about asking him name to repeat it.**

  > *I'm sorry I didn't understand your name and I'd like to know it. Would you mind repeating it?*

Using titles

When you introduce peers, use a person's title only when you introduce an older person or someone with status.

> *Mrs. Peters, I'd like you to meet my friend, Donna Randall. Donna, this is Mrs. Peters, my supervisor.*

Memory lapses

If you want to make an introduction and can't remember a person's name, don't be embarrassed and neglect to make the introduction. We all get brain cramps at one time or another. Here are a couple of tactful ways to fake it:

> *First I needed glasses, now my memory seems to be failing me. I can't recall your name.*

or

> *Listen everyone. This is the wonderful gentleman who just became the president of the Ace Chemical Company. I'd like you all to meet him.* (Before long, he'll be going around to the guests, shaking hands and introducing himself, and you don't have to worry about not knowing his name when you introduce him.)

Using first or last names

If you have to think about which name to use, use the last name or full name. Some people feel it lacks respect if you're too familiar and use only a first name; others prefer it. Generally, a younger person will call an older person by his last name, unless asked to do otherwise. It's better to err on the side of being too formal. Check out Chapter 19 for introducing people from other countries and cultures.

Using nicknames

Some names hang on from childhood and can be embarrassing in certain business situations. Don't use a person's nickname, unless that's what the person is normally called. There's nothing wrong with *Charlie* for Charles, *Jim* for James, or some other form of the person's name. But *Butch, Junior, Cookie,* or *Kitten* may not be appropriate in some settings.

Introducing Yourself

If you don't have Ed McMahon ready to jump in and say, "And heeeere's Johnny," introduce yourself. You can stimulate conversation by stating your name (obviously) with a tagline that connects you to the other person. For example, you were all invited by the host because of some commonality and you probably know what it is.

> *Hello, I'm Jim Smith from the San Francisco office.*

> or

> *Hello. I'm Jim Smith. This is my first meeting with the Chamber of Commerce. Are you a member?*

Don't just hide out in a safe spot next to the hors d'oeurves. Mingle. Otherwise, you're missing the opportunity to meet new and interesting people. And who knows, there may be someone next to you wishing you'd rescue him from anonymity.

The Golden Handshake

In the United States, the handshake is the classic business greeting. Handshakes create a link between two people. Following are great opportunities to shake hands and establish relationships:

- ✔ Being introduced to someone
- ✔ Greeting a visitor to your office
- ✔ Running into a business associate outside your office
- ✔ Firming up a deal
- ✔ Saying goodbye

Giving the right impression

Always extend your right hand for a handshake and look the person directly in the eye. Use a handshake that's of medium strength and hold the shake for three to four seconds. People tend to think that your handshake matches your character, so don't let it be too weak or too strong. A weak, limp handshake suggests mousiness, and a strong bone crusher suggests superiority. Plus, it hurts the other person's hand.

Handshake etiquette

When you greet a business associate in your home or office, *you* should be the one to extend your hand. On neutral ground, do what's comfortable; it doesn't matter whether you're a man or a woman. Here's some handshake etiquette:

- ✔ **Juggling a drink.** If you're holding a drink, you may want to hold the drink in your left hand so your right hand won't be cold or wet when you need to extend it.

- ✔ **Wearing gloves.** If you're wearing gloves, remove them before shaking someone's hand. No one can feel the warmth of your hand through fabric. If you're wearing gloves at a formal celebration, however, don't remove them.

- ✔ **Dealing with a special situation.** If you're unable to shake someone's hand and the reason is obvious (your arm's in a sling), you don't need to explain. If the reason isn't obvious, offer an explanation. For example, *I'm sorry I can't shake your hand; my carpal tunnel is acting up.*

Rising to the occasion

When you're introduced to someone . . . stand up, step forward and smile, extend your hand for a handshake, say, *Hello,* or, *How do you do,* and repeat the other person's name. If you can't stand because you're stuck in a tight corner, rise slightly from the chair and extend your hand. When you don't stand or make the effort to stand, you may give the impression that you don't think the person is important.

The Art of Conversation

Conversation is the social dialogue that surround all business interactions — whether you're talking with a supervisor, direct report, client, supplier, or John Q. Public. Conversation involves not only the way you speak to someone, but your tone of voice, body language, and choice of words. Being a good conversationalist means *speaking* as well as *listening.* Remember, we have two ears and one mouth. We should use them in equal proportion.

Some people are natural-born speakers, but poor listeners. Others are just the opposite. If you want to be considered a good conversationalist, you must do both well.

Rating your conversational skills

A great conversationalist is an asset to any company. He can persuade, encourage, praise, charm, motivate, comfort — and, in the process, further his career. Conversation is a skill everyone can learn. See how many of these skills you already have. (This isn't a test, so it's not a matter of how many you get right. It's a matter of what you need to work on.) The more boxes you check, the better your conversational skills are.

I always or generally

- ❏ Accept and deliver compliments gracefully
- ❏ Can discuss a wide range of *safe* topics
- ❏ Display a sense of humor
- ❏ Maintain eye contact
- ❏ Make people smile
- ❏ Question without prying
- ❏ Show interest in other people

I never

- ❏ Burst someone's bubble
- ❏ Correct someone's grammar or pronunciation
- ❏ Exclude anyone present from the conversation
- ❏ Interrupt someone who's speaking
- ❏ Switch subjects unless it's appropriate
- ❏ Pretend to be an expert on a subject

Speaking

Some people are just natural-born talkers; others struggle to make conversation. One thing I have learned in my years in business is never to confuse shyness with aloofness. Some people merely need to be encouraged.

Break the ice with small talk

When you're introduced to someone, you may be slightly uncomfortable as you stand there tongue-tied not knowing what to say. Small talk involves any noncontroversial topic: news events; the latest corporate takeover;

gardening; books or magazines; movies, TV programs, or local performing arts; travel; sports; and much more. After you master the art of small talk, you have a valuable talent. Small talk is conversation that does the following:

- ✔ Fills distressing silent moments
- ✔ Puts people at ease when getting acquainted
- ✔ Breaks tension
- ✔ Builds relationships
- ✔ Maximizes career opportunities

Avoid issues that deal with controversial current events, confidential business issues, politics, harmful gossip, your health and personal misfortunes, how much things cost, sex, religion, or anything of questionable taste. Here are some great ways to break the ice:

- ✔ **Identify commonalties.** You're all assembled because you have something in common. Use the commonality as an opener.

  - *I understand that we're all financial planners.*

  - *What do you think of the new [medical breakthrough] we're here to learn about?*

  - *Have you ever used this type of software before?*

- ✔ **Ask open-ended questions.** After you initiate small talk, avoid dead-end questions that have yes-or-no answers. Instead, start your questions with what, who, when, where, or why.

  - *What have you seen in the city since you arrived?*

  - *Where are you staying?*

  - *How long are you staying in New York after the seminar is over?*

- ✔ **Engage the person in a conversation about himself.** People are basically egotistical and love to talk about themselves. If there's no icebreaker or known common interest, don't stand there like a dummy. Think of where you are and why you're there. Here are a few icebreakers to stimulate conversation:

  - *Where did you first meet Jim?*

  - *What's your involvement with the XYZ Company?*

  - *How do you feel about the upcoming merger?*

Perhaps you're at a social business function seated next to the non-working spouse or partner of a business associate. Ask the person about his hometown, profession, or anything else that's neutral. In addition to being a good listener, you may learn a thing or two about your business associate.

✔ **Try neutral openers.** If all else fails, here are a few standards:

- *Isn't this wonderful weather we've been having?*

- *How did you find the traffic getting here?*

- *That's a very nice [article of clothing] you're wearing.* (This line is especially well suited for one woman to say to another.)

✔ **Avoid negativity.** Avoid negative statements such as, *Isn't the food lousy* or *This conference center is really a dive.*

✔ **Converse with foreigners.** If you've just been introduced to a foreigner, avoid topics that may be construed as inappropriate. Check out Chapter 19 for more details.

Know what's going on around you

If you can only talk shop, you'll be labeled a bore. Know what's going on in the world and your industry. Read the local newspaper and a news magazine. Be prepared to discuss business, sports, science, literature, performing arts, and non-controversial current events. Here are some tips for scanning the newspaper:

✔ Skim the headlines to get the gist of the news.

✔ Read the business and sports sections.

✔ Read the lifestyles section if you're in a city other than your own. It will tell you what's hot in the area so you can talk about it.

Accepting compliments

Give compliments that are sincere and make someone smile. When someone pays you a compliment, never downgrade the praise. Accept it graciously with a *thank you.* We all need praise and should be able to give and receive it gracefully.

Listening, not just hearing

Of all your communication skills, listening is perhaps the most important and the most neglected. You don't learn anything if you do all the talking. People who don't listen often miss the subtleties and signals that could result in being passed over for a promotion.

Listening isn't a process of just hearing. It's a process of internalizing, decoding, and interpreting what you hear. You must mentally do something with the sound, not let it go in one ear and out the other (as my mother used to say). This is true whether you're involved in an intimate conversation with a small group of people or you're part of a large audience. How good a listener are you? Check off any boxes that apply to you:

❏ I listen mainly for the facts.

❏ I'm critical of the speaker's delivery.

❏ I interrupt when I don't disagree.

❏ I pretend to listen when I'm bored.

❏ I avoid listening to difficult material.

If you checked any of these boxes, you have some work to do! Here are some tips for becoming a skilled listener:

✔ **Know what makes a poor listener:** Are you listening to the speaker or biting your tongue waiting for your turn to speak? Poor listeners are easy to spot, as you see in Table 12-1.

✔ **Be an active participant.** Listening isn't a passive activity; it's an active one. A good listener is physically and emotionally ready to get involved in the conversation when the timing is appropriate. He makes a conscious effort to listen to the message, process it, and decide what makes sense.

✔ **Use speaking and listening to your advantage.** The average speaker talks at the rate of about 125 to 150 words per minute (wpm). That's not a steady pace. Words rush out. The speaker hesitates. He pauses. The human being can think at the rate of 500 to 800 wpm. So, while the person is speaking you have time to plan, reflect, and even daydream. Use that time to your advantage. Perhaps the suggestions that follow will help you stay tuned and focused.

• Focus on the idea and anticipate what the speaker may say.

• Keep track of supporting material to clarify the ideas.

• Identify your feelings. Does the speaker make you feel comfortable or uncomfortable, happy or angry? Try to understand why.

• Analyze the quality of the ideas. Perhaps you wish the speaker would expand an idea or offer some alternatives.

Remember the words of Calvin Coolidge: *Nobody ever listened himself out of a job.* (They didn't call him *Silent Cal* for nothing.)

Table 12-1	Identifying Poor Listeners
In small groups, they . . .	*In large audiences, they . . .*
Change the subject	Criticize the speaker
Interrupt	Get sidetracked
Look at their watches or out the window	Compose needless rebuttals
Avoid eye contact	Shape what they're hearing

Body Language

A lot of our body language is dictated by our personalities. Some people are inherently casual; others, more formal. Therefore, you must be aware of the signals you send. For example, assume you're a laid back person and you attend a business meeting called by a more formal person. You're slumped down in your chair, your hands are folded on your stomach, and your legs are stretched out. Although you may be listening to every word the speaker is saying, the speaker may interpret your body language as not being actively involved. It's helpful, therefore, to take body language cues from the speaker and mimic them.

Being aware of the signals you send

Never dismiss the old adage, "Actions speak louder than words." Your body language can shriek "I'm hanging on every word," or "I'm bored to tears." Table 12-2 shows some ways to decipher the message.

Table 12-2	Reading Between the Lines	
Action	*Body Language*	*Message*
Shaking hands	Firm (but not knuckle-breaking grip)	You're confident
	Weak	You're not confident
Listening to the speaker	Maintaining eye contact	You're interested
	Eyes roaming around room	You're disinterested

(continued)

Table 12-2 *(continued)*		
Action	*Body Language*	*Message*
Sitting while listening to someone talk	Sitting attentively without slumping	You're paying attention
	Crossing and uncrossing your legs or fidgeting	You're preoccupied or bored
As the speaker, making a point	Sitting straight or standing tall	You're saying something of importance

Working the Room

You may recall the words of your mother: *Never talk to strangers.* This warning makes sense for a defenseless five-year-old (for safety reasons). But a professional has nothing to fear. Don't squander the chance to make valuable professional and social contacts. That's what working the room is all about.

Working the room is an old political phrase that used to invoke the image of obese, cigar-smoking politicians cutting deals in backrooms. Today, however, it means attending a gathering of people and mingling. Even if you were the high school wallflower, you can learn to schmooze and emerge as the Prom King or Queen.

You're not working an entire room, just one or two people at a time. Here are a few things to ease the pain:

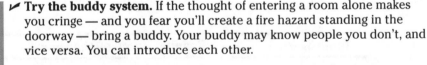

- ✔ **Try the buddy system.** If the thought of entering a room alone makes you cringe — and you fear you'll create a fire hazard standing in the doorway — bring a buddy. Your buddy may know people you don't, and vice versa. You can introduce each other.

  You and your buddy shouldn't be joined at the hip. Split up as soon as you meet new people. Otherwise, you defeat the purpose of going to the gathering.

- ✔ **Understand the payoffs.** Before you attend a business function, understand how you may benefit — professionally and socially. Personally you gain confidence, feel good about yourself, have fun, and meet new people. Professionally you establish new contacts, enhance your career opportunities, gain new information, and increase your contact sphere.

✔ **Realize that even bores need love.** We've all met bores and have had our ears chewed off. Excusing yourself may be difficult, but there are a few lines you may try. Finish what you're saying, then smile and politely state:

- *Please excuse me, I'd like to refresh my drink.*

- *Excuse me, there's someone over there I must say hello to.*

- *Excuse me, it's been nice talking to you.*

If you can't find a means of escape, play a mind game with yourself. Think about how awful it would be to work with this person every day or to wake up next to him each morning. Then thank your lucky stars you don't have to. Knowing your boredom is temporary may ease the pain.

✔ **Notice someone you've met before.** If you see someone you've met before, this is a great opportunity to engage in conversation. If you don't recall the person's name, don't be shy about asking. Approach the person, extend your hand and say:

> *I don't recall your name. But didn't I meet you at the Bergstein's office last month?*

Do's and taboos for working the room

When you work a room, it's important for people to know who you are. (Check out Chapter 22 for ways to wow people with your name badge.) Following are some do's and taboos for working a room:

Do's

Following are some things to remember when you work a room:

- ✔ Look for people with white knuckles. They're more hesitant than you are.

- ✔ Bring a lot of business cards and distribute them liberally.

- ✔ Be open to new people and new ideas.

- ✔ Bring your sense of humor.

- ✔ Dress appropriately.

Taboos

Following are things to avoid when you work a room:

- ✔ Don't sit on your rump. You can't work a room sitting down.

- ✔ Don't smoke. Many people find it offensive.

✔ Don't wear strong-smelling perfume or after-shave lotion. Many people also find that offensive.

✔ Don't get drunk. This is a business function.

✔ Don't barge in on conversations that are in progress.

You can schmooze in gyms, airplanes, banks, restaurants, supermarkets, or just about anywhere. You often make new friends and business relationships in the strangest places! Don't limit yourself.

What's Hot on the CD-ROM

Here's what you'll find on the CD-ROM:

✔ 12-1: Introducing Yourself and Others

✔ 12-2: Shaking Hands Properly

✔ 12-3: Becoming a Good Speaker and Listener

✔ 12-4: Reading Body Language

✔ 12-5: Working a Room

Chapter 13

Wining and Dining

- -

In This Chapter

▶ Reserving a table

▶ Minding your table manners

▶ Ordering food and alcohol

▶ Paying for the meal

▶ Tipping

▶ Eating a variety of food with class

- -

In Mexico we have a word for sushi: bait.

— José Simon, American scholar

*B*usiness entertaining is a multibillion-dollar business, and much of it revolves eating, drinking, and talking business. Whether you're the host or the guest . . . whether you're trying to close a big deal or land a job . . . whether you're in the United States or abroad . . . your table manners and attention to detail can make or break a deal. This chapter focuses on how to shine during all aspects of a business meal.

Making Reservations

When you host a business luncheon or dinner, pick a restaurant that sets the tone for the meeting and be sensitive to the person you host. For example, if you're trying to win the business of a start-up company that has limited capital, opt for a nice, conservative restaurant. On the other hand, if you have a long-standing relationship with a client whose business is prospering, a lavish restaurant may be just what the doctor ordered.

Always call ahead and let the restaurant know your needs. For example, you may say, *Hello, this is John Doe from ABC Company. I'd like to reserve a table for four in the Colonial Room, for [date] and [time].* With this simple statement, you accomplished more than reserving a table. You identified yourself as a person with authority, established which table will be "yours," and informed the restaurant you're planning a special meal.

After you do this a few times at the same restaurant, the person who makes the reservations will recognize you. If you tip well, you ingratiate yourself with the servers. Find out more about tipping later in this chapter.

It's a good idea to call the restaurant a day or two in advance to confirm the reservation. On the big day, arrive before your guests. You may wait at the bar, at the table, or in the waiting area.

When you host a business meal, take care of all gratuities, including the coat check. Let your guests know that they're not responsible for tipping or anything else.

Checking Your Coat

When you enter a fine restaurant, leave your coat, briefcase, umbrella, or other paraphernalia with the coat room attendant. If you'll be conducting business and need your briefcase, place it next to you, not on the table or empty chair. The man generally takes care of checking a lady's coat; however, some women object to this. If you're a woman who objects, politely smile and say, *Thank you. I'll take care of it.*

Greeting Guests

When you host a dinner or luncheon for a large number of people, wait for the first of your guests to arrive, and escort them to the table. The maitre d' or head waiter escorts the stragglers. If your guests don't know each other, be sure to make the introductions. This is something people often neglect or take for granted. If you find yourself being an unintroduced guest, introduce yourself. Check out Chapter 12 for tips on making introductions properly.

Using Your Napkin, Not Your Sleeve

As soon as you're seated, place your napkin on your lap. At a formal dinner or at an elegant restaurant, the server may do that for you. After the meal is finished or if you leave the table for any reason during the meal, place the napkin on the left side of your dinner plate. If your plate has been removed, place the napkin where the plate was.

Oops! Although it's embarrassing, we all get messy once in a while. If you drop or spill something and the mess is minor, discreetly use your napkin to clean it up. If the mess is major, call for the server for help. Here are a few napkin taboos:

- ✔ Never tuck your napkin into your collar, belt, or shirt buttons.
- ✔ Don't crumple or refold your napkin after you finish your meal. Place the napkin down in loose folds near the dinner plate.

Placing Your Order

The server generally takes the women's orders first. Here are a few ordering tips:

- ✔ **When you're a guest, be sensitive to prices and to the pocketbook of your host.** Ask the host what she's having, and then let that price be your guide. In very fancy restaurants, the guests may get a menu without prices. So just order what looks good and isn't too messy, such as stringy spaghetti!
- ✔ **When in doubt, order the special.** Chefs take a great deal of pride in preparing special meals, so specials are generally a good choice.
- ✔ **Don't hesitate to ask the server to explain any item you're not familiar with.**

Ordering cocktails

Here are some tips for ordering cocktails:

- ✔ If you're waiting to be escorted to your table, you can order cocktails at the bar.
- ✔ If you're already seated at the table, you can order cocktails while you're waiting for the other guests to arrive.
- ✔ If you're a nondrinker, order a soft drink.

Pecking order

Here's the pecking order in a fine restaurant:

- **Maitre d':** Seats you at your table.

- **Captain:** Takes your orders and supervises your table service. He lights the souffle, tosses your caesar salad, filets your fish, and so forth.

- **Sommelier (wine steward):** Takes your wine order.

- **Server/ Waitstaff:** Takes your order and is responsible for giving you good service. The terms "waiter" and "waitress" are passé.

- **Busboy:** Fills the water glasses and clears the table.

Ordering wine

When you dine in a fine restaurant, order your wine from the sommelier, or wine steward. (In a less fancy restaurant, the server takes your order from the wine menu.) The sommelier presents the wine to the host. Here's what happens next:

1. **The host checks the label to make sure the wine is correct.** If it is, she gives the green light with a nod. If it's not, she discreetly points out the discrepancy.

2. **The sommelier opens the wine, pours a small amount in the host's glass, and again waits for the green light from the host.** Getting a bad bottle of wine is rare, but if you do, discreetly explain the problem to the sommelier and ask for another bottle.

3. **After the host approves, the sommelier pours the wine into the glasses of the guests.** The sommelier usually starts by serving the women first. Or the sommelier may pour the wine in order around the table, saving the host for last.

None for me, thanks

If you don't want the server to pour you a glass of wine, touch the rim of your glass with your fingertip as an indication that you don't want any. Don't order another wine instead of drinking what the host has selected; that's rude.

What goes with what

Following are some suggestions for wine to compliment your meal. You don't have to stick to the old rules of ordering white wine with poultry and red wine with red meat. Order what you like. If you're fussy about which wines work well with certain foods, check out *Wine For Dummies,* 2nd Edition, by Ed McCarthy and Mary Ewing-Mulligan, published by IDG Books Worldwide, Inc.

- ✔ **Cajun:** White wine or champagne

- ✔ **Chicken and pasta:** Red or white, depending on the sauce (options are Merlot, Cabernet Franc, or sparkling wine)

- ✔ **Chinese:** White Zinfandel

- ✔ **Lobster:** Chardonnay or Viognier

- ✔ **Mexican or Indian:** Beer or Chardonnay

- ✔ **Poultry and fish:** Red wine, such as Pinot Noir or French Burgundy

- ✔ **Shellfish:** White wine, such as Chenin Blanc, Pinot Grigio, or German Riesling

- ✔ **Stew and game:** Red wine, such as Zinfandel or Cabernet Sauvignon

- ✔ **Sushi:** Sake or Sauvignon Blanc

I'd like to propose a toast

The host (or designated person) proposes the first toast before the meal to welcome the guests. If there is a guest of honor, the host proposes a toast to the guest over dessert. The guest of honor then toasts the host.

Clinking glasses is a custom that dates back to the Middle Ages, when doing so offered a chance to pour some of your drink into someone else's glass in case that person was trying to poison you. So, unless you think someone wants to poison you, don't clink glasses.

When someone proposes a toast to you, you don't take a sip. Raise your glass, smile, and nod. Drink later.

Minding Your Table Manners

Polite eating habits separate us from animals and say a lot about our behavior in other aspects of our lives. Displaying good table manners gives you an edge in business.

Reaching across the table

Reaching across the table may be okay, provided you're not reaching across someone else or sticking your sleeve in the salsa. If something isn't within your reach, simply say, *Jim, would you please pass the cream.*

Summoning a server

Always find out the name of your server and remember it. One server can remember who's having what for a party of twelve, but twelve people don't often remember the name of one server. Many servers find it rude to be called as "waiter" or "garçon" (the French word for "boy").

If you need to summon your server, try to establish eye contact or use body language. If that doesn't work, summon her by name. If you can't remember her name, you can fudge it by saying, *Excuse me, would you please . . . .*

Handling utensils

You can generally tell Americans from Europeans. Americans change the fork from the right hand to the left after cutting food. Lefties, of course, do the opposite. Europeans leave the fork in their left hand after cutting meat.

- ✔ If you're not sure which utensil to use, start from the outside and work your way in toward the plate. For example, use the small fork on the outside for the salad, and the large one next to the plate for the main dish.

- ✔ If you drop a utensil on the floor, leave it there and ask the server or busboy to replace it.

- ✔ If a dirty utensil is part of your place setting, don't wipe it. Call the server and ask for a clean utensil.

- ✔ After you finish the main course, place the knife and fork next to each other on the dinner plate, diagonally from upper left to lower right.

Letting the server know there's a fly in your soup

A man was dining in a fine restaurant when he noticed a fly in his soup. "What's that fly doing in my soup?" he asked the server. "The backstroke," the server answered. Alien life forms can appear in food even in the finest restaurants. If this happens, deal with it inconspicuously. Call for the server and ask for a new serving.

Even if your meal was finger-licking good, avoid the temptation. Licking your fingers is gauche. If you need to clean your fingers, excuse yourself and go to the washroom. If you're at an informal restaurant and in the company of colleagues you know very well, you may lower your water glass below the height of the table and dampen the corner of your napkin by tilting your water glass slightly.

Dining do's and taboos

Following are several dining do's:

> ✔ **You can lean your elbows on the table during a conversation, but not during the meal.** It's appropriate before or after the meal or between courses when you're talking.

> ✔ **Keep the noise level to a minimum.** Other people in the restaurant are trying to enjoy their meals so talk in moderate voice levels. And don't sit at the table and chat on your cell phone. If you must use the phone, excuse yourself and go somewhere where you won't disturb anyone.

> ✔ **Dress appropriately.** If you're uncertain as to what attire is proper, call the restaurant in advance.

> ✔ **Fold paper (such as sugar wrappers) into a small unit.** Then tuck the paper under the rim of your plate.

> ✔ **If you receive the wrong food order or your food isn't prepared as you requested, summon the server before you eat too much.** Don't complain after you finish your meal. If the food isn't up to the quality you expected, discreetly mention your disappointment to the server so she can pass the information along to the chef.

> If your food isn't prepared the way you requested, it isn't the server's fault. Don't take your frustrations out on the server when you leave your tip.

> ✔ **Eat foods such as vegetables and potatoes directly from the plates on which they're served.** Don't pile them onto your dinner plate.

Following are things to avoid:

> ✔ **Don't ask to taste someone else's food.** This is only appropriate when dining with friends or others with whom you're extremely close. Otherwise you risk getting your hand stabbed with a fork.

> ✔ **Don't push your plate away from you when you finish eating.** Leave the plate where it is until the server removes it.

> ✔ **Don't drink a beverage while you have food in your mouth.** Not only is it rude, you're difficult to understand.

> ✔ **Don't cut up your entire meal before you eat.** Cut each piece of food just before you eat it.

> ✔ **Don't mix potatoes and veggies on your plate.** If you want to mix them, take small portions of each on your fork.

> ✔ **Ladies, never place your handbag on the table.** Depending on its size and shape, place it on your lap, on the floor, or sling it across the back of your chair.

Paying the Check

When you're the guest, turn your head away while the host is taking care of the bill or engage in conversation with other guests. When you're the host and are treating, arrange in advance with the maitre d' (or server) for the check to be presented to you. (The check will be presented face-down in a small plate or in a small folder.) Without letting your guests see the check, review it quickly. Put the meal on your credit card so your guests don't see money being exchanged.

Dealing with an error in the check

If there's something wrong with the amount of the check, ask for the head-waiter and discreetly discuss the problem. If the problem can't be straight-ened out easily, pay the bill and discuss the matter afterward, asking your guests to wait in the lobby. You don't want to spoil an otherwise good meal by making a scene.

Tips on tips

I've heard it said that the word *tip* comes from an innkeeper's sign: "To insure promptness." When patrons would enter the establishment and put a few coins on the table, they'd get fast service. Today, tips aren't paid in advance, they're paid after the meal as a reward for good service. If the service is poor, you're not compelled to leave a tip. Following are some tipping hints for food and drinks:

- **Drink at a bar:** 10 to 15 percent of the tab
- **Drink in a cocktail lounge:** 15 percent of the tab
- **Steward/sommelier:** 10 to 15 percent of the cost of the wine
- **Server at sit-down meal:** 15 to 20 percent of the tab, depending on the quality of the service and the restaurant
- **Server at buffet:** 10 to 15 percent of the tab, depending on the quality of the service and whether she served parts of the meal (soup, coffee, dessert)
- **Coatroom attendant:** $1 per coat. If two coats are on one hanger, add $.50.

Tipping practices often differ from country to country. In many countries, the bill includes service. You see it listed as a separate entry. When the tip is included, you may consider leaving the foreign equivalent of $2 to $5 in the local currency in addition to what's included.

✔ In Europe, you leave the tip on the table, just as you would in the U.S.

✔ In parts of the Far East, you tip very discreetly.

✔ In the Arab countries, you tip with great fanfare.

Eating a Dinosaur

Some foods are meant to be eaten with your fingers. Finger foods are especially popular at stand-up parties (cocktail parties and buffets) because you don't have to juggle eating utensils. Finger foods include small sandwiches, fruits, and small cakes. If you're are hosting a party and serve finger food, always provide plates for holding the food. Don't expect your guests to hold the actual food in their fingers.

Table 13-1 lists in alphabetical order how to eat the foods most people wonder about.

Table 13-1	How to Eat Messy Foods
Food	*How to Eat It*
Apple	Place the apple on your small plate. Quarter it with your knife. Cut out the core and eat each quarter with your fingers.
Artichoke	Pull off one leaf at a time and dip into the sauce. Scrape each leaf through your teeth. Discard the leaves on a plate. After most of the leaves have been removed, cut away the remaining leaves with a knife. Use a knife and fork to eat the remainder of the artichoke.
Bacon	Eat crisp bacon with your fingers. If the bacon isn't crisp, use a knife and fork.
Baked potato	Use one hand to steady the potato, and slit it lengthwise with a knife that you hold in your opposite hand. Use your fingers to push the slit open so that the steam can escape. Eat the pulp of the potato with your fork. When the pulp is finished, use your fork to cut the skin into bite-sized pieces and eat the skin. If you prefer, you may just leave the skin on your plate.

(continued)

Table 13-1 *(continued)*

Food	How to Eat It
Banana	At a formal dinner, peel the entire banana. Place it on a plate and cut it into bite-sized pieces. Eat each piece with your fork. At an informal gathering, peel the banana halfway and eat it from your hand.
Bread and butter	You'll generally have a separate plate for your bread and butter. Cut the bread into pieces and place a slice on your plate. Take butter from the main butter tray and place the pat on your butter plate. You can also use your butter plate for carrots, celery, or pickles.
Caviar	Put a small portion on your plate along with toast, crackers, or garnishes. Spread the caviar on the toast and eat it in several bites.
Cherries	If the cherries aren't in syrup, you can eat them with your fingers. Discreetly remove the pit by dropping it into your slightly closed fist and replacing it on your service plate. If the cherries are served in syrup, eat them with a dessert spoon. Place the pit in the spoon by bringing the spoon to your mouth. Return the pit to the service plate.
Chicken	Use a knife and fork. Eat chicken with your fingers only at a barbecue or outdoor picnic.
Corn on the cob	Although a popular barbecue item, this will rarely be served at a formal dinner. When you eat corn, use both hands. Hold one end of the ear with your right hand, the other with your left. Butter and salt only a few rows at a time. (If the ear is very large, consider breaking it into small pieces.) You can eat straight across or around the ear, whichever suits you.
Crabs	Crab dishes are popular in the middle section of the East coast of the U.S. The server places a large piece of brown paper on your table and dumps out the crab. It's messy but lots of fun. If you're eating a soft shell crab, the entire crab is edible. Cut it up with a knife and fork, and enjoy. If you're eating a hard shell crab, try this: Pull the legs off with your fingers. Remove the meat with a fork or suck it out. Remove the undershell with a small fork. Use your fingers for the rest.

Food	*How to Eat It*
Fish (noncrustaceans)	A noncrustacean is a fish that doesn't have a hard shell. Use your knife to slice along the center back. Lift one slice of fish off to the side of your plate. Using a fish knife and fork, carefully lift the meat off the spine. Flake off the skin.
French fries	Cut each fry into bite-sized pieces and eat with your fork. If you use ketchup, pour a small amount on your plate and dip each fry. Never pour the ketchup over the fries unless you're at a fast food restaurant.
Gravy	Gravy is primarily intended for meat but can be used over potatoes. When gravy is passed in a gravy bowl with a ladle, spoon it out with the ladle. If no ladle is available, pour the gravy directly from the bowl. Sopping up gravy with bread is one of those gray areas. If you do, put a small amount of gravy on your plate. Place a piece of bread down on the gravy and eat the drenched bread with your fork as you would any other food.
Lemon	To keep the lemon from squirting in the eyes of the person sitting across from you, shelter the lemon in one hand. Pierce it with your fork (thereby rupturing the cells) and squeeze. Some classy restaurants put a little net over the lemon to protect your eyes and the eyes of the people sitting across from you.
Lettuce	Cut large pieces of lettuce with a knife and fork.
Lobster	Probably the only time you'll see an adult wearing a bib is when she's eating a lobster in New England. This gustatory delight is well worth the messiness. Twist the claws off with your hands. Crack each claw with a nutcracker or special lobster cracker. Use a pick or small lobster fork to remove the meat. Break the tail off with your hands. (It should already be split.) If not, break the back flaps with your hands and push in with a fork. Twist off the legs. Gently suck out the meat. Use a fork to reach the small pieces of meat in the body. Use your fork to eat the tomalley (the liver that appears as green matter) and the roe. Although it looks awful, it is edible.
Meat	If the service is family-style and platters are passed around, take one slice at time. Wait for the platter to come around again before taking another slice.
Melon	Use a fork to pick up a melon ball. Use a spoon to eat a melon wedge. If you're eating watermelon, use a fork to remove as many seeds as possible.

(continued)

Table 13-1 *(continued)*

Food	How to Eat It
Orange	Peel the orange with a knife and leave the peels in your plate. Eat the orange in sections with a fork or your fingers.
Pasta	Never cut pasta. Many people eat pasta by holding a fork against a spoon and wrapping the pasta around the fork. Here's a more appropriate way: Wrap a few strands around your fork until you wrap all the long strands. Then lift the fork to your mouth. Never slurp or let long strands of the pasta hang from your mouth.
Pickles, celery, and the like	Never take these items from the tray and place them directly in your mouth. Transfer them to your bread and butter plate first.
Pizza	In New York, people fold the pizza in half lengthwise. In other parts of the United States, people hold a slice of pizza flat while eating it. In Italy, people eat pizza with a knife and fork.
Sandwich	If you're eating a club sandwich or one that is exceptionally thick, cut it into small portions.
Shrimp cocktail	If possible, spear the shrimp with your shrimp fork and eat it in one bite. If the piece is too large, grasp the cup firmly with your left hand (the opposite for lefties) and cut the shrimp as neatly as possible with your fork.
Soup	Eat soup with a soup spoon. Tip the bowl slightly away from you as you scoop. Move the spoon away from you as you fill it. Never slurp soup. If it's too hot, blow it gently. Never place crackers in your soup, and don't dip them. The exception to this rule is oyster crackers, which you may add to chowder, a few at a time.

Working your way around the buffet table

People generally walk around a buffet table clockwise. Loading your plate isn't necessary, because you can return for second and third helpings. At some buffets, the server brings soup, salad, coffee, and dessert at your table. If those courses are on the buffet table instead, take one course at a time and return to the buffet table for each additional course. A server will come around to remove your dirty dishes.

What's Hot on the CD-ROM

Here's what you'll find on the CD-ROM:

- 13-1: Making Reservations
- 13-2: Checking Your Coat
- 13-3: Greeting Guests
- 13-4: Using Your Napkin, Not Your Sleeve
- 13-5: The Pecking Order at a Restaurant
- 13-6: Placing an Order
- 13-7: Minding Your Table Manners
- 13-8: Paying the Check
- 13-9: Eating Different Kinds of Food
- 13-10: Going "French"

Heimlich to the rescue

The universal sign that you're in trouble is to move your hand or fingers across your throat. If someone is choking, never let that person go off alone. She is in need of immediate assistance.

Use the Heimlich maneuver on any person who is choking or is suspected of choking on a piece of food.

To perform the maneuver on someone else, follow these steps:

1. Make the person stand up, if possible. Stand behind the victim and wrap your arm around her waist.

2. Make a fist with one hand, pressing your thumb against the person's body in the place where the rib cage forms an inverted V. Grasp the fist tightly with the other hand.

3. With a quick upward thrust, jab your fist into the person's abdomen. Repeat this procedure until the piece of food has been dislodged.

To perform the maneuver on yourself, follow these steps:

1. Press your body against a chair, sink, or other low object that will give your body stability.

2. Repeat steps 2 and 3 above.

Chapter 14

It's Better to Give

In This Chapter

▶ Giving gifts that show creativity

▶ Selecting special-occasion gifts for colleagues

▶ Sending and exchanging gifts

▶ Being savvy with foreigners

▶ Saying "no thanks" with panache

▶ Sending notes of thank you

The excellence of a gift lies in its appropriateness rather than in its value.

— Charles Dudley Warner, American editor and writer

Gift giving can be a daunting experience. When you select a gift, it speaks to your taste and expresses your feelings toward the person receiving it. There's no better way to show appreciation from your heart than to express "Thank you," "You did a great job," "I'm sorry," "I miss you," "Happy holidays," "Had a wonderful time," "Congratulations," or just about anything else. When you give a gift, be certain to give it in the right spirit and don't expect anything in return.

Putting On Your Creative Cap

Do you give the same old boring gift year after year? If you do, put on your creative cap and try something different. In the following sections, I provide some tips for breaking out of the box (so to speak).

Cybershop

Find your favorite store on the Internet and browse through the e-catalog. (Check out Chapter 5 for information about electronic commerce.) Here are a few Web addresses you may want to check out:

- ✔ www.artisangifts.com (handcrafted items)
- ✔ www.brookstone.com or hammacher.com (innovative gifts)
- ✔ www.gifts24.com (gifts for specific occupations and lifestyles)
- ✔ www.watchzone.com (major brands of watches)
- ✔ www.1800flowers.com (flowers)
- ✔ www.amazon.com (books, music, and more)

Everyone loves books and magazines

A book or magazine subscription is a great gift when you know the person's interests and taste. Inscribe something personal in the book and it becomes a treasure. And a magazine is the gift that keeps on giving all year long.

Seedlings grow up

Flowers and plants make wonderful gifts to someone in the hospital, a hostess, an administrative assistant, a coworker, or a thank you. Rarely is there a wrong time to give flowers or plants. These gifts aren't just for women; men enjoy them, too.

Just like grandma used to make

If you have a special talent, make it a treasured gift. Consider giving something you baked, grew, canned, wrote, painted, knitted, embroidered, or carved.

Playing it safe

If you don't know what to buy, consider a gift certificate. You can purchase a gift certificate for any amount of money. Don't limit yourself to gift certificates to local department stores. Consider a gift certificate to a health club, bookstore, flower shop, boutique, or art store. How about a one-year membership to a museum?

For the traveler

Many people mix business with pleasure and spend extra time visiting a new and exciting area. Following are some gifts for travelers:

- Binoculars
- Diary
- First aid kit
- Guidebook and/or foreign dictionary
- Camera (disposable with wide angle)
- Hidden money belt
- Jewelry case
- Lingerie case (for women)
- Passport holder (leather)
- Photo album or picture frame
- Raincoat (lightweight and easy to pack)
- Sewing kit
- Stationery and stamps
- Travel iron or steamer (with adapter, if necessary)
- Umbrella (folding)

Giving the gift of "thank you"

A gift isn't always money. It can be a turkey for Christmas, a gift certificate to a great restaurant, or tickets to a ball game or concert. Even something as simple as a handwritten note or letter, such as the one shown in Example 14-1, expresses appreciation.

Dear

DiamondSoft is proud of people such as you whose contributions are responsible for the company's success the past year. Without your efforts, we wouldn't be providing such high-quality services to our customers. Thank you for your hard work and great accomplishments.

Congratulations!

Name

Example 14-1: A thank you letter is a gift of expression.

Gift for your supervisor

Birthdays and holidays are often thought of as gift-giving times. The average supervisor is often embarrassed to receive a gift from a direct report, so be sure to determine whether gift giving is appropriate. If it is, consider a gift for your supervisor only if you have a very close relationship or if he has already set the tone by giving you one. Limit the gift to $25 and shun anything personal. Here are a few things that make super gifts for supervisors:

- ✔ Book or magazine subscription
- ✔ Bookends
- ✔ Bottle of wine
- ✔ Desk accessories
- ✔ Home baked goodies
- ✔ Tie or scarf

Be careful about having something monogrammed. After you've had something momogrammed, you can't return it. If you think there's a chance that you'll need to return the gift for any reason, give it un-monogrammed. You or your supervisor can always have the monogram added.

Gift for your administrative assistant

Supervisors often give gifts to administrative assistants for birthdays or holidays. Most appreciate the recognition and deserve it! Here are a few great suggestions:

- Box of candy
- Flowers (Not roses, however. They're a sign of love.)
- Gift certificate
- Goodies from a gourmet shop
- Theater tickets
- Tie or scarf

Don't forget your administrative assistant on Secretary's Day, which falls in mid-April. (I hope someday soon the calendars will update the name of this occasion to be more in line with the times. But for now, many administrative assistants enjoy being remembered during this time.)

Mixing Business and Pleasure

There are many occasions when you give gifts to colleagues. These occasions start at the birth of children and go through the cycle of life. They touch many of the rites and rituals we all enjoy.

If someone takes up a collection for a colleague, you're not obligated to contribute. You may say, *No thank you* or *I'm sorry, but I can't make a contribution at this time.* Most people understand.

It's a boy! It's a girl!

Baby showers have become commonplace in the office, and they're being given for the soon-to-be dads as well as the soon-to-be moms. Here are some nifty gift ideas:

- Baby blanket
- Baby clothes (Don't buy newborn sizes. Babies outgrow them too quickly. Buy sizes for 6 months or older.)
- Children's book(s)
- Feeding plate (with sections and a warmer)
- Furniture (a good chip-in gift)
- Mobile for a crib or playpen
- Music box
- Photo album or picture frame
- Savings bond

- ✔ Silver cup
- ✔ Silver fork and spoon
- ✔ Vaporizer

April showers

Showers in the modern office have more to do with the wedding than the bride; these showers are also given for grooms. After all, the groom is half of the happy couple. Here are some gift suggestions to get them started off right:

- ✔ **Kitchen:** Small appliances (toaster, Crock-Pot, blender); a basket of small utensils (spatula, strainer, measuring cups, cork screw, and so on); a basket of pharmaceutical supplies (bandages, aspirins, cold capsules, ointments, and so on); baking pans, cookie sheets, pie plates, and so on; a canister set; cookbooks; a bread maker; a fire extinguisher; a wok; a spice rack and spices.

- ✔ **Linens:** Bed sheets (for this gift to work, you need to know the size of the bed, of course – double, queen, or king); bath towels and mat; electric blanket; thermal blanket.

If the couple has been sharing a household, they already have many of the basics. Consider some of the gift ideas at the beginning of this chapter.

Here comes the bride — and groom

Brides and grooms often invite business associates to their wedding. The cost of a wedding gift should reflect your closeness to the person and what you can afford. Many couples register with a wedding consultant or a local store, so purchasing a gift through a registry is a matter of deciding how much you want to spend. Check out these ideas:

- ✔ Art object (lithograph, print, sculpture, and so on)
- ✔ Cash, savings bond, or stock certificates
- ✔ Entertaining piece (wine glasses, silver cake server, serving bowl, and so on)
- ✔ Household furnishings
- ✔ Practical items (vacuum cleaner, food processor, and so on)

If you give cash, a bond, or a stock certificate, give it at the wedding. If you buy a gift, consider sending it to the bride's home before the wedding. If you decline a wedding invitation, you don't have to give a gift. Do, however, send a congratulatory note.

By invitation only

Invitations are slightly off the topic of gifts, but I'd feel remiss if I didn't mention them. *Never bring uninvited guests to a wedding.* It causes embarrassment and hard feelings for everyone involved.

When my husband and I got married, we wanted a very intimate wedding. We planned an elegant Sunday morning brunch for 32 close friends and family members — four tables of eight.

We sent an invitation to a colleague of Jon's, a man who was single and not in a relationship. He responded that he was coming. When he showed up with an unexpected date, I had to scramble around to accommodate this additional person. We created a table of nine, which caused everyone at the table to eat with nine elbows sticking in their faces.

Jon also invited his administrative assistant with her husband. Instead of showing up with her husband, she opted to bring her teenage daughter. This caused hard feelings on the part of friends, whose teenage children we didn't invite because of the limited space.

Again, *never bring uninvited guests to a wedding.* If you feel compelled to alter the invitation in any way, call the hosts and ask if there's a problem with that.

Sending a Gift through the Mail

Timing is everything. When you send a gift, plan ahead so it arrives on time. A gift loses some of its thoughtfulness if it arrives after the occasion. Following are some tips for sending gifts through the mail:

- **If the gift has value, insure it.** Many carriers automatically provide insurance of up to $100 without additional cost. Check it out.

- **If you buy the gift at a store and the store mails it, the store is responsible.** Save the tag and receipt in the event of damage or loss. Report a problem to the store immediately.

- **If a catalog company or e-tailer mails the gift, it is responsible.** Keep a record of your confirmation number.

When the Shoe Doesn't Fit

We've all been given white elephants that we store in the closet and pull out when the giver visits. A gift is supposed to be pleasurable, so keeping something you don't want or can't use is foolish — unless you know the giver will be upset.

Don't mix and match

Several years ago the people I worked with gave me a bridal shower. One of my colleagues gave me a gift wrapped in a Lord & Taylor box. I wasn't able to use the item and went to Lord & Taylor to exchange the gift. You can imagine my embarrassment when the store clerk told me that Lord & Taylor doesn't stock that item. I found out through the grapevine that my colleague bought the item at a bargain store.

The moral of this story is: *Never put a gift in a labeled box if the label doesn't reflect the store from which the item was purchased.* This will save you and the recipient much embarrassment.

Exchange the gift for something you'll enjoy and tell the giver you've done so. Also, let the him know how much pleasure you're getting from the new gift.

When I give someone a gift, I always save the price tag and receipt until I'm certain the recipient is satisfied. When I give the gift, I generally give the recipient a chance to save face by saying one of two things:

If you'd like to exchange this, I bought it at . . . .

I'd be glad to exchange this for something you'd rather have.

Giving to Foreigners

As Americans, we pride ourselves on cultural diversification. Yet it's amazing how uninformed we are about other cultures. Then we wonder why foreigners often have the perception that Americans tend to be crude, materialistic, and thoughtless. When you give a *thoughtful* gift, you help to dispel the myth. A thoughtful gift says you're thinking about your colleague, not about yourself. Make sure your gift is of the highest quality.

Foreigners are generally familiar with names such as Tiffany's, Saks Fifth Avenue, Cartier, Neiman Marcus, and the like. Your foreign colleague will appreciate something you bought in the United States, not something you picked up in his country.

Gift-giving do's

If you're not sure about the appropriateness of a gift, ask a business colleague who's been to the country, a business person from the country who lives in the U.S., or an official at the consulate. No matter what you select, wrap the gift nicely because presentation is important. And buy something that isn't too costly so it's not mistaken for a bribe. Following are some gift ideas:

- Classical music, jazz, or folk music (stay away from rock and rap)
- Coffee-table book from the United States, your state, or your region of the country
- Crystal, china, or porcelain
- Fine box of stationery
- Liquor (except in Arab countries)
- Local handicrafts or nonperishable foods that typify the United States
- Pen and pencil set, with refills for the pen
- Something that reflects your colleague's special interest or hobby
- Specialty item unique to your area (maple syrup from Vermont or a piece of silver from the Southwest, for example)

Gift-giving taboos

Never give anything that's personal, such as a shirt, lingerie, or the like. And don't bring a gift from your company with a logo bigger than life. That's not a present, it's an advertisement and crass commercialism.

Before you give a gift to a colleague in a foreign country, always check with a business colleague who's been to the country, a business person from the country who lives in the U.S., or an official at the consulate. Customs differ from one country to another and finding out what to give and how to present it is important. Here are some gift-giving taboos for specific countries:

- **Arab countries:** Don't bring liquor or wine. Alcohol is illegal in Islamic countries and will be confiscated at the airport. Also, don't bring food items because they may be construed as reproach of your host's hospitality.
- **Argentina:** Never give a set of knives because it suggests your wish to "cut off" the business relationship.
- **China:** Chinese law prohibits people from accepting personal gifts. If you do feel the need to give a gift to someone with whom you have a personal relationship, give it privately. Suggestions may be an art book, a lithograph, ceramic piece, or something representing the United States.

✔ **France:** Don't bring a bottle of wine if you're invited to dinner. The host undoubtedly already made the selection and may be insulted. Don't give chrysanthemums because they're placed on graves on All Saint's Day. And don't give yellow flowers; they symbolize infidelity.

✔ **Germany:** Don't give Germans beer unless you brewed it yourself or it's from your home state. Germans are beer connoisseurs. And don't bring a heather plant to a home in North Germany. Heather is put on graves and represents bad luck.

✔ **India:** Never give a gift of cowhide to a Hindu. The cow is sacred.

✔ **Japan:** The Japanese are enthusiastic gift givers and receivers. Never give a Japanese colleague a gift in front of others unless the gift is to be shared by everyone, such as food or liquor.

✔ **Spain:** Don't give dahlias or chrysanthemums; they're for funerals. And don't give a gift that's purple and black. Those colors as associated with the processionals during Holy Week.

Refusing a Gift

Refusing a gift is always awkward, but occasionally you may have to. For example, certain companies and branches of the government deem it inappropriate to accept gifts because the sentiment may be viewed as an impropriety.

If you're in a position to return or refuse a gift, exercise great tact. If the gift is handed to you, you may simply say, *I very much appreciate your thoughtfulness, but it's against my company policy to accept any gifts.* If the gift is mailed, return it with a handwritten note explaining why. See Example 14-2 for a suggestion.

Dear

How kind of you to remember me. I certainly appreciate your thoughtfulness and generosity and know that a great deal of thought went into selecting the [gift]. However, it's against company policy to accept any gifts from clients. It's with the greatest regret that I must return it to you.

I want to wish you a very wonderful holiday and success for the new year.

Warmest regards,

Name

Example 14-2:
Sorry I can't accept your thoughtful gift.

Thanks a Million

You learned at your mother's knee to say *thank you* when someone gives you something. Little did you realize how well your mother was preparing you for the real world. Consider handwriting the note; it adds a personal touch of warmth.

You've got great taste

When someone gives you a tasteful gift, writing a note of thanks is easy. Examples 14-3, 14-4, and 14-5 are samples of a few.

Dear

Thank you so much for your thoughtfulness. I can't tell you how much I'm going to enjoy the beautiful [gift]. You'll be in my thoughts every time I use it.

Sincerely,

Name

Example 14-3:
A simple expression of thanks.

Dear

The Belgian chocolate you brought was luscious. It was such a huge assortment that it fed my entire family of "chocoholics." Next to having given me a winning lottery ticket, there is nothing we could have enjoyed more.

Sincerely,

Name

Example 14-4:
Thanks for nature's most nearly perfect food.

Dear

Your new software is first-rate. It was easy to install, easy to use, and performed exactly as we had hoped it would. I'm sure your company has a winner with this one.

Thanks for allowing us to try your software. It did exactly what we needed it to do. Please feel free to use this letter as an endorsement.

Sincerely,

Name

Example 14-5: Thanks for the software.

Acknowledging an inappropriate gift

When someone gives you an inappropriate gift or one you think is in bad taste, you should still acknowledge it. Notice, however, the difference between the following thank you and the ones for appropriate gifts:

The book you gave me was a pleasant surprise. I appreciate the thought. Thank you.

Trade show treasures

Sales and marketing people can get a lot of mileage from promotional items that are well made and well designed. The items often bear the company's name and/or logo. (The smaller you make the logo, the more appreciated the gift will be.) The giveaway may be just another tee shirt for you, but you're a walking advertisement every time you wear it. Here are some of the giveaways I've enjoyed getting over the years. Even though they had the company logo, they were useful items.

- Calendars
- Clocks
- First aid kits
- Highway emergency kits
- Key chains
- Map cases
- Memo pads
- Mugs
- Pen and pencil sets
- Playing cards
- Stop watches
- Sweat bands
- Tennis hats
- T-shirts

What's Hot on the CD-ROM

Here are the files on the CD-ROM:

- ✔ 14-1 Web Sites for Creative Gifts
- ✔ 14-2: Gifts for Supervisors
- ✔ 14-3: Gifts for Administrative Assistants
- ✔ 14-4: Baby Gifts
- ✔ 14-5: Gifts for Weddings
- ✔ 14-6: Giving Gifts to Foreigners
- ✔ 14-7: Trade Show Giveaways

Chapter 15

When Worlds Collide: Men and Women in the Workplace

In This Chapter

▶ Getting rid of stereotypes
▶ Using gender-neutral terms
▶ Ending sexual harassment of both sexes
▶ Dealing with office romances

There is more difference within the sexes than between them.

— Ivy Compton-Burnett, *Mother and Son*

Since the beginning of time, men and women have had clearly defined roles and responsibilities in the workplace and in the home. Men brought home the bacon; women cooked it. Everyone knew what was expected of them based on tradition and perceived strength and ability. After all, it was Moses whom God sent up to Mt. Sinai to schlep down the heavy tablets containing the Ten Commandments, not Moses's sister, Miriam.

SHERYL SAYS

In days of old

My father was an accountant. I can recall going to his office — the first office I ever saw. It was a bullpen-type office he shared with several men of different professions: an attorney, a meat packer, and another accountant. Each man had a desk, file cabinet, and part-time secretary. My father had an honest to goodness roll-top desk, which was home to his green blotter, his rotary phone, his stack of papers, and his hand-cranked adding machine. Next to his desk, my dad had a metal typewriter stand for his Underwood Noiseless typewriter (early 1900's vintage) on which his part-time secretary (my mother) typed his letters. It truly was a "man's world."

During World War II, while men were off serving their country, women were practically the entire workforce. When the war ended, women went home and started re-thinking their roles. It wasn't until the 1960's, however, that everything went haywire and the twilight of a new era was ushered in. As women entered the workforce in record numbers and started shattering glass ceilings, men assumed greater responsibility in hearth and home. All of a sudden, all of the rules went out the window.

Say Goodbye to Stereotypes

Stereotypes about men and women are as old as the Garden of Eden and as new as the Internet. Differences between men and woman do exist, of course. And in many ways I say, "Viva la difference." Perhaps you've heard these stereotypical expressions:

- **Real men don't ask directions.** Perhaps that's the reason Moses roamed the desert for 40 years.

- **Real women don't change flat tires.** Maybe that's why we have the American Automobile Association (AAA).

Say goodbye to stereotypes, because there *are* men who ask directions and there *are* women who change tires.

In today's professional environment, treat men and women as professionals and talented employees – not as males and females. Men are often in a quandary as to whether to hold the door open for women, whether to walk a woman to her car in a deserted parking lot, and other courtesies. This section addresses many of these nebulous issues.

For men only

As a professional woman, I do enjoy the little niceties of having doors held and so forth, provided the man doesn't go overboard. Men who have been surrounded by women (mothers, sisters, wives, daughters) often fall back on what's comfortable and tend to treat women in the workplace with paternalism. Don't confuse good manners with a "father figure."

My advice to men is this: Don't always feel as though you're walking on ice that's thinner than filament. Do what's respectful and what comes naturally and comfortably. This isn't a first date.

Following are a few tips for courtesy toward women in the workplace and beyond:

- ✔ **Walking:** When you walk down the street with a woman, walk toward the curb to keep the woman from getting splashed. If you're in a dangerous neighborhood, however, walk closest to the building.

- ✔ **Elevators:** When entering an elevator, you enter first to clear the way. When exiting, the person closest to the door exits first.

- ✔ **Coats:** Offer to hang up a woman's coat in a restaurant.

- ✔ **Chairs:** Hold a woman's chair out in a restaurant.

- ✔ **Dinner checks:** If a woman invites you to dinner, let her pay the check if she offers. If you invite her, you offer to pay. It's also appropriate to split the check if it makes you both more comfortable.

- ✔ **Conversations:** Never exclude a woman — or a man — from a conversation, and avoid cussing or foul language.

A female isn't a girl, a dame, or a chick. She's a woman. Instead of saying, *There are two girls working in the mail room,* say, *There are two women working in the mail room.* Better yet, use their names: *Lucy and Ethel work in the mail room.* Check out the following sections for more about sexist language.

For women only

Don't get hung up on words in the English language that appear sexist. Many words that have become commonplace contain the word *man* — even wo*man* has the word *man* in it. There's sports*man*ship, *man*power, *man*hours, and more. I met a woman who wanted to change the name of the round disk covering a hole in the road known as a *man*hole cover to *person*hole cover. I told her to get a life.

Real men don't ask directions

There may be a biological reason why men don't ask directions and women stop at every gas station between Point A and Point B. Dr. Matthias Riepe, a neurologist of the University of Ulm in Germany, discovered that men and women use different parts of the brain to process information about the spaces around them.

One difference involves the *hippocampus* (the navigational part of the brain). Everyone has these banana-shaped structures on the left and right side of the brain. Both sexes use the right hippocampus to negotiate space. However, men also use the left hippocampus, whereas women use the right prefontal cortex instead.

What does all of this mean for you? Essentially, women relate better to landmarks. (*Turn left at the cinema on the corner, then take the next right at the pharmacy.*) Men relate to geometry, such as the kind you find on a road map. Are these differences learned or biologically programmed? Unfortunately, we'll have to wait for more studies to get the answer.

Following are a few general tips for women:

- **Doors:** Open your own doors and hold the door open for other men and women.

- **Foul language:** Don't participate in off-color jokes or use foul language just to fit in with the men.

- **Femininity:** Professionalism and success have nothing to do with femininity. If you wear a feminine dress or a pinstripe suit and a tie, you're still a woman. Always look and act the part of a professional and don't expect any special favors because of your gender.

- **Compliments:** Many compliments are meant sincerely and you should take them in that way. For example, if you dress conservatively and suddenly come to the office in an ultra-feminine dress, chances are you'd appreciate being noticed. Not ogled at, but noticed. You may appreciate a simple statement from a male co-worker such as, *You look especially nice today.*

- **Anger:** Woman tend to have shriller voices when they become angry. (This isn't a sexist remark; it's a fact.) Therefore, when you want to get your point across, always exercise good manners and speak directly and firmly. Never shout in a business situation. This applies to both men and women.

Some women fall into the trap of blaming anything negative that happens in the office on the fact that they're women. Instead of reacting emotionally and impulsively, put yourself in the other person's place. Yes, there are sexist words and deeds in an office, but don't blame everything on sexism.

Use Gender-Neutral Terms

One way to show respect for both sexes is to use gender-neutral terms. Table 15-1 shows some that are worth considering.

Table 15-1	Gender-Neutral Substitutions
Instead of this . . .	*Use this . . .*
Forefather	Ancestor
Chairman	Chairperson, chair, moderator
Cameraman	Cinematographer
Delivery boy	Delivery person, messenger

Instead of this . . .	Use this . . .
Fireman	Firefighter
Fisherman	Fisher
Steward, stewardess	Flight attendant
Mankind	Humanity, human race
Insurance man	Insurance agent
Postman	Letter carrier, mail carrier
Clergyman	Member of the clergy
Weatherman	Meteorologist
Layman	Nonprofessional
Policeman, policewoman	Police officer
Newsman	Reporter, journalist
Salesman	Salesperson, sales representative
Repairman, repair woman	Service technician
Spokesman	Spokesperson
Stock boy	Stock clerk
Man-made	Synthetic
Workman	Worker

Sticky Wickets

Following are sticky situations and tactful ways to address them:

- ✔ **Smoking.** Although many companies have banned smoking in the workplace, there are places where smokers congregate. If there isn't a room set aside, smokers generally congregate outside the building. One courtesy men still extend is to light a cigarette for a woman when he lights one for himself.

- ✔ **Revolving doors.** Who goes first? Who pushes? Use common sense. Revolving doors are often difficult to push, so the person who's stronger should push and go first.

- ✔ **Parking lots.** A man should walk a woman to her car in a parking lot or any area where there is a potential danger. He should also be certain that she pulls away safely. This attitude isn't a chauvinistic one; women are more likely to be victimized than men.

- ✔ **Standing to shake hands.** Men and women should always stand to shake the hands of other men and women.

Sexual Conquistadors Need Not Apply

It's illegal to make anyone in the workplace feel uncomfortable. Women have traditionally been the targets of sexual innuendoes, blatant comments, and actions. Men also experience sexual harassment, but less often. Not only is sexual harassment insulting and unwelcome, it's illegal. There's no place in the office for the sexual conquistador.

What is sexual harassment?

Sexual harassment occurs whenever unwelcome conduct — on the basis of gender — affects an employee's job or performance. Years ago this meant males harassing females, but since women have broken through the glass ceiling and have high-level positions, it also relates to women harassing men and to same-sex harassment. Employees who commit sexual harassment may be subject to severe disciplinary action, which can include the notorious pink slip. Here are some signals of sexual harassment:

- ✔ Someone in authority threatens you with termination, demotion, or intimidation for refusing sexual advances.

- ✔ Someone creates an abusive or hostile work environment or interferes with your job performance through words or actions.

You create a hostile environment verbally by commenting on a person's physical attributes, telling off-color jokes, using demeaning or inappropriate terms and nicknames, discussing sexual activities, ostracizing employees because of gender, using crude or offensive language, touching someone unnecessarily, using suggestive gestures, or hanging sexually aggressive displays in your office.

If you're the victim of harassment and the offense is minor, try handling it yourself. Tactfully let the predator know you're offended. If the predator refuses to take the hint or the offense is serious, don't dismiss the offense. Bring the situation to the attention of your supervisor. If the offender is your supervisor, go another level up.

Buzzing at the watercooler

The watercooler and fax machine seem to be places where people congregate to exchange the who, what, when, where, and why of others' private lives. Although gossip has become the meat and potatoes of office life, it's often unkind and damaging.

Gossip is the information virus of the office and spreads like wildfire! Never engage in or repeat gossip. When you do, you run the risk of being known as *Gossiping Gerry* — the office equivalent of *Typhoid Mary*. When someone initiates this type of conversation, simply say, *I prefer that we don't talk about others.*

Responsibilities and procedures

Supervisors can help prevent sexual harassment by setting the example and maintaining a productive work environment. Should a report of harassment occur in your work area, assist in the investigation and resolution of the complaint.

If you're a victim, report the incident to your immediate supervisor. If your immediate supervisor is the perpetrator, discuss the incident with your supervisor's manager or with someone in the human resources department.

Bringing false charges against anyone is unconscionable, and looking for innuendoes in everything you hear and see is inappropriate.

Don't Be a Stupid Cupid

I'm sure this comes as no shock, but *romance* and *the office* aren't mutually exclusive. You spend so much time at work that it can be a natural and ideal place to meet someone you'd like to spend time with outside the office. For many single people, socializing with coworkers is not as threatening as socializing with complete strangers because you generally know the person and have a common base. There's nothing wrong with people meeting, falling in love, and marrying. But keep your private life private. Here are some suggestions:

- ✔ **Never let your relationship interfere with business.** Even if the romance is on the up and up, be discreet during office hours.

- ✔ **Never get involved with a member of the opposite sex who's married.** That spells disaster.

> ✔ **Avoid talking about your sex life to other people in the office.** If you need a support system or sympathetic ear, find a friend who works someplace else.
>
> ✔ **Don't engage in unwanted flirtations.** If someone initiates it, a simple statement such as, *This isn't the place for that* or *I'm happily married* should suffice.

Be very careful about getting involved in relationships with your supervisor or with someone with whom you have day-to-day dealings. If the relationship doesn't work, imagine how you'd feel if you continued to work with that person on a regular basis. If it gets too uncomfortable and one of you has to leave, it may have to be you. Think before you act! Also, some companies don't believe in nepotism, so if you marry someone from the office, one of you may have to find employment elsewhere.

Shaking hands or kissing

There are seldom situations in business when more than a handshake is appropriate. Some exceptions might be when you congratulate a colleague you know particularly well on a promotion, marriage, or birth of a child. If someone offers to kiss you and you aren't receptive, just turn your head away or smile and take the person's hand and squeeze it affectionately.

Dealing with a roving eye

Being gawked at makes most people uncomfortable. If this happens to you, notice if you're wearing clothes that are particularly tight or revealing. If the answer is yes, get a new wardrobe and stop looking for trouble. (Check out Chapter 24 for tips on dressing for business.) If the answer is no, politely say something to the offending person. Perhaps something such as, *I seem to have lost your attention.*

Supervisors and Assistants

The person who assists a supervisor isn't the *secretary,* the *girl,* or the *boy* — that person is the *administrative assistant* (sometimes called an *AA, assistant,* or *admin*). Without a good assistant, many supervisors may very well be on the bread lines. Here are common scenarios in the supervisor/assistant relationship:

> ✔ male supervisor/female assistant
>
> ✔ male supervisor/male assistant

> ✔ female supervisor/female assistant
> ✔ female supervisor/male assistant

This section focuses primarily on the male supervisor/female assistant relationship, because it's the most common and the one that seems to create the greatest amount of uncertainty.

Do's for the male supervisor

As the supervisor, you set the standards in your department or office.

> ✔ **Let your assistant know from the beginning — and the job interview is not too soon — what her responsibilities will be.** This way, there will be no surprises for either of you.

> ✔ **Refer to your assistant by name when you speak to other people.** *Please call Jennifer Smith tomorrow,* or *Please call Jennifer, my assistant.*

> ✔ **When you give instructions, make certain they're clear.** Your assistant isn't a mind reader. It's your responsibility to guide and direct.

> ✔ **If your assistant is busy or on the phone, wait a few minutes — just as you would expect her to do for you.** It's rude to interrupt anyone who's engaged in a conversation.

> ✔ **Be tactful when offering criticism.** Your purpose is to bring about a change in attitude or behavior, not to intimidate.

> ✔ **Keep the lines of communication open.** Always encourage her input.

Praise your assistant for a job well done. A good assistant is hard to find; don't take her for granted. You may show your appreciation at Christmas-time or on Secretary's Day with a scarf, plant, book, local handicraft, or gift certificate to her favorite store. (Check out Chapter 14 for other great gift ideas.) Let her know that the gift is an expression of your appreciation, not a present.

Taboos for the supervisor

Here are some things supervisors must avoid:

> ✔ **Don't assume when your assistant is on the phone it's a personal call.** Besides, an occasional personal call isn't out of line. We all need to make them once in a while.

- ✔ **If you share an assistant with another supervisor, don't put her in the position of deciding whose work is more important.** You and the other supervisor(s) need to assume that responsibility.

- ✔ **Even though you and your assistant work closely together, don't talk about too many personal issues.** This relationship is centered around business; she's not your therapist.

- ✔ **Never allow your spouse to "pump" your assistant for information.** If this happens, tell your spouse that she's putting your assistant in an awkward situation.

- ✔ **Never expect your assistant to do housekeeping chores.** After all, she didn't sign on as the cleaning staff.

- ✔ **Never criticize your assistant in front of others.** That holds true for anyone who reports to you.

Do's for the female assistant

Do any of these complaints sound familiar? I constantly hear assistants complaining about, what I've termed, the Rodney Dangerfield syndrome:

- ✔ I don't get any respect.

- ✔ I might as well be part of the furniture.

- ✔ I'm tired of buying birthday and anniversary presents for his wife or girlfriend.

First and foremost — if you want to be respected — be proud of who you are and what you do.

- ✔ **If you want to be treated as a professional, look the part.** Pattern your dress after female professionals you admire.

- ✔ **Always ask your supervisor to clarify something that isn't clear.** *I'd like to make sure I'm understanding. You asked me to . . . .*

- ✔ **If you want to give your supervisor a gift at Christmas-time or on another appropriate occasion, it doesn't have to match in value gifts he's given you.** Check out Chapter 14 for appropriate gifts.

- ✔ **Cover for your supervisor, when it's appropriate.** He may be delayed at a meeting and will be late for his next appointment. (However, if you're put in uncomfortable situations because of indiscretions, don't suffer in silence. Simply say, *It makes me uncomfortable when . . . .*)

- ✔ **If you feel you've been treated unfairly, ask to have a private conversation.** Never yell and don't harbor grudges. Calmly state your feelings.

Treat yourself with respect and you'll get respect. I personally know one woman (in her early thirties at the time) who worked her way up the corporate ladder in a major Fortune 500 corporation. She had a bachelor's degree in marketing and started out as an administrative assistant. Within seven years, she was Vice President of the Marketing Department. She got ahead through hard work and dedication. She took her admin's job seriously, made suggestions, showed initiative, and got several promotions which led to a $175,000-a-year position.

Taboos for the assistant

Following are tips for the administrative assistant:

- ✔ **Never discuss classified or confidential information or your supervisor's private life with anyone.** This information isn't to be shared with coworkers, friends, or family.

- ✔ **Show good manners at the front desk.** Don't smoke, chew gum, or eat lunch at your desk.

- ✔ **If you're not very busy and opt to read a magazine or book, do so discreetly.** Putting a file folder around the reading material may be helpful, so that when a client enters the office, you can close the folder and still maintain a professional image.

The Good Old Girls' Network

Over the years, men have had the advantage of close associations with clubs, schools, sports, and other activities that tie them into the "good old boy network." So when it has come to upward mobility, the wheels of the network have ground into motion.

Historically, women haven't had networking advantages. As women are now playing more vital roles in colleges and universities, sports, community activities, and boardrooms, many networking opportunities are opening up to them. The women of today have a responsibility to set a good example for the women of tomorrow. Here's some advice:

- ✔ Join organizations where both men and women congregate.
- ✔ Attend professional meetings.
- ✔ Serve on committees.
- ✔ Donate your time to community activities.

Check out the *Encyclopedia of Associations,* which can serve as a broad-based source of organizations you may consider supporting. Involvement in these organizations can be a springboard to your own career development. And consider learning to play golf. A lot of business is done on the golf course.

What's Hot on the CD-ROM

Here's what's available the the CD-ROM:

- ✔ 15-1: Tips for Men Only
- ✔ 15-2: Tips for Women Only
- ✔ 15-3: Gender-Neutral Terms
- ✔ 15-4: Sticky Wickets
- ✔ 15-5: Appropriate Behavior for Supervisors and Assistants
- ✔ 15-6: The Good Old Girls' Network

Part V
Be a Fearless Road Warrior

The 5th Wave   By Rich Tennant

"Does our insurance cover a visit from Mike Wallace?"

In this part . . .

There are two basic types of travelers: Those who plan and those who fly by the seat of their pants. The fly-by-the-seat-of-your-pants group often gets ripped off on air fare, winds up in second-rate hotels, doesn't have their travel papers in order, and commits blunders in foreign countries.

Whether your travels take you to some mundane part of the United States or to some exotic country abroad, there's no need to feel like Dorothy (from *The Wizard of Oz*) who just got blown in from Kansas. Make your trip hassle free, not turbulent. This part shows you how!

Chapter 16

Air Travel: Up, Up, and Oy Vey!

. . . .

In This Chapter

▶ Finding the best deals

▶ Avoiding the big bump, delays, and cancellations

▶ Exercising while flying

▶ Overcoming jet lag

▶ Earning free flights

▶ Navigating international airports

. . . .

When the captain has turned off the overhead seat belt light you may move your seat to a reclining position. If you cannot figure out how . . . ask the person in front of you whose head will be resting in your lap once they're in a reclining position.

— Brutally Honest Flight Attendant Announcement, *Mad* magazine

Three cheers for Orville and Wilbur! These inventors and pioneers in aviation never finished high school, yet they gave mankind the first powered man-carrying airplane that ultimately shaped the way we do business. The Wright brothers also paved the way for flight delays, long check-in lines, fare wars, lost luggage, jet lag, and air sickness. This chapter tells you how to combat these woes and more. It gives toll-free numbers, hot Web sites, and tips for everything from booking your flight to exercising the kinks out of your cramped body.

Booking Your Flight

There are several ways to book a flight. You may call a travel agent, call the airline directly, or use the Web:

- ✔ **Travel agents.** Call a travel agent (your own or your company's). Travel agents can book your entire trip including airlines, hotels, car rentals, and more. They'll also prepare your itinerary. Travel agents typically charge $10–$15 when they book a flight because the airlines have greatly reduced their commissions.

- ✔ **Toll-free numbers.** Use a toll-free number in Table 16-1 to book your air travel. One advantage to making your reservations with the airline by phone is that if your flight changes (due to bad weather, for example) the airline calls you directly. Table 16-2 lists the toll-free numbers for popular car rental agencies. Some airlines have relationships with specific car rental agencies and will reserve a car for your trip at the time you book your flight.

- ✔ **The Web.** You find the best airfares on the Web and generally get the best rate if you book your trip as far in advance as possible. The best discounts come to those who reserve at least 14 to 30 days ahead. To encourage online reservations, many of the airlines offer great deals such as lower fares, bonus frequent flyer points, and more.

Table 16-1	Toll-Free Airline Numbers
Airline	*Toll-Free Number*
Air Canada	800-776-3000
Alitalia	800-223-5730
America West Airlines	800-235-9292
American Airlines	800-433-7300
British Airways	800-247-9297
China Airlines	800-227-5118
Continental Airlines	800-525-0280
Delta Airlines	800-221-1212
Delta Express	800-325-5205
Finnair	800-950-5000
Iberia Airlines of Spain	800-772-4642
Japan Airlines (JAL)	800-525-3663
KLM Royal Dutch Airlines	800-438-5000
Korean Air	800-438-5000
Lufthansa	800-645-3880
Midwest Express	800-452-2022

Airline	Toll-Free Number
Northwest Airlines	800-225-2525
Qantas Airways	800-227-4500
Sabena Belgian World Airlines	800-873-3900
Southwest Airlines	800-435-9792
Swissair	800-221-4750
Trans World Airlines (TWA)	800-221-2000
United Airlines	800-241-6522
US Air	800-428-4322
Virgin Atlantic	800-862-8621

Table 16-2	Toll-Free Car Rental Numbers
Car Rental Agency	**Toll-Free Number**
Alamo Rent A Car	800-GO-ALAMO
Avis	800-831-8000
Budget Rent A Car	800-527-0700
Dollar Rent A Car	800-800-4000
Enterprise	800-736-8222
Hertz	800-654-2210
National Car Rental	800-CAR-RENT
Rent A Wreck	800-535-1391
Thrifty Car Rental	800-367-2277

Getting the best deal

Here are some ways to get more for your dollar if you're willing to be flexible:

✔ **Avoid traveling between Monday and Friday; opt for the weekend instead.** Mondays through Fridays are notoriously crowded by business travelers, so discount fares are limited on those days.

> ✔ **Stay over on a Saturday night.** Airlines might cut fares as much as 60 percent for those who stay over on a Saturday night.
>
> ✔ **Consider flying in or out of a smaller airport.** Low-fare competition is driving down prices in smaller airports.

You can also get good buys at the last minute by booking with the airline online. (This doesn't mean you shouldn't purchase in advance, however, because last-minute deals are based on availability.) Airlines hold seats expecting harried travelers to pay top dollar to fly across the country. Then they sell the leftover tickets at greatly reduced prices online. Their theory is that a low fare is better than no fare.

Of course, there's nothing like the comfort of flying first class. My husband was flying home from Brussels and didn't have a reserved seat. When he asked for a window seat, the woman behind the counter told him all the window seats were taken. My husband half jokingly said, *I'll take first class instead.* He got it! You may not get bumped up to first class, but you lose nothing by asking.

Visit www.smarterliving.com to sign up for a weekly e-mail that summarizes the Web fares of 20 different airlines. Or visit your favorite airline directly. If your favorite isn't listed here, do an Internet search using the name of the carrier.

> ✔ **America West:** www.americawest.com
>
> ✔ **American:** www.americanair.com
>
> ✔ **Continental:** www.flycontinental.com
>
> ✔ **Delta:** www.delta-air.com
>
> ✔ **Northwest:** www.nwa.com
>
> ✔ **Southwest:** www.southwest.com
>
> ✔ **Trans World Airlines (TWA):** www.twa.com
>
> ✔ **United:** www.ual.com
>
> ✔ **US Airways:** www.usair.com

Safeguarding your tickets

When you get your tickets, photocopy them and keep them in a secure place. If your tickets are stolen, immediately report the loss to the issuing airline and/or travel agent. Having a photocopy on hand hastens your replacements.

Go site seeing

The Web is a great place to get deals. Many of the carriers even give bonus frequent flyer points when you book online. Here are a few of the hot sites to check out for great deals on airlines, hotels, and other travel-related deals:

✔ For full service sites surf
www.biztravel.com,
www.internettravelagency.com,
or www.itn.com.

✔ For discount auction sites try
www.priceline.com,
www.travelclearinghouse.com,
or www.bid4travel.com.

✔ Or go directly to the Web site of the airline of your choice.

Avoiding the perils of electronic tickets

Many airlines offering electronic ticketing, which is sort of a ticket for a ticket. On one hand, electronic tickets are great because you don't have to worry about your tickets getting lost or stolen; they're not actually tickets. On the other hand, if you have to switch to a different airline because of a canceled flight or delay, you can't do it with an electronic ticket.

Here's a suggestion I got from a booking agent: Opt for an actual ticket during heavy travel times such as Monday mornings, Friday evenings, or holidays. Airlines are more likely to overbook during these peak travel times. Otherwise, you may consider electronic ticket.

Special needs

If you have a physical disability, ask to be booked in a bulkhead seat — those in coach that have no seats in front of them with plenty of leg room. The airline can't always guarantee you a bulkhead when you make your reservation, but if you arrive at the terminal early enough, you can generally get one.

Here's how to contact the Society for the Advancement of Travel for the Handicapped (SATH) to find out about special travel services:

SATH
347 Fifth Avenue, Suite 610
New York, NY 10016
212-447-7284
E-mail: sathrave@aol.com
www.sath.org

Avoiding the Big Bump

There's always a chance you may encounter the dreaded "B" word – *bumped*. Getting bumped means you're left without a seat because the airline over-booked, which they do regularly. The reason is that many people make reservations and fail to show, and the airline doesn't want to be left with empty seats. So, they try to estimate how many no-shows they'll have for each flight. Here's how to reduce your chance of getting bumped:

- ✔ **Call the airline the day before your flight and ask if the plane is full.** If it's only 70 percent full, don't worry. If it's more than that, be sure to arrive at least one hour early.

  When you travel internationally, call the airline at least 24 hours before your flight to reconfirm it. Arrive two hours before your flight is scheduled to leave.

- ✔ **Get a seat assignment when you make your reservation.** That's generally a good way to ensure you'll have a seat.

When the airline overbooks, the flight attendant generally dangles a carrot and asks for volunteers who are willing to take a later flight. The volunteer is given money or a round-trip ticket for a later date. If no one volunteers, the airline has the right to bump passengers. If you're chosen, you'll be offered compensation, provided you have confirmed reservations and checked in at the specified time.

Fight Flight Delays and Cancellations

Despite their best efforts, airlines can't always get you to your destination on time. Flight delays and cancellations are as much a part of flying as lost baggage and turbulence.

Getting to the church on time

There are some things you can do to reach your destination even when your flight is canceled or delayed:

- ✔ **Run (don't walk) to the nearest pay phone.** If you booked your flight through a travel agent, call the agent's emergency number. (If he doesn't have one, find another travel agent before your next flight.) If you booked directly through the airline, call the airline's reservation department and get yourself rebooked on another flight. Calling will keep you from waiting on long lines with the rest of the irate detainees. If you have a cell phone, pull it out immediately.

✔ **Find another carrier.** You may get a more timely departure with another carrier. Carriers try to honor each other's tickets during flight delays and cancellations. *You can't do this, however, if you have an electronic ticket.*

✔ **Fly to a nearby destination.** Consider booking on a flight that takes you a little out of your way (perhaps to a nearby city) and renting a car to drive to your destination.

✔ **Fly out of a nearby airport.** For example, if you're booked on a flight out of JFK Airport in New York, you may try to rebook on a flight out of LaGuardia or Newark airports, neither of which is very far away. You can transfer to the other airport via a shuttle that runs between airports. In many cases, if you rebook with the same airline, you won't pay any additional airfare.

Make sure your luggage flies with you. If your luggage doesn't arrive at your destination, find out what arrangements the airline will make to get your luggage to you.

Making the connection

If your plane arrives late, causing you to miss a connecting flight, immediately reserve a seat on the next available flight. If you can't get rebooked on a flight within a reasonable period of time, the airline may be required to provide you with hotel accommodations and book you on a flight the following morning. Of course this isn't going to help you if you have a pressing engagement, but this isn't a perfect world.

Flight Etiquette

Air travel is quite casual and rather impersonal. People sitting together don't necessarily drum up conversations, except during meals or snacks if they choose. If the person sitting next to you is reading or otherwise occupied, don't interrupt with conversation. Also, don't monopolize the time of your flight attendants. They're there to serve all the passengers, not just you.

Lounging around

You don't have to be a VIP or hold a special card to use an airport executive lounge. You can get a priority pass by calling 800-352-2834 or surf the Web at www.prioritypass.com. For just $295 a year you get unlimited access to lounges at more than 300 airports around the world. You can also get a one-time lounge pass for $20 to $30.

Don't waste a trip

Years ago I made a business trip from New York to Wisconsin. My plane left at 6:00 in the morning, and I was to be in Wisconsin just for one day. I arrived for my appointment only to find that the man I was supposed to meet with had to make an emergency trip to Dallas to attend a funeral. He didn't know how to reach me to tell me not to come.

The moral of the story is: *Always give your hosts a phone number where they can reach you if they need to break the appointment at the last minute.* I would rather have had the gent awaken me in the middle of the night and save me the hassle of flying to a meeting that we had to reschedule.

TIP

The airlines will provide service for most special needs if you let them know in advance how they can help. This includes things from wheelchairs to special meals (vegetarian, kosher, or something else).

Working Out the Kinks

Don't let an aching back or muscle fatigue ruin your trip. Following are some things to help you reduce fatigue and stiff muscles caused by long or crowded flights. Some of them may make you look weird, but at least you won't feel like a mummy.

- ✔ **Move around as much as you can.** Walk up and down the aisles and prop your feet on a small travel bag.

- ✔ **If you're relaxing or falling asleep, use a pillow.** Never sleep with your head cocked to one side. That's a recipe for a stiff neck.

- ✔ **Relieve facial tension.** Open your mouth as wide as you can and let your tongue hang out. At the same time, open your eyes as wide as possible. This looks gross so you may want to do this in the lavatory. Otherwise, the pilot may make an emergency landing and have you carted off.

- ✔ **Loosen your shoulder and neck muscles.** Shrug your shoulders and hold the shrug for the count of ten. Roll your head forwards from side to side. Try this five times.

- ✔ **Exercise your feet.** Sit with your feet flat on the floor. Lift your heels ten times keeping your toes on the floor. Then reverse that, lifting your toes ten times keeping your heels on the floor. Also, rotate your ankles clockwise ten times, then counterclockwise ten times.

> ✔ **Flex your hands.** Hold your arms in front of you and spread your fingers as wide as you can. Rotate your wrists clockwise ten times, then counterclockwise ten times.

> ✔ **Stimulate your buttocks and abdominals (stomach muscles).** Sit tall. Contract your abs, then release. Do this five times. Then do the same exercise by contracting and releasing your buttocks.

Overcoming Jet Lag

The human body ticks on an internal clock known as the *circadian rhythm,* which controls bodily functions. This clock is set by a variety of cues such as light, food, caffeine, and exercise. The shift of time zones sends conflicting signals to the brain. Road warriors agree that eastbound flights produce more jet lag than westbound trips because you lose part of the day going east. Whichever direction you fly, however, here are a few tips to help you win the battle of travel fatigue.

Before the flight

You can take some preventative measures before flying:

> ✔ Get to the airport in plenty of time so you don't start your trip hassled.

> ✔ If you're flying across multiple time zones, try to build in a recovery day.

During the flight

Once you're in the air, try these tips:

> ✔ When your plane takes off, set your watch to the time at your destination. This gets you mentally prepared.

> ✔ Grab a snooze followed by a standing stretch.

> ✔ Drink lots of water or decaffeinated beverages, but no alcohol.

> ✔ Eat light meals. (Heavy meals tend to zap your energy.)

I'm all ears

If you tend to suffer from earaches due to changes in aircraft cabin pressure, here are a few things you may try:

- Close your mouth and hold your nose while you attempt to blow through your nose. This

forces the air pockets out of your Eustachian tubes and may relieve the discomfort in your ears.

- If that doesn't help, ask your doctor about taking a decongestant before you take off.

To get more information on jet lag, contact the U.S. Department of Energy and ask for its free copy of "Feast-Fast Jet Lag Diet." Send a self-addressed, stamped envelope to the following address:

Aragonne National Laboratory
9700 South Cass Avenue
Aragonne, IL 60439

You Can Get Something for Nothing

Whoever said "there's no such thing as a free lunch," didn't know how to fly. Join an airline's *frequent flyer club* and earn free trips, upgrades, and hotel accommodations. You can even pass your points to friends and relatives to give them the benefit of free airline flights.

Earning frequent flyer points

Many companies used to ask you to turn in your frequent flyer miles so they could reuse them. However, most companies now give these points to the traveler as a perk for making the trip. Here are a variety of ways to earn frequent flyer miles:

- Each time you fly, you earn one point for each mile so try to stick to one or two airlines.
- Look for special offers from phone services such as MCI or Sprint.
- Earn points for hotel stays and car rentals.
- Get a credit card that partners with an airline and earn one point for each dollar you charge. (If you pay off the balance each month, you won't pay any interest. It's a win-win situation.)

You often need to make reservations far in advance because airlines allow a limited number of frequent flyer seats per flight. Airlines also reserve the right to block out peak travel times for frequent flyers.

Managing your miles

There's more to the equation than just accumulating frequent flyer miles; you must manage them properly. Airline statements aren't always clear as to how many miles you have and when they expire. So, of course, the Web comes to the rescue. Check out www.airease.net and www.maxmiles.com to help you manage your miles.

Also know when it does and doesn't pay to use your miles. Sometimes it's more cost effective to pay for an inexpensive trip and save the miles for an expensive one. For example, if you accumulate 25,000 miles (often enough for a free trip within the U.S.), does it pay to spend those miles on a flight that would cost only $120? Probably not — unless your miles are about to expire.

Getting a free trip

Here are two ways my husband and I got many free trips:

✔ Shortly before I was about to make reservations for a trip to Europe, one of the major airlines sent me a pre-approved application for a major credit card. Two of the perks were 5,000 bonus points and a free companion ticket to anyplace the airline flies. I signed up for the card, my husband got a free companion ticket, and I earned enough miles from the European trip to get a free trip to California to visit my son. Additionally, every time I charge to the card, I continue to get bonus points.

✔ When my husband and I were building our home, we charged all our large purchases (appliances, furniture, and other things) to our credit card. We got enough points for several free trips. If you're a business owner, you can earn lots of points when you charge purchases.

Navigating International Airports

Most international airports are geared to handle the needs of travelers and have signs in multiple languages, including English. So getting around most foreign airports isn't much of a problem. You can always follow the pictograms or the other passengers. Here's what to expect when you arrive at a foreign airport:

✔ **Immigration.** Immediately head to immigration where you show your passport (and visa, if necessary). This process is painless. It's merely a matter of the immigration agent verifying that you're the person the passport was issued to.

✔ **Luggage.** Reclaim your luggage and schlep it to customs.

✔ **Customs.** This is generally a formality, and the officer waves you through. On occasion, the officer may do a spot check to make sure nothing comes into the country illegally, so don't be alarmed if he rummages through your underwear.

If you have any problems at all, it may be after you leave the airport and try to hail a taxi. Two expressions you must learn in the native language are *How much?* and *That's too much.* In some countries taxi drivers are notorious for taking advantage of innocent foreigners. If you can't converse in local currency, take out a pencil and paper and use that as a means of connecting. Numbers are recognized internationally.

What's Hot on the CD-ROM

Here's what you can find on the CD-ROM:

✔ 16-1: Getting the Best Deal when Flying

✔ 16-2: Web Sites for Airlines and Booking Services

✔ 16-3: Toll-Free Numbers for Airlines and Car Rental Agencies

✔ 16-4: Special Services for the Disabled

✔ 16-5: Avoiding the Perils of Electronic Tickets

✔ 16-6: Avoiding Getting Bumped

✔ 16-7: Dealing with Flight Delays and Cancellations

✔ 16-8: Exercises to Work Out the Kinks

✔ 16-9: Reducing Earaches from Changes in Air Pressure

✔ 16-10: Overcoming Jet Lag

✔ 16-11: Getting Free Flights

✔ 16-12: Navigating International Airports

Chapter 17

Please Come Inn

In This Chapter

▶ Checking out the star ratings

▶ Getting the best deal

▶ Personalizing your room

▶ Keeping yourself safe

All saints can do miracles, but few of them can keep a hotel.

— Mark Twain, *Notebook*

Historians suggest that people traveled as far back as 4000 B.C., and it was then that tourist homes were first recorded. These homes provided shelter and rest to bone-weary travelers. Although travel has changed dramatically since then, the original premise remains the same. Today's business travelers look for shelter and a place to rest their weary bones. Hotel owners still know the importance of being in the right location and identifying the traveler's route. However, competition is stiff and today's hotel owners provide lots of amenities.

Star Gazing

Hotels are internationally classified by a system of stars on a scale of one to five. The primary criteria are cleanliness, maintenance, physical conditions, services, and degree of luxury. Remember that people's expectations of luxury vary depending on whether they're staying at a dude ranch in the Southwest, a historic inn in Cape Cod, or the Four Seasons Hotel in Boston. Here's how to read the stars without going to an astrologer:

✔ **Five-star hotel:** The most deluxe and luxurious. You'll be treated like a VIP and can expect superior restaurants, luxurious lobbies, and a meticulously groomed landscape.

✔ **Four-star hotel:** A cut above the average. You can expect a good restaurant, nice-looking lobbies, and an appealing landscape.

✔ **Three-star hotel:** Average. It should include everything in a two star plus other amenities. A three-star hotel offers you a very pleasant stay.

✔ **Two-star hotel:** More than a one-star. You may expect a TV in your room, direct-dial phones, 24-hour desk service, but little in the way of luxury.

✔ **One-star hotel:** The most economical and frugal. You know what's important to you, what your budget is, and what you're willing to settle for. At the very least, you should expect a clean and comfortable room.

Using the Hotel's Toll-Free Number

With toll-free numbers, comparison-shopping is easy. Don't be fooled by discounts, however. One hotel may advertise a 50 percent discount, but a comparable hotel's everyday rate may still be lower. Get the real dollars. Also, ask about frequent guest programs, special weekend rates, AAA and AARP discounts, corporate or government rates, and any other special rate offerings. Table 17-1 shows the toll-free numbers for some popular hotels.

Table 17-1	Toll-Free Numbers for Popular Hotels
Hotel	*Toll-Free Number*
Best Western Hotels	800-528-1234
Comfort Inn	800-244-8181
Crowne Plaza Hotels and Resorts	800-2CROWNE
Wooster Inn & Suites (formerly Days Inn)	800-932-3297
Doubletree Guest Suites	800-222-8733
Embassy Suites Hotels	800-362-2779
Hilton Hotels and Resorts	800-HILTONS
Holiday Inn Hotels	800-HOLIDAY
Hyatt Hotels and Resorts	800-233-1234
Marriott Hotels	800-228-9290
Radisson Hotels Worldwide	800-333-3333
Ramada Inn	800-228-2828
Ritz-Carlton Hotels and Resorts	800-241-3333
Sheraton Hotels	800-325-3535
Susse Chalet Inn	800-524-2538
Westin Hotels and Resorts	800-228-3000

You may also check out a hotel's Web site or get information from an online service such as www.priceline.com.

Getting the best deal

You may not always get the best rate when you call a hotel's toll-free number. The reservationists aren't empowered to negotiate. Instead, consider calling the hotel directly. Ask very politely for the absolute lowest rate they have. If you want to push a little more, ask for an upgrade or a suite. You know you've pushed enough when the operator is about to hang up.

If you book a room in advance and want it held for late arrival, prepay for the room with your credit card. If your plans change, you can generally cancel without penalty within hours before. Ask about the hotel's cancellation policy. If you do cancel, get a cancellation number.

If you book a room in a foreign country where the dollar is weak, consider paying in advance in U.S. dollars. Paying in advance can be a gamble, but if the dollar remains weak, your room will be cheaper than if you paid on-site in foreign currency.

Getting a room without a reservation

If you don't have a reservation and arrive early in the day, you have a better chance of getting the accommodations you want, where you want them. Noon is generally a good time to find a room because hotels know by then who's checking out. If you think a hotel may be booked or you're unsure of what's available in the area, take advantage of hotel booking services found at airports, train or bus terminals. Or call the hotel directly and make your own reservations.

What can you do if you get you to your destination late and you don't have a room? Here's where a guidebook is handy. Hail a taxi and ask the driver to take you to the closest hotel on your list. If the desk clerk tells you that all the rooms are booked, ask her to find you a room in a nearby hotel. Most desk clerks want to maintain good will and are glad to accommodate you.

Getting a room with a view

Not all rooms are created equal, and the meek inherit the worst. So be assertive. Hotels are anxious to please. The more hotels understand your needs, the easier it is for them to accommodate you. Following are some issues that may concern you:

✔ **Smoking.** Do you require a smoking or non-smoking room?

✔ **Noise.** Do you want to be away from the bar or ice machine? Do you mind having a room over the bar?

✔ **Bed.** Do you want a double-, queen-, or king-sized bed?

✔ **Amenities.** Do you want a whirlpool, a double sink, lots of closet space?

✔ **Floor.** Do you prefer an upper or lower floor? Higher floors are often less noisy.

✔ **Views.** Do you prefer a room with a view of the mountains, the pool, the golf course?

Check Out Before You Check In

Your hotel is your home away from home. Therefore, "safety first" must be the mantra of all savvy travelers. Following are ways to check out the safety of a hotel before you make a reservation and tips for staying safe once you're there.

Shopping for safety before you book

How safe is your hotel? This information *is* available to you, so comparison shop for safety — not just for prices and amenities. Any hotel that prides itself on safety and security will be glad to answer your questions:

✔ **Are there rooms that open to the interior of the building only?** Avoid easy-access rooms that open to the outside, such as those that have patio doors.

✔ **How secure are the doors to the rooms?** Do they have peepholes? Are there deadbolts, latches, or chains?

✔ **What kind of keys are used?** Avoid hotels that offer metal keys. Metal keys can be reused, sometimes by the wrong person. Instead, look for a hotel that offers card keys. Although they might be more difficult to use because you often have to jiggle to get them in properly, card keys *are* safer. Most of the hotels change the code on the card key or issue a new card keys for each new guest.

✔ **Are there telephones in the room?** Most hotels do have telephones in the rooms, but don't take it for granted, especially if you stay at a one-star hotel. Also, ask for a complete list of emergency numbers.

✔ **Is there 24-hour staffing?** Most hotels do offer round-the-clock staffing, but don't take that for granted either.

✔ **Is there adequate lighting?** Find out about parking lot lighting and corridor lighting.

Many hotels have special floors for women where there's extra security. If you're a woman and this is important you, check it out. As an added bonus, the rooms for women are generally decorated with a more feminine motif.

Staying safe after you arrive

Following are some safety tips to ensure a safe stay at the hotel:

- ✔ **Don't open your door without verifying who is there.** If a person claims to be an employee, call the front desk and ask if they sent someone from their staff to your room. If they didn't, never open the door. If the person is indeed a member of the hotel staff, he or she won't mind waiting.

- ✔ **Use the main entrance of the hotel, especially when returning to your room after dark.** Also, be observant and look around before entering parking lots. Have your room key ready. Take it out before you reach your room, so you're not fumbling at the door for your key.

- ✔ **Take precautions when you leave for the day.** Turn a light on so you'll return to well-lit, comfortable surroundings. Also, don't leave the sign on the doorknob requesting maid service; it's an advertisement that you're not there. Leave the message at the front desk instead.

- ✔ **Lock the door securely even when you're in your room.** And make sure you lock sliding doors, windows, and connecting room doors as well.

- ✔ **Be wary of strangers.** If you make a new acquaintance you'd like to meet for dinner or drinks, do so in a public place – never in your room.

- ✔ **Protect your valuables.** If you have valuables, get a hotel safe. Make a list of the contents and the value of each item, and be certain that a hotel employee signs a verification. Also, be certain your valuables are actually being stored in a safe. In some smaller hotels, the "safe" may be the cubbyhole beneath the desk.

- ✔ **Be aware of what's around you.** If you see anyone or anything that looks suspicious, report it to the hotel management immediately.

This may sound slightly paranoid, but if you're traveling alone, before you leave your hotel room, write down your destination, the people you're planning to meet (along with their phone numbers), and the time you expect to be back. Leave the note in a visible spot in your room. If for some unexplained reason you don't return, the police will have a starting point to search for you.

Puttin' on the Ritz

The Ritz hotel chain is revolutionizing the industry by catering to the new techno-driven consumers who are willing to pay for the best of everything. For example, if you travel to Boston and stay at the Fifteen Beacon Street hotel, you can call the 24-technology butler at two in the morning if your computer is acting finicky.

You can get business cards printed on the spot with your personal phone and fax number so your calls can be forwarded to voice mail or a cell phone. You can control the surround-sound system by pushing a button from your bed.

Catering to the young Internet millionaires, even the minibar is stocked with energy bars, ginseng, high-protein drinks, and Krug champagne. Yes, all the comforts of home (not mine, of course).

Business travelers often disqualify hotels that aren't *wired*, so many more hotels are jumping on the techno-bandwagon. In fact, hotels who want your business employ a *comp-cierge*, a computer concierge who responds to technical needs and problems.

Hotel Savvy

If you stay at a hotel that offers valet service, make your life easier and use it. For a tip of a dollar or two ($5 in a swanky hotel), you don't have to schlep your luggage.

For the sake of safety, desk clerks generally write down your room number, rather than announcing it to the immediate world. If the desk clerk calls out the number of your room and others overhear it, ask for another room assignment. Be certain that your room assignment isn't on the first floor — another safety precaution.

Checking out your room

When you arrive at the hotel, ask to see the room you've been assigned. If you don't like it, politely assert yourself. For example, you might say, *This room is awfully dark. Do you have something that's sunnier?* Hotels often push the lousy rooms first. This is especially true in foreign countries, where the worst rooms often go to foreigners.

If another room is available, you'll probably get it. Otherwise, you might just have to grin and bear it. If you're on business travel and your company does a lot of business with the hotel, you might tactfully convince the hotel manager that you're entitled to superior accommodations and service. If you don't get satisfaction, try to stay elsewhere on your next trip.

Staying on the club floor

The club floor is a special section in a hotel offering perks. Safety and privacy are the main draw of the club floors, but it may add as much as 20 percent to your bill. You can enter the club floors only with a guest's elevator key. The room doors often have high-security coded locks. The floor usually has private lounges for dining. Other amenities may include complimentary hors d'oeurves, express check-in and check-out, and frequent traveler discounts. Many of the leading hotels have club floor services, so check with your hotel if you're interested.

Personalizing your room

Even if you're staying for just a few days, why live with a utilitarian look? You'd be surprised at how much more pleasant your room is when you personalize it. Bring from home a favorite photo or favorite (replacable or inexpensive) object that's special. Display these treasures on the dresser or some other visible place. Even though you'll be away from your hotel room most of the day, seeing something familiar when you open the door makes the room more homelike.

Concerning the concierge

The term *concierge* is synonymous with *service*. The concierge looks after guests by suggesting restaurants, getting tickets to theaters and sporting events, providing directions, and disseminating information about happenings in and around the area. The concierge is an amenity provided by the hotel, so you aren't required to tip.

If the concierge pulls off a minor miracle, however, a tip is befitting. Guests sometimes feel uncomfortable giving money, but a small gift is appropriate. Flowers, a fine box of candy, perfume, or cologne are common examples of gifts given to the concierge.

You should tip the people who make up your room. One dollar per night is customary. You can leave the tip on a nightly basis or accumulate it for when you check out.

Talk is (not always) cheap

Before making calls from your room, check with the front desk to find out if you'll be charged an access fee for using the hotel's phone system. Some hotels participate in agreements with international phone companies such as

AT&T and MCI that limit access fees. If there is a charge, don't hang up after each call. Instead, press the pound sign (#) between calls to eliminate additional access charges.

If you have a calling card, use it. Chances are you'll save on the access fees many hotels tack on to phone calls. Some hotels offer free local service and charge only for long-distance calls. Find out in advance. Be aware, however, of calling card surcharges. Some carriers tack on a charge if the call originates out of the calling area.

If you really want the best deal, use a pay phone. Check out Chapter 2 for tips on keeping the costs down when using pay phones.

What's Hot on the CD-ROM

Here are the files on the CD-ROM:

- 17-1: Hotel Star Ratings
- 17-2: Toll-Free Numbers for Popular Hotels
- 17-3: Shopping for Safety Before You Book a Hotel Room
- 17-4: Staying on the Club Floor
- 17-5: What's Important in a Room
- 17-6: Minimizing Telephone Expenses

Chapter 18

Getting Your Papers in Order

· ·

In This Chapter

▶ Applying for a passport

▶ Getting a visa

▶ Knowing when you need an international driver's license

▶ Dealing with health issues

▶ Getting a shot in the arm

▶ Knowing how to handle money

· ·

When You Look Like Your Passport Photo, It's Time To Go Home

— Erma Bombeck's popular book

*A*rmchair travel is hassle-free. You sit in your favorite armchair and watch your favorite travel video. Or you pore through the pile of papers on your end table — magazines, brochures, maps, and more. When you venture out for the real experience, however, you may have more paperwork than you imagined. You know you need a passport to travel abroad, but have you thought of getting a visa, an international driver's license, health forms, and more?

Your Passport to Paradise

When you travel outside the United States (other than to Canada, Mexico, the West Indies, the Caribbean, and some South and Central American countries) you need a passport. A passport lets you leave the U.S., get protection in a foreign country (should you need it), and return to the U.S.

SHERYL SAYS

My birth certificate expired?

Applying for my first passport was an interesting experience. I went to the local passport office with my birth certificate in hand. The woman behind the desk looked at my birth certificate and promptly said, "I can't accept this birth certificate. It expired." "Expired?" I questioned. "Yes," she answered, "It expired." "But, birth certificates don't expire," I retorted. I pinched myself to make sure I was still alive, and I hadn't expired. "Do you mean I've been paying taxes all these years for nothing?" I quipped. She didn't appreciate my attempt at humor.

To make a long story short, of course, my birth certificate hadn't expired. Birth certificates don't expire. When the city of New York issued my birth certificate a hundred years earlier, the clerk who issued the certificate didn't place an embossed seal on it. The passport office stopped accepting birth certificates without embossed seals a few years earlier.

The lesson learned is . . . *be certain your birth certificate has the embossed seal* or you too may expire prematurely.

If you don't have a passport, get one now. You never know when you may have an opportunity to travel abroad. If you have a passport, you can save yourself the stress and expense of applying for one at the last minute.

If it's your first time, be gentle

When you apply for your first passport, appear in person at a state department passport agency; a designated Federal, state, or county courthouse; or a designated branch of the U.S. Post Office. Not all post offices issue passports, so call ahead. Here's what you need to bring with you:

- ✔ **I.D.:** A valid form of identification, such as a driver's license or government I.D. card.

- ✔ **Proof of citizenship:** Your original embossed birth certificate, certificate of naturalization, certificate of citizenship, or report of birth abroad if you're a U.S. citizen. If you don't have any of these, bring a baptismal certificate, voter registration, elementary school records, or insurance papers.

- ✔ **Photos:** Two identical 2 x 2-inch photos that were taken within the last six months. The photos can be either color or black and white. Check the Yellow Pages to find out which photo shops or travel agencies take passport pictures.

- ✔ **Fee:** Your check for $65 for the initial passport, and $55 for renewals by mail. (This amount is subject to change, so check ahead.)

Many foreign governments require that your passport be valid for at least six months from the date you enter the country. So it's wise to renew your passport a year before it expires.

Renewals

A passport is valid for ten years. If you had a passport in the past and want to renew it, visit your local passport office or participating post office, or mail in your application. Include an application form, your old passport, two new photographs, and the appropriate fee.

An ounce of prevention

After you get your passport, photocopy two copies of the first page. Take one copy (plus the original passport) with you when you leave the country. Leave the other copy with someone you can contact in the event your passport is lost or stolen. Make sure you record on a separate sheet of paper the serial number, the date your passport was issued, and the city in which it was issued. Keep the photocopy in your suitcase or pocket just in case you and your passport should be separated.

You must have your passport in order to leave a foreign country. If you lose it, you'll be floating around looking for the U.S. Embassy, chanting, "Beam me up, Scotty." Actually, you won't become a permanent resident of never-never land, but the ordeal could be extensive.

Keep your passport on you (not just with you) at all times. Don't leave it in your hotel room, your suitcase, or your pocketbook. A safe way to carry your passport is to use a money belt or special passport holder that's attached to your body. If you're going to the beach or some other place where that isn't possible, take your passport or lock it in the hotel safe.

Despite all these precautions, here's what to do if your passport is stolen. This is where having an extra copy of the pertinent information is handy. Proceed to the U.S. Embassy or consulate, and they will issue you a new passport. If you don't have this information, you may have to wait several days before the State Department in Washington authorizes a new passport.

Visitor's Visa

A visa is an endorsement made in your passport that allows you to enter the country you're visiting. It testifies that your passport has been examined and is in order. A visa permits you to visit the country for a specified (usually limited) period of time.

Some countries require visas, but not all. Call your local consulate office or your travel agent. When you're visiting a country that requires a visa, you can get one issued by the consulate of that country. You can get a visa by submitting your passport, an application, and any necessary fees. Some countries require a letter of reference or proof that you have transportation in and out of the country, and some will restrict the length of your stay. Here's how to get more information on visas:

> PVS International
> 1700 N. Moore Street
> Rosslyn Center, Suite 310
> Arlington, VA 22209
> 800-556-9990

International Driving Permit

Some countries honor American driver's licenses; others require a local one written in the native language. For information about an international driving permit, call the American Automobile Association (AAA) at 800-222-8252. This number tends to be busy, so you may want to check with your local AAA office.

International Certificate of Vaccination

Some countries in Asia and Africa request certificates of vaccination for diseases. You can get forms through local or state public health offices or passport agencies. The form requires a doctor's signature and the health department's stamp. If you're planning to visit a country that requires immunizations, allow at least ten days between the final shot and the date of departure to give the vaccine time to take effect and to allow for any adverse reactions you may have. Following are two sources for getting more information:

> Health Information for International Travel
> Publication No. (CDC) 81-8280
> Superintendent of Documents
> Washington, DC 20402

Centers for Disease Control
888-232-3228
cdc.gov/travel/index.htm

Here's to Your Health

If you have health problems that may require special attention, ask your doctor to prepare your medical history to take with you. Have him include your medical history, blood type, medications and dosages, allergies, and any other relevant information. Following are a few other health-related things worth looking into:

✔ **MedicAlert.** This is a nonprofit foundation that maintains your health records to be retrieved by phone from around the world. You can get a medical alert card, I.D. bracelet, or necklace. It costs $35 to enroll, and there's a $15 annual renewal fee. Here's how to contact the foundation:

MedicAlert
Box 1009
Turlock, CA 95381
800-344-3226
www.medicalert.org

✔ **Health insurance:** Check with your health care provider to understand what your policy does and doesn't cover when you're out of the state or country. If your policy doesn't cover you where you'll be traveling, ask your travel agent or insurance carrier about short-term health or emergency assistance policies. Short-term policies are generally inexpensive and may be worth the cost. (Medicare doesn't cover you outside the U.S.)

✔ **Medication:** Leave your medication is its original container and make sure it's labeled. Ask your doctor for the generic name of your medication so you can get a supply in a foreign country, which may use a different brand name. And never pack your medication in your suitcase; carry it with you at all times.

If you need emergency medical or dental services while you travel, contact the U.S. embassy or consulate. However, it's always a good idea to carry with you the names of medical people you can contact in case something unexpected happens. Here's how to contact the International Association for Medical Assistance to Travelers (IAMAT) for that information:

IAMAT
417 Center Street
Lewiston, NY 14092
716-754-4883
www.sentex.net\~iamat

Money Matters

Whenever you visit a foreign country, take along a calculator. No matter where you travel and what kind of payment you use, a calculator helps you convert your foreign currency into U.S. dollars. (For example, in countries such as Italy or Turkey, where you have endless zeroes on the price of a stick of gum, the amounts can be intimidating. After you do the math, it never seems so bad.) Also bring along a supply of $1 bills. They come in handy for tips.

Foreign currency

More than 1,700 years ago, the Roman Emperor, Diocletian, put forth a noble effort to establish a single currency in Europe to try to unite his disparate subjects. The single-currency concept fell after 16 years following Europe's many bouts of bloodshed. More than 2,000 years later, the euro (the currency found in most of Europe) once again reigns supreme. (Check out Chapter 19 for more about the euro.) Following are some tips on exchanging money in a foreign country:

- ✔ Before you leave the U.S., purchase a small amount of foreign currency for buses, taxis, telephones, tips, and other small expenses.

- ✔ When you're abroad, you get your best rate of exchange at local banks or American Express offices. Kiosks and hotels milk you for outrageous exchange fees.

- ✔ Don't exchange more money than you anticipate needing because you incur an additional fee for converting back to U.S. currency. Use your best guess as to what your out-of-pocket expenses will be. Each time you exchange money, you pay an exchange fee.

- ✔ In some countries you break the law if you enter or exit with that country's currency. Check with the country's embassy or consulate before you leave home.

Credit cards

If you travel a lot for business, consider having one credit card that you dedicate to business travel. That makes it easy to track your expenses. If your credit card is lost or stolen, report it to the company immediately: Table 18-1 gives you phone numbers of the popular card companies for the U.S. and abroad.

Table 18-1	Reporting Lost or Stolen Credit Cards	
Card	*Dial from the U.S.*	*Dial Collect from Abroad*
American Express	800-528-4800	910-333-3211
Diner's Club	800-234-6377	None
Discover	800-347-2683	Not accepted outside the U.S.
MasterCard	800-622-7747	303-278-8000
Visa	800-336-8472	410-581-7931

Note: Not all countries accept the American Express card. If American Express is your only credit card, you may consider getting another as a backup.

Traveler's checks

Even though you have local currency and credit cards, it's a good idea to bring along traveler's checks. Record the serial numbers, the denominations, and the name of the bank or office that issued them. Keep one copy of this information in a safe place (perhaps with someone in your home office) and another one with you (obviously not with the checks themselves).

If your traveler's checks are lost or stolen, notify the issuing company immediately. Table 18-2 gives you the phone numbers to report lost or stolen traveler's checks for the U.S. and abroad.

Table 18-2	Reporting Lost or Stolen Traveler's Checks	
Bank	*Dial from the U.S.*	*Dial Collect from Abroad*
American Express	800-221-7282	800-221-7282 (or contact the nearest American Express office)
Citicorp	800-645-6556	813-623-1709
Thomas Cook MasterCard	800-223-7373	609-987-7300
Visa	800-227-6811	410-581-5353

If you need immediate cash, call your local bank or Western Union. Get the number of the Western Union office nearest you by calling 800-325-6000.

What's Hot on the CD-ROM

Here's what's on the CD-ROM:

- ✔ 18-1: Papers You Need to Get a Passport
- ✔ 18-2: Information on Visas
- ✔ 18-3: Getting an International Driving Permit
- ✔ 18-4: Information on Vaccinations
- ✔ 18-5: Phone Numbers for Major Credit Cards
- ✔ 18-6: Phone Numbers for Traveler's Checks

Chapter 19

When in Rome . . .

In This Chapter

▶ Representing America well

▶ Enjoying Europe

▶ Amazing Asia

▶ Loving Latin America

▶ Meandering in the Middle East

▶ Knowing when holidays are celebrated in other countries

When You Start to Look Like Your Passport, It's Time To Go Home.

— Erma Bombeck, writer

As the world continues to shrink and the world market continues to grow, business people are becoming vigilant and skillful in searching out and seizing new growth markets. As a result, business travel to foreign countries abounds. Foreign travel is exciting. It exposes you to new and different cultures and broadens your horizons. Each country has its own culture, language, customs, and pace. Enjoy these new experiences. Let the pleasure of these new customs enhance your business pleasure and your world.

Notice the Rose in the Vase, Not the Dust on the Table

Don't consider standards in the United States a guideline by which you measure life elsewhere. And don't judge. Things *are* different elsewhere. Different doesn't make them better or worse; they're just different. Enjoy the differences and think of them as a way to learn about a new and exciting culture. When you see Tibetan tribesman greet each other by sticking their tongues out or Latin Americans greet each other with a firm hug (known as an *abrazo*), that's part of the culture and perfectly normal.

Unifying Languages

Since the Tower of Babble, people have been searching for a common way to communicate. English is the language of business, and most people in the business world have some command of the English language.

Hablo Esperanto, monsieur?

One attempt to unify languages was in 1887 with the advent of an artificial language called *Esperanto*. It's artificial because there's no country or region from which it originates. Esperanto was intended to create a solution to the disparate languages spoken around the world. Although about 2 million people speak, read, and write this language, we can't be sure how widespread its usage has become.

Esperanto has no gender (subjects aren't male or female as they are in other languages). From the following words, you may see a similarity between Esperanto and other languages you know:

- amik-o: friend
- pan-o: bread
- kaf-o: coffee
- trink: drink
- te-o: tea
- latk-o: milk

Computers to the rescue

Translation software has helped bridge the gap in communications. An international group of computer scientists advanced speech-technology research to the point that it can translate among English, French, German, Italian, Japanese, and Korean on the fly. For example, an English-speaking person telephones a colleague in Germany. Both people speak in their native languages and the software keeps the conversation alive by recognizing the speaker's language and digitally speaking to the listener. As the Web spans time and oceans language barriers will become insignificant.

There are folks living in the United States who may as well be in a foreign country when they leave their homes. Following is a letter Ann Landers published from a reader who lives in Herbert Hoover's home state: "We live in Des Moines. When we traveled East a few years ago, we were appalled that a number of people had never heard of Iowa. They didn't know that Iowa is a great agricultural state. . . . A New England woman asked my wife where we were from. When my wife said, 'Iowa,' the Connecticut Yankee replied crisply, 'We pronounce it Ohio in this part of the country.'"

You're an Ambassador

When you travel outside the United States — whether or not you realize it — you're an ambassador for your country. The image you create reflects the way those you meet will view *all* Americans. Take the time to learn all you can about your host country.

If you know nothing about the customs or language, you insult your hosts. The message you communicate is that they aren't worthy of your taking the time to learn about them. To get information about a host country, contact the country's embassy or consulate, get a travel guide, or tap into the Internet.

Open doors with key words

When you learn a few key words in the language of the host country, you transform yourself from a stuttering, gesticulating gringo to a savvy professional. Here are some common words and expressions (in addition to hello and good bye) to learn in the native tongue that will be helpful in social and business situations:

Please	Thank you	Excuse me
Good morning	Good day	Good evening
I'm sorry	Yes, I understand	No, I don't understand
Just a moment	Chairman	President
Vice-President	Director	

General do's

The following tips may keep you from standing out like a wort. You find more information about most of these tips later in this chapter.

- ✔ Compliment your host about the beauty or accomplishments of the host country or city.

- ✔ Become familiar with the dress code for business and after hours (formal, casual, or in between). Check out Chapter 24 for more information.

- ✔ Know the religious taboos, if there are any.

- ✔ Know the proper way to greet your hosts and make introductions.

- ✔ Understand what gifts are appropriate. Check out Chapter 14 for information on gifts.

- ✔ Be aware of current events that surround the country or area, and be sympathetic to their problems.

- ✔ Find out as much as you can about artistic, cultural, and sports figures.

- ✔ If appropriate, learn about the metric system.

- ✔ Bring plenty of business cards. Place your name, company, and address on the reverse side in the language of the host country. Offer the card with the native-language side showing.

- ✔ Be cognizant of a person's personal space. Some cultures foster physical closeness; others shun it.

- ✔ Respect a country's monetary unit. It is *real* money. On overseas trips, I've heard comments such as, "What does this cost in real money?" or, "This is just like Monopoly money!" Those comments are not only rude, they make the speakers sound like idiots.

Lost in the translation

When you say something in a foreign language, be sure it translates properly. Following are some signs that were translated into English to accommodate Americans:

- ✔ **Bangkok dry cleaners:** Please drop your trousers here for best results.

- ✔ **Acapulco hotel:** The manager has personally passed all the water served here.

- ✔ **Budapest zoo:** Please do not feed the animals. If you have any suitable food, give it to the guard on duty.

- ✔ **Paris elevator:** Please leave your values at the front desk.

- ✔ **Paris boutique:** Dresses for street walking.

- ✔ **Czech tourist agency:** Take one of our horse-driven carriage tours. We guarantee no miscarriages.

In their native tongue

During World War II, the Americans became desperate as the Japanese proved to be extremely adept at breaking military codes. Communications teams chosen from the 3,500 Comanche Indians serving in the armed forces were assigned to communicate via battlefield radios. They relayed orders in their native tongue, which only a few outsiders knew.

The Japanese were thrown into confusion because Comanche was probably the only tongue Japanese intelligence couldn't master.

The American forces were able to move forward, protected by the use of a strange language that tribal tradition had kept alive for hundreds of years.

On November 30, 1999, Charley Chitbitty, the last survivor of this elite group known as Comanche "code talkers," received a special award from the Army for his extraordinary service.

General taboos

We've all heard of the Ugly American, and I've personally met many of them. They're offensive, ill-mannered, and insensitive. During a trip to Italy, I was having dinner at a fine restaurant. I was enjoying the ambience, the strolling guitar players, and the wonderful food. Then, lo and behold, Ugly Americans reared their ugly heads at the next table.

One American was complaining about the slow service. Another loudly announced to the waiter that Italian food tastes better in the United States. One woman ordered *pasta verde* then complained because her pasta was green. Perhaps these people should stay home and eat in fast-food restaurants.

During another trip I took, this time to Russia (in the Communist era), some Americans were making a scene because the street signs weren't bilingual (Russian and English). Where did these people think they were? Following are blunders to avoid:

- ✔ **Gestures.** Know what gestures to avoid. For example, in many parts of the world, giving someone a thumbs-up or pointing your index finger is rude or obscene.

- ✔ **Conversation.** Avoid "cute" remarks that might be misinterpreted as social blunders. For example, if you're in Greece, you shouldn't tell your host that "in America, all diners are owned by Greeks." And never tell dirty stories or use profanities.

- ✔ **Language.** Unless you're asked to do so, don't correct a foreigner's English.

- ✔ **Photos.** Don't take people's pictures without their permission. (That's true in the U.S. as well.)

✔ **Electrical gadgets.** Bring along the correct converter or adapter for your hair dryer, electric razor, and other electrical gadgets or else you run the risk of blowing out the hotel circuits.

Mixing Business with Pleasure

There's no need to be a prisoner in your hotel room once your meetings are over. If time allows, venture out and see the area. Of course, you should exercise reasonable precautions just as you would in the United States. Stick to well-trafficked and well-lit areas, and avoid questionable areas. The hotel staff can be a great source of do's and taboos in this regard.

Following are handbag tips for women:

✔ If you carry a shoulder bag, fling it diagonally across your body.

✔ If you carry a handbag or clutch bag, secure it under your arm.

✔ Always have your bag facing away from the curb so that it can't be snatched by someone in a slow-moving vehicle.

Asking for directions

Finding your way around a foreign country isn't always easy, especially when you're not looking at a recognizable alphabet. Here are a few tips I picked up in my travels:

✔ **Have someone (from the hotel perhaps) write your destination in the native language.** If you get lost, locals can point you in the right direction even if they can't understand you.

✔ **Always carry something with your hotel's address and phone number.** A matchbook or piece of stationery work well. I was lost in a large underground train station in Tokyo and couldn't find my way to the street level in order to get a cab back to my hotel. Luckily I thought of taking a matchbook with me. I kept showing it, and people pointed me in the right direction.

✔ **Carry a local area map and a transportation map.** These are invaluable, especially in countries where you recognize the alphabet.

✔ **If you need to ask directions of people with limited English, don't cast your question in the negative.** When people don't speak English well, this form of questioning may be confusing. Instead of asking, *Isn't this the direction to the Zona Rosa?* ask, *Is this the direction to the Zona Rosa?*

✔ **Don't rely on the nod of a head to confirm a *yes* or *no* answer.** Local gestures vary. Get a verbal response.

In your face

Americans often like a field of about 18 inches around their bodies in order to feel comfortable. Otherwise, they feel intruded upon. That's not true of people in some other cultures. For example, Middle Eastern and Latin American folks tend to stand closer than some Americans like. Just remember, they're not trying to be in your face; it's just part of the culture.

Being Respectful of Holidays

If someone from another country planned to visit you for business and requested a meeting on December 25, you'd probably think of her as naive. After all, didn't she bother to learn that December 25 is Christmas — a national holiday? When you visit someone in a foreign country, you must be respectful of their holidays as well.

Not all the holidays around the world constitute the closing of business. The following table lists many of the holidays celebrated in foreign countries as well as those celebrated in the United States. (Although I have taken great care to compile this list, I can't accept responsibility for any errors or omissions. Use the table as your guide, but always double check with your host, a guidebook, or someone in the know.)

		Belgium	Canada	France	Germany	Great Britain	Italy	Mexico	Netherlands	Spain	Switzerland	United States	Japan	Hong Kong	Indonesia	Singapore	South Korea	Taiwan
New Year's Day	Jan 1	•	•	•	•	•	•	•	•	•	•	•	•	•	•	•	•	•
Martin Luther King Jr. Day	Jan 18											•						
Chinese New Year	Varies													•				
Lunar New Year	Varies																	•
Constitution Day	Feb 5							•										
National Foundation Day	Feb 11												•					
Lincoln's Birthday	Feb 12											•						
Presidents' Day	Varies											•						
Ash Wednesday	Varies											•						
Washington's Birthday	Feb 22											•						
Independence Day	Mar 1																•	
St. Patrick's Day	Mar 17											•						
St. Joseph's Day	Mar 19						•			•								
Spring Equinox	Mar 21												•					

		Belgium	Canada	France	Germany	Great Britain	Italy	Mexico	Netherlands	Spain	Switzerland	United States	Japan	Hong Kong	Indonesia	Singapore	South Korea	Taiwan
Juarez' Birthday	Mar							•										
Palm Sunday	Varies	•	•	•	•	•	•	•	•	•	•	•						
Passover	Varies											•						
Ching Ming	Varies													•				•
Good Friday	Varies	•	•	•	•	•	•	•	•	•	•	•						
Easter	Varies	•	•	•	•	•	•	•	•	•	•	•						
Professional Secretaries Day	April 21		•									•						
Liberation Day	April 25						•											
Greenery Day	April 29												•					
Queen's Birthday	April 30								•									
Mohammed's Ascension	April-May														•			
Labor Day	May 1	•		•	•			•		•	•							
Constitution Day	May 3												•					
May Day	May 3					•												
Children's Day	May 5												•					•
Ascension Thursday	Varies	•		•	•				•		•							
Vesak Day	Mid May															•		
Whitsunday (Pentecost)	Varies	•	•	•	•	•	•	•	•	•	•	•						
Whitmonday	Varies			•														
Victoria Day	May 24		•															
Memorial Day	Late May											•						
Spring Holiday	May 31					•												
Dragonboat Festival	Early June													•		•		•
Republic Day	June 2						•											
Corpus Christi	June 3							•			•							
Memorial Day	June 6																•	
Flag Day	June 14											•						
National Unity Day	June 17				•													
Saints Peter and Paul Day	June 29							•		•								
Canada Day	July 1		•															
Independence Day	July 4											•						
Bastille Day	July 14			•														
Constitution Day	July 17																•	
National Day	July 21	•																
St. James Day	July 25									•								
National Day	Aug 9															•		
Assumption	Aug 15	•		•			•			•	•							
Independence Day	Aug 17														•			
Labor Day	Early Sep											•						
Rosh Hashana	Sep											•						
Respect for the Aged	Sep 15												•					
Independence Day	Sep 16							•										
Yom Kippur	Sep											•						

		Belgium	Canada	France	Germany	Great Britain	Italy	Mexico	Netherlands	Spain	Switzerland	United States	Japan	Hong Kong	Indonesia	Singapore	South Korea	Taiwan
Autumnal Equinox	Sep												•					
Thanksgiving	Sep-Oct																•	
Physical Culture Day	Oct 11												•					
Columbus Day	Oct 11											•						
Thanksgiving	Oct 11		•															
National Day (Columbus Day)	Oct 12									•								
Deepavali	Oct-Nov															•		
All Saints' Day	Nov 1	•		•			•			•	•							
All Souls' Day	Nov 2	•					•											
Culture Day	Nov 3												•					
National Unity Day	Nov 4						•											
Armistice Day	Nov 11	•		•														
Veterans' Day	Nov 11											•						
Remembrance Day	Nov 11		•															
Dynasty-Kings Birthday	Nov 15		•															
Repentance Day	Nov 20				•													
Anniversary of the Revolution	Nov 20							•										
Thanksgiving	Late Nov											•						
Hanukkah	Dec											•						
Immaculate Conception	Dec 8						•			•								
Our Lady of Guadalupe	Dec 12							•										
Emperor's Birthday	Dec 23												•					
Christmas	Dec 25	•	•	•	•	•	•	•	•	•	•	•		•	•	•	•	•
Boxing Day	Dec 26		•			•								•				
St. Stephen's Day	Dec 26									•								

Enjoying Europe

The advent of the European Union (EU) or European Community (EC) has created perhaps the largest single business market in the world. To the business traveler, that means having to show your passport when you first enter Europe, rather than at each country's borders. There are many customs that are common to the EU and others that are unique to each country. As a general rule, Europeans are more formal than we and are very sensitive to good manners.

Shake, bow, or hug?

Greetings in most European countries are similar to greetings in the U.S. — a handshake for greetings and departures. Observe the same rules of etiquette as you would in the United States. If you're unsure of protocol, observe those around you. Europeans tend to shake hands frequently, so be prepared to shake often.

Don't call people by their first names, unless you're invited to or know them well.

Topics of conversation

Be sensitive to topics you discuss. It's appropriate to talk about art, sports, the weather, and topics that don't have historical or political implications. Although most of Europe is happy to talk about events that have blurred their borders, *you* must be careful. (It's like talking about your loved ones. *You* can say negative things about them, but no one else can dare!) Here are some additional tips:

- Don't ask business acquaintances about their families, unless you know them well. Europeans tend to be private.
- Don't discuss money or the cost of living.
- When talking to someone — even casually — don't keep your hands in your pockets. Although we view this as casual, Europeans may view it as disinterested.

Tips on tips

Most restaurants and bars add to the bill a 10 to 15 percent tip, and additional tipping isn't required. If the service is extraordinary, you may want to include an additional 5 percent or round the bill up to the next highest unit of currency.

Staying current on currency

On January 1, 2002, the euro will become the legal currency of the EU, and local currency will be phased out over a period of six months. As of this writing, however, the euro is legal tender for business transactions only. Stocks are traded in euros; wires, drafts, and traveler's checks are issued in euros. Table 19-1 lists European currencies in effect through December 31, 2001:

Table 19-1	European Currencies
Country	*Currency*
Belgium	Franc
Britain	Pound
Denmark	Krone
France	Franc
Germany	Mark
Greece	Drachma
Ireland	Punt
Italy	Lira
Luxembourg	Franc
Netherlands	Guilder
Norway	Krone
Spain	Peseta
Sweden	Krona
Switzerland	Franc
Turkey	Lira

Looking like a native

Most of the guidelines that apply in the United States hold true in Europe. However, some exceptions do exist. For example, Europeans aren't big on pantsuits for women. Dress with common sense and wear what's appropriate.

- ✔ If in doubt, dress conservatively.
- ✔ When dining at an elegant restaurant or attending the theater, women wear skirts or dresses and men wear business suits.
- ✔ At theaters, you might be expected to check your coat in the cloakroom rather than take it to your seat.
- ✔ For business dealings, women wear suits or dresses.

If you're at a beach resort, err on the side of conservatism. Women shouldn't parade around in bikinis or go topless and men shouldn't wear Speedo-style swimsuits. Don't confuse business travel with personal travel.

Something to remember

Shopping abroad can be a real treat if you know how to do it. The country's embassy or consulate can answer specific questions, but here are a few generalities:

- **Comparison shop.** Have an idea what you're willing to spend and shop around. Prices may be better in small towns than in large cities.

- **Keep your receipts.** Make sure the name, address, and prices are printed clearly. You'll need receipts to clear U.S. Customs.

- **Deal with value-added tax (VAT).** If you're traveling in countries that have VAT, you may be eligible for a tax refund before you leave the country. Find out the dollar amount. Check with the consulate or store.

- **Beware of duty-free shops.** *Duty free* doesn't mean that you pay less. It merely means the shop didn't pay import or local tax on the merchandise because they aren't used in the country where the shop is located. And beware of airport shops that call themselves duty free because that may be an advertising ploy. Know your prices.

- **Buying art.** If you purchase art, be sure it's an item you may take out of the country. Also, be aware of the customs duty on the item because it may jack up the price to more than you want to spend.

Minding your table manners

It's critical to display good table manners. In the United States, *you* are judged by your manners. Abroad, all Americans are judged by your manners. Following are some things to keep in mind:

- Europeans hold their forks with the tines down, and they don't switch their knives and forks after cutting. If you want to eat like a European, hold your fork in your left hand and your knife in your right to cut your food. (Lefties do the opposite.) And don't switch to eat.

- Use your knife to push your food to the back of your fork, and hold your knife in your right hand. (Lefties do the opposite.)

- Keep your wrists on the table and don't put your hands on your lap.

Value-Added Tax (VAT)

European governments impose a value-added tax of 15 to 25 percent on most transactions, including hotels, transportation, meals, exhibition/conference costs, professional fees, and other travel charges. The tax is designed to be borne by local taxpayers, not visitors or companies doing business with

European companies. VAT can, therefore, often be reclaimed. If you make large purchases and intend to reclaim the VAT, keep original invoices, register receipts, or credit card receipts.

How do you get VAT refunded? Sometimes you can reclaim the VAT at a bank in the international departure lounge of the airport. Or, if you submit the proper form to a customs officer as you leave the country, you might get the refund mailed. (But in some countries, don't hold your breath.) If you're an occasional traveler, check with the consulate of the destination country.

If you're a prolific traveler or part of a company doing business in Europe, there are many companies that will help you reclaim your VAT for a percentage. Check the Internet and search under the search word *VAT.*

Amazing Asia

When many of us think of Asia, we conjure up the image of *The King and I* and *Madame Butterfly.* Those images couldn't be farther from the truth. Asia is a distinct and remarkable part of the world. Each Asian country is unique; the customs, lifestyles, and religious beliefs may be quite different. Learn all you can about the country or countries you plan to visit before you go.

Be politically correct. The Asian people are *Asians,* not *Orientals* or *Far Easterners.*

Pleased to make your acquaintance

Greetings differ among Asian countries. In most Asian countries, you greet the oldest person in the room first. Table 19-2 shows you proper ways to greet and address colleagues in Asian countries.

Table 19-2	Greetings in Asia
Country	*Appropriate Greeting*
China	Shake hands
Hong Kong	Shake hands (Older people will clasp their own hands, shake them, and bow.)
India	Hold palms together at chin level and nod
Japan	Bow and hold your head down (Japanese business people who are used to doing business with Americans may shake hands.)

Table 19-2 *(continued)*	
Country	*Appropriate Greeting*
Korea	Bow slightly
Malaysia	Shake hands
Philippines	Shake hands
Singapore	Shake hands

Dressing and blending in

Unless you're Asian, you can't blend in. People's attitude toward you, however, won't depend on the color of your skin or your hair. Their attitude will depend on other initial impressions, such as your manners and the way you dress. To avoid stares — other than those of mere curiosity — be conscious of what you wear.

✔ Err on the side of being too conservative.

✔ Avoid sleeveless garments, mini skirts, halters, and other items of clothing that might be too revealing.

✔ Dress up for an evening on the town, such as theater and dining.

A yen for conversation

The following tips can be useful in casual conversation:

✔ Asians can be expected to ask personal questions, even if they don't know you well. Don't be surprised if you're asked your salary or your age.

✔ Asian people tend to deny compliments paid to them, so if you're paid a compliment, deny it graciously.

✔ Avoid any topics about politics or World War II.

Shop 'til you drop

If you have copious free time, you'll find the Asian countries are meccas for shoppers. In the markets and bazaars you can expect to haggle over prices, but prices are fixed in department stores and boutiques. Asia is not the shoppers' paradise it once was, so shop around for your best buys. Try any mechanical items (watches, cameras, and so on) to make sure they work. And ask for an international guarantee. If you're planning to have clothing custom tailored, visit the tailor early in your trip to allow time for alterations.

For your dining pleasure

Dining in many of the Asian countries can delight the senses. Of course, you can head for the nearest Kentucky Fried Chicken or McDonald's — and they're all over — but why would you? Be an intrepid diner and experience local culinary delights.

Religious dietary laws influence the foods people eat. For example, many Muslims don't eat pork; Hindu's don't eat beef; and Buddhists tend to be vegetarians.

Asian cuisine

Rice is a staple in Asian countries and it's served at every meal, even breakfast. Tea is the standard beverage. The Asian food you eat in the United States may be quite different from what you'll eat in Asia. For example, in China, fried rice is white. Here are some things to enjoy while you're out and about:

- ✔ **China:** There are four major regional styles of Chinese food. *Cantonese* dishes are stir-fried or steamed in light oil to keep the natural flavor. Favorites are sweet and sour. *Peking-style* is often deep fried, and is hot and spicy. *Shanghai cooking* is sweeter and more oily than the first two, and often consists of fish. *Hunan-Szechuan* can be hot and fiery.

- ✔ **India:** Food may be liberally spiced with curry, cinnamon, cumin, ginger, cardamom, and peppers and chilis. *Tandoori*-style is often chicken based and not too spicy.

- ✔ **Indonesia:** Indonesian food is famous for its *rijsttafel* (rice table), a throwback from the Dutch colonials. Expect chicken, meat, seafood, vegetables, coconuts, tropical fruits, and assorted relishes.

- ✔ **Japan:** Japan is well known for *sukiyaki* (thin pieces of beef, noodles, mushrooms, and bamboo shoots), *tempura* (deep fried fish or shrimp and vegetables) and *sushi* (raw fish).

- ✔ **Korea:** While in Korea, try *kimchi*, which is a vegetable (generally cabbage) that has been pickled with garlic, red peppers, and onions.

- ✔ **Malaysia:** S*atay* is marinated chicken, beef, or mutton on a bamboo stick that's roasted over a charcoal grill and dipped in peanut sauce.

- ✔ **Philippines:** A favorite in the Philippines is *abodo,* which is chicken, pork, or squid that's simmered in a marinade.

Using chopsticks

Although you can request a fork and spoon in most restaurants, many Asians will appreciate your attempt at chopsticks. You won't need a knife because your food is generally cut into small pieces. Example 19-1 shows how to eat with chopsticks.

Pick up one chopstick as if you were picking up a pen, leaving your index finger free to act as a lever.	
Pick up the other chopstick and place in parallel to the first one. Hold it firmly with your thumb and index finger.	
The first chopstick should remain firmly in position in the crook of your thumb, held by your third and fourth finger. Use the top chopstick as a lever. Never cross them.	

Example 19-1:
Using
chopsticks.

Tipping

In some Asian countries, tipping is not expected and might be taken as an insult. However, I found that many people do appreciate tips. It's best to look around and notice what others are doing, ask a local, or read a guidebook.

General business practices

Asians have a great deal of respect for age, wisdom, and experience. Therefore, if you send a business delegation to one of the Asian countries, it might be wise to include some of your more mature staff members. Also, Asians tend to form personal relationships before business relationships. So, your first meeting might be a getting-to-know-you session involving very little business.

Doing business in Japan

Japanese business people take protocol and customs very seriously. Following are tips from Henry M. Seals, author of *Making It In Japan: An Insider's Journey to Success.*

Distribute business cards. Give and accept business cards with both hands. When you accept a business card, look at it, touch it, and keep it in an obvious spot. Never stuff the card in your pocket or write on it in front of the person who gave it to you.

Let's make a deal. Japanese rarely make business decisions right away. When you're invited to an initial meeting, the people you meet with are probably there to evaluate you and your business, not to make the deal. They'll take the information back to their superiors, and you'll be invited back if negotiations are to continue.

Take a bow. Japanese business people bow to show deference and respect; they don't shake hands with each other. Japanese business people bow 60 degrees; the chief executive bows 45 degrees. As an American, you should bow deeply.

Seals states, "To the Japanese, manners and etiquette are very important. . . . If you can perform correctly, if you know the rules of etiquette, then the feeling is that you can be trusted to act prudently in another environment, the business environment."

Loving Latin America

Latin American people tend to be very warm and open. Spanish is the primary language, except in Brazil, where they speak Portuguese. (If you speak Spanish, you may be able to understand some Portuguese; there are many similarities.)

Latin Americans aren't as casual about greetings as Americans. When people stop to say, "Hello, how are you?", they often shake your hand and genuinely wait for a reply. It's also a more touchy-feely society, and it's not uncommon for men to embrace or throw their arms around each other's shoulders.

Naming names

In Spanish, mother's and father's family names are important. Following a person's given name or Christian name, is the father's surname followed by the mother's family name. For example, when you see the name Eduardo Martinez Lopez, his father is a Martinez, and his mother is a Lopez. You address him as *Señor Martinez.* A married woman is *Señora,* and an unmarried woman is *Señorita.*

In Portugese, the mother's family name comes before the father's. Many business people simplify their names by using only a first and last name. Address a Portugese male as *Senhor,* a married woman as *Senhora,* and an unmarried woman as *Senhorita.* The "h" is silent.

Confirming appointments

When you have a business appointment, always confirm it a day or two in advance. Meetings don't necessarily start on time, but you should arrive on time. Latin Americans tend to make small talk before actually getting down to business and may sit and schmooze over a cup of coffee. Refusing a cup of coffee is considered rude, so sip if you must.

Getting around

Driving in many Latin American countries isn't easy. Traffic is a nightmare in major cities, roads are poor in rural areas, and driving in mountainous areas can be downright scary. Here are a few of the pros and woes of getting around:

- ✔ **Airplanes:** If you're flying between countries, always reconfirm your flight at least 24 hours before departure. Get to the airport well in advance of your departure time because planes may leave before schedule.

- ✔ **Trains:** In some Latin American countries, train systems are old and service is limited. Some services are better than others, so check with a travel agent or other knowledgeable person.

- ✔ **Buses:** Bus transportation may be the best way to get from place to place. Major routes often have first-class services and provide air conditioning, reclining seats, and more. Buenos Aires, for example, is known for outstanding bus facilities to a wide variety of destinations.

Not all buses have bathroom facilities, but they do make stops along the side of the road. If you have a weak bladder, check before you book. You may have to curtail your consumption of liquid before and during the trip. (Men, of course, have an easier time with these stops than women. One woman I met travels with an oversized rain poncho so she can extend it around her for a little privacy if she has to squat at the roadside.)

Border crossings

Crossing the border may not be as simple or as friendly as it is in other parts of the world. For example, many Latin American countries close shop for a three-hour afternoon siesta. In some places you may also encounter an unexpected fee at the border known as *modida*. In plain English, it's a bribe. One way to deal with this is to hold several dollar bills in your hand and walk casually so the bills are obvious. Someone may whisk the money out of your hand, and you'll be on your way. Don't be alarmed if you see a heavy presence of armed guards or military personnel at border crossings; they're commonplace.

Border crossings are easier when you are outwardly friendly. A minor pleasantry such as *Buenos dias* (Good day) and a warm smile will go a long way.

Eat, drink, and be merry

A typical breakfast may consist of coffee with hot milk, rolls with butter or jam, eggs with bacon and sausages. The midday meal — which is the main meal of the day — may consist of staple foods such as beans, corn, and rice. The evening meal is a scaled-down version of the midday meal. Always bring along a pocket menu guide so you know what to order.

If you're in a restaurant that's not fancy, don't be surprised to see locals clapping their hands or banging silverware to get the attention of the wait staff. In cosmopolitan cities you find very elegant restaurants that may serve European-style food. If you don't like spicy food — and stay away from it if you don't — say *No muy picante, por favor,* which means "Not too hot, please."

Some restaurants tack on a cover charge *(cubierto)* in addition to a service charge.

In major cities that use purified water, you'll have no problem. However, if you're unsure, stick to bottled water. Avoid fruits and vegetables that may have been washed with unpurified water, and anything else that's questionable, such as ice cubes.

Mingling in the Middle East

Many people avoid the Middle East because parts have been in conflict or war. However, these events are random and have little effect on daily life. By and large, the Middle East is a safe place to travel. Crowds enjoy freedom of movement at all hours. Most people speak English, so language is rarely a problem.

Mainly meals

Many hotels and restaurants cater to tourists and offer international food; therefore, it's not uncommon to find Western and Oriental food on menus. A staple food in the Middle East is pita bread, also known as pocket bread. It's much the same as what you find in the U.S. Here's what you may expect at mealtimes:

- **Breakfast:** Coffee and tea are standard, accompanied by pita bread with white cheese, jam, and honey. You may also expect scrambled eggs or omelets.

- ✔ **Main meal:** Middle Easterners prefer to eat their main meal at midday, although hotels serve main meals in the evening also. Favorite appetizers are *hummus* (a dip made of ground chickpeas), *tahini* (a paste of sesame seeds with lemon juice and garlic), *tabbouleh* (a mixture of bulghur or cracked wheat with chopped tomatoes, onions, parsley, and mint leaves with olive oil and lemon juice dressing).

- ✔ **Popular main dishes:** These include *shish kabob* (skewered and grilled cubes of meat or chicken and vegetables) and *kofta* (a popular Arab dish of minced meat, onion, seasonings shaped into balls then grilled, baked, or fried). Fresh vegetables are abundant, especially eggplant, cabbage, green peppers, onions, peppers, zucchini, and tomatoes.

- ✔ **Desserts:** You must try *muhallabihay,* a rice pudding that's part of every Arab cook's repertoire. You may also expect dessert to be fresh fruits including apricots, dates, figs, watermelon, and oranges.

If you eat in an authentic Arab restaurant, you'll see a communal wash sink in the entrance way. You wash your hands as you enter the restaurant and again when you leave. Watch what others do.

Although many Muslims have adopted a 20th-century lifestyle, *strictly observant Muslims don't drink alcohol.* It's wise to refrain from drinking in their presence.

Cashing in on currency

You may not be able to purchase all Arab currency in the United States because some currencies fluctuate regularly. Some countries have very strict regulations about not taking currency out of the country. Check with an embassy or consulate.

When in Israel

Israel's population is about 85 percent Jewish. Other citizens are Arabs (Christians and Muslims). Israelis are rather casual in dress and style. A traditional greeting is *Shalom* ("Peace"), which means both "hello" and "goodbye." Many Jews don't do business on Sabbath (from sundown on Friday to sundown on Saturday).

Religious Jews observe special dietary laws. In Israel, you'll see lots of *kosher* food, which means food that is proper within the Jewish law.

Jews don't eat pork or shellfish, and they separate dairy from meat. They cook dairy in separate pots and eat dairy from separate dishes.

Religions Jews don't cook on the Sabbath, so some dishes are made in advance. A popular dish is *cholent,* a stew of meat, barley, and legumes. Popular dinner and lunch beverages are *mitz* (bottled orange or grapefruit juice) and *gazoz* (bottled soda water).

Getting down to business

When you visit on company business, you may need to present a letter of introduction that was sent from a high-level member of your company to the host. After you present the letter, immediately give the host your business card with the Arabic side up.

Arabs don't rush business, so be prepared for a lot of preliminary chitchat over tea, coffee, or a cold drink before you get down to business. You may experience *majlis* (meaning, "audience"), which is based on an ancient custom where a citizen may approach the ruler to discuss personal concerns. It's still practiced in some offices. Therefore, the host may give each person a chance to explain a problem, then offer an answer. This may seem confusing to an outsider, but follow the lead of the host.

Homeward Bound

When you return from abroad, you'll have to go through customs as soon as you enter the United States. Customs agents look for merchandise that's brought in illegally and any items on which you have to pay duty, so be certain to keep handy any receipts for items you purchased abroad. You're allowed to bring back $400 worth of duty-free merchandise and will be taxed 10 percent on the next $1,000. There are other regulations that apply in special situations, so contact the U.S. Customs Service for a free booklet on rules and regulations entitled "Know Before You Go." Write or call for the booklet at the following address or phone number:

U.S. Customs Service
Box 7407
Washington, DC 20044
202-927-6724

When you bring your own valuable items on a trip abroad (computers, cameras, and the like) bring receipts or other proof of ownership. If you don't have receipts, get Form 4457 from the U.S. Customs Office *before you leave the United States* to register your valuables. Doing so will help you avoid the hassle of a customs agent trying to impose a duty on your stuff, thinking you bought the merchandise abroad.

When nature calls

Leave at home any preconceived ideas about plumbed facilities. If you visit a major city and stay in a first-rate hotel, you probably find business as usual. When you venture out, however, be prepared to either exercise camel-like staying power or set aside all cultural biases. Following are some of my experiences:

- People in other countries don't always recognize the words *restroom* or *bathroom*. They do recognize *toilet, WC* (for water closet), or some equivalent in their native language.

- Be prepared to use unisex toilets. Men are often less intimidated by this than women. But I try to look on the bright side: I always chuckle when I see a man waiting in line. (Women do it all the time in the U.S.)

- Always bring from home a role of toilet paper. In some facilities you don't find any; in others, you find an attendant willing to sell you a 3-x-3-inch sheet for pocket change.

- You may have to adjust your position as well as your thinking. In some parts of the world, you find toilets that are level with the floor. (The word *squat* takes on an entirely new meaning.) For flushing, you find anything from a pull chain to a bucket of water. If you see a wastepaper basket next to the toilet, use it to discard your toilet paper or else you risk clogging up the works. (I learned the value of packing nose clips.)

In Belgium, I found the most modern toilets I've seen anywhere. The toilets had a small handle to flush small jobs, and a large handle to flush big jobs. The amount of water dispensed depended on what was needed.

This section isn't meant to discourage you from experiencing another way of life, but it always pays to remember the Boy Scout motto: *Be prepared.*

What's Hot on the CD-ROM

Here's what you'll find on the CD-ROM:

- 19-1: General Do's and Taboos When Travelling
- 19-2: Handbag Tips for Women
- 19-3: Shopping Tips
- 19-4: Enjoying Europe
- 19-5: Amazing Asia
- 19-6: Loving Latin America
- 19-7: Mingling in the Middle East
- 19-8: Going Through U.S. Customs

Part VI
Conducting Meetings People Relish

The 5th Wave   By Rich Tennant

"GET READY, I THINK THEY'RE STARTING TO DRIFT."

In this part . . .

Technology has changed the way people relate to each other. Whether you hold meetings face-to-face, electronically, or a combination of the two, this part shows you how to abide by the guidelines of protocol and etiquette. And you also learn to make dynamite presentations that propel your career and leave your audience clamoring for more.

Chapter 20

This Meeting Will Now Come to Order

In This Chapter

▶ Planning an efficient meeting

▶ Presiding over a meeting

▶ Accomodating the attendees

▶ Videoconferencing

If Michelangelo wasted as much time in meetings as most business executives today, he would never have found time to take on the Sistine Chapel job. They would have given it to that da Vinci fellow. . . .

— John Cleese

Americans suffer from a rare condition called *meetingitis*. Do you have any idea how many meetings are held in the United States each day? Exclusive of seminars and educational conferences, I've heard numbers ranging from 750,000 to over 12 million. Meetings are either very productive or marathon sessions that leave you with an empty head and full bladder.

We've all attended chaotic meetings that may just as well have been planned by the Mad Hatter from *Alice in Wonderland*. The Mad Hatter spoke utter nonsense; he had no clear purpose. The March Hare was ill-mannered. And the Doormouse was so bored, he snoozed. Many of us have seen characters just like these in modern-day business meetings.

Well-planned and well-conducted meetings can be magic. They bring out the best in us — the best ideas and the best decisions. With the following guidelines, you can plan action-oriented meetings that are so meaningful, participants will be energized, rather than mentally packing for their vacations to Hawaii.

The Proof Is in the Planning

Never call a meeting merely because you haven't called one in a while or because you feel compelled to assemble people each week. It's a waste of everyone's time and costs the company money. Just think of the salaries of the participants and how much work isn't getting done because they're at your meeting. Before you call a meeting, ask yourself these questions:

- Is the meeting really necessary?
- Can the information be communicated in a better way (by e-mail, memo, telephone, or conference call, for example)?

It's appropriate to hold face-to-face meetings for any of the following reasons:

- Analyze or solve a problem
- Brainstorm
- Communicate essential information
- Demonstrate something
- Ensure that everyone has the same understanding of a situation
- Gain support for acceptance of an idea, program, or decision
- Reach a decision in which group judgment is required
- Foster team spirit
- Reconcile clashing viewpoints or ideas

The long and short of it

A meeting should last long enough to accomplish the business at hand — not a moment longer. Remember that productivity tapers off after 1½ hours and falls dramatically after 2 hours.

If your meeting lasts longer than 1½ hours, consider breaking it into several sessions. If that's not possible, never go longer than 1½ to 2 hours without a 15-minute break to allow people to use the restroom. Some meetings impose their own timing. For example, you may need an immediate decision on something and have to gather people on the spot. If you do have flexibility, remember:

- People are most alert in the mornings.
- Try to avoid early Monday morning meetings or late Friday afternoon meetings.
- Unless it's unavoidable, don't call a meeting that's close to quitting time.
- Avoid meetings on religious holidays.

Your blueprint for success

George J. Lumsden, former manager of sales and training at Chrysler Corporation, said, "We don't prepare food without recipes or build houses without blueprints. Why should we expect meetings to be successful without plans?" Your agenda is the blueprint of the meeting. Without it, the meeting clearly lacks order and may never accomplish its purpose. Here's the value of the agenda:

- ✔ When you've put the agenda down on paper, you've invested time thinking about the meeting's purpose and priorities.
- ✔ It's a good leadership tool that keeps the meeting on track.
- ✔ It's useful to the attendees so they can gather their thoughts and be prepared to make a contribution.

When you prepare your agenda, express opportunities, not problems. Make your agenda upbeat and inclusive. Following are items to include in an agenda:

- ✔ **Times:** The time the meeting will start and end, breaks, and length of presentations.
- ✔ **Place:** If the meeting is off site, attach directions.
- ✔ **Purpose:** List objectives and intended outcome, if there is one.
- ✔ **Attendees:** A list of everyone who's expected to attend.
- ✔ **Responsibilities:** What attendees need to bring or prepare.

Think out of the box (or conference room)

If you have the budget or the inclination, dare to be different and consider something besides the same-old, same-old meeting place.

Restaurants are good choices when you're having a meeting for a dozen people or less. Consider holding a breakfast or luncheon meeting at one of your favorite restaurants.

Hotels make great meeting places for large groups. They generally include basic equipment, such as projectors, jacks, podiums, microphones, and the like, as part of the amenities.

Most of your major hotels have special groups set up to accommodate you. Check the Web site of your favorite hotel. If you host a large convention, prices are generally negotiable.

Airport lounges are a great place to meet with out-of-town attendees for a one-day meeting. You may contact Continental Presidents Club at 800-322-2640 or the American Admirals Club Executive Center at 800-237-7971.

Don't plan a meeting with multiple objectives unless every attendee has a vested interest in all the topics *and* you can deal with each topic quickly.

When to distribute the agenda

For small meetings that don't involve a large number of people, send the agenda at least two days ahead. Example 20-1 shows an informal agenda sent as an e-mail message. For more elaborate meetings, allow a week or two. If you're inviting people from out of town, give them as much notice as you can.

Location, location, location

Selecting a meeting room is somewhat like choosing a gift box. If it's too small, your gift gets squished; if it's too big, it rattles around. You have many options to consider when selecting a room. Be guided by the reason for the meeting, your budget (if that's an issue), and how many people you expect.

Subject: PR Mtg. May 15, 2–2:30, Rm. 205

Hi Guys,

Purpose

• Jim and Ernie will be coming to review the text for the brochure.

• They'll also show us the visuals they've created.

Objective

To finalize the PR campaign so we can launch in July.

Action Item

Be sure you've reviewed the copy they gave us at the last meeting and have your comments ready. This will be our last chance to give our input.

See you there. Thanks.

Jillian

Example 20-1:
Come one —
Come all!

An office or conference room offers a convenient and no-cost place to hold a meeting. An off-site facility (such as a nearby hotel or restaurant) serves as a change of scenery and emphasizes the importance of the topic at hand. Sometimes the choice isn't yours. But if you can choose the location, here are some things to keep in mind:

- **Convenience:** Be sure the location is easy to reach.

- **Neutrality:** If you're having the meeting to resolve a conflict, aim for a neutral spot that isn't the office of one of the combatants.

- **Politics:** Know what's involved and who needs to be there. For example, if you're making a presentation to a customer, it may be wise to visit the customer's site.

- **Budget:** Know what you can and can't afford.

- **Needs:** Carefully evaluate your needs and the needs of your audience.

  - Are the acoustics appropriate?

  - Does the lighting need to be controlled?

  - Will there be any distractions from adjacent rooms or the outside?

  - Is ventilation adequate?

  - Is there access to the back of the room so latecomers can enter without being disruptive?

  - Can the temperature be controlled? (68 degrees is ideal.)

  - Are there accommodations for the disabled?

When you can't have the room of your choice because it's not available or within your budget, do some tweaking. If you're meeting with a few people in a large room, make the area feel cozy by sitting in a corner. Or use partitions to make any large room appear smaller.

Banging Down the Gavel

An hour before the meeting begins, be certain that everything is ready. This includes handouts, equipment, water on the table, name tags, and anything else. Although you expect people to be punctual, decide how long you're willing to wait for stragglers (if at all). If participants know you mean business when you give a starting time, they'll learn to be there on time. Here are a few tips:

✔ I've been to meetings where people were strongly encouraged to arrive and return from breaks on time. One person hosting an all-day meeting announced that anyone who returned late from the break would have to enter the room telling a clean joke or singing a song. After the first break, one person arrived late and was humiliated when he had to enter singing. No one came late after that.

✔ At another meeting, stragglers were told they had to pay a $5 fine if they came back late. One group of four came back late. The meeting host collected $20 and put it toward a round of drinks after the meeting ended.

Getting started

When you call a meeting, take charge:

Distribute the agenda

Even though you send each participant an agenda, some may not have brought it. If everyone has an agenda on the table, it's easier to keep the meeting on track.

Make sure all the participants know each other

If the meeting involves only a few people, make the appropriate introductions. If the meeting is large (12 or more people) and most of the members don't know each other, conduct a getting-to-know you session. You can do that in a variety of ways:

✔ Pair new acquaintances and have them get to know each other through a series of questions and answers. (Name? Job? How did they become part of this team?) Then each person introduces his "new best friend" to the rest of the group.

✔ Go around the room and have members introduce themselves, giving a brief description of what they do.

I was at a company meeting attended by people from different departments who never interacted with each other on the job. They had to introduce themselves by telling of a special interest that few people knew about. It was a delightful way for coworkers to get to know each other on a more personal level. Several people formed friendships based on common interests. For example, two of the guys were amateur magicians.

Create a productive environment

Set the tone and direct the flow of business by channeling the discussion. Create an environment for problems to be solved and new issues to be aired and shared. Be a facilitator, not a boss. Facilitating involves asking and defining questions, examining issues, selecting criteria for evaluating suggestions, suggesting solutions, and encouraging participation. Make participants feel comfortable to communicate, cooperate, give and receive *constructive* criticism.

> ✔ Never call people names such as *immature, unprofessional, inept,* or *irresponsible.*
>
> ✔ Don't be judgmental.
>
> ✔ Avoid words such as *bad, worst, should have, would have,* and *could have.*

End on time

At the end of the meeting, review the action items and the outcome by recapping who, what, when, and where. If applicable, highlight the events of the next meeting and decide when it will be held. If you indicated an end time on the agenda, stick to it. *It's okay to finish earlier, but not later.*

Express appreciation

Acknowledge people who made special contributions, and be certain you don't leave anyone out. Be sure to thank all the participants in a meaningful way: *Thanks for your input. It's been very productive and I appreciate your help. I want to thank you all for coming.* This is more courteous than merely saying, *Thanks for coming.*

Following the leader

As an attendee of a meeting, you play a vital role and bear the responsibility for the outcome of the meeting. Being an effective group member takes knowledge, skill, and common sense.

Do your homework. Come prepared with whatever data you need and be ready to participate.

Sit in a different seat. If you attend regular meetings (weekly, monthly, or whatever), play musical chairs. Don't be part of a clique and don't always sit near the same people.

Keep an open mind and a positive attitude. If someone suggests something you don't approve of, say, "What I like about your suggestion is.... However, my concern is that...."

Accept constructive criticism. If any of your ideas are criticized, don't take the criticism as a personal attack.

A word of caution: Although you fall in love with your own ideas (and who doesn't?), you must always be respectful of others. Don't be the *murmurer,* who whispers and chats to your neighbors; the *big mouth,* who knows it all; the *squabbler,* who needs to take on the world; the *interrupter,* who doesn't give anyone a chance; the *broken record,* who loves to hear himself ramble on; or the *mule,* who doesn't listen to reason.

Staying on track

As the leader, it's your responsibility to keep the meeting on track. Some people respond to body language such as eye contact, a look, a gesture. Others need a more direct approach. If body language doesn't work, Table 20-1 lists some things that do.

Table 20-1	Keeping a Meeting on Track
Situation	*Getting Back on Track*
Cross-conversations	*Please, we can only hold one meeting at a time"* If the conversation persists, nominate several speakers: *Jim, you may speak first; then. . . .*
Long periods of silence	*I need some help here* Kiddingly say, *Are you all asleep or are you just thinking?*
Critical topics are being bypassed	*We have plenty of time left to resolve this issue. Let's not rush into something we may regret later on this critical matter.*
Energy is ebbing	*We just have a few more points to cover. Let's finish so we can get on with our morning.* or *Perhaps we should take a quick break and get some coffee.*
Group gets stuck	*Okay, this is where we are. We just finished. . . .* or *It appears as if we're getting bogged down. Let's back-track slightly.*
One-person filibuster	*Why don't we hear from someone else?* or *It's time we moved on. If we have time we can discuss this later.* or *Let's discuss this off line.*
Someone is unclear	*Would you mind clarifying that?* or *Can you please be more concise?*
Clear-cut differences	*I'd like to see a show of hands of those who support. . . .*
Time is getting short	*Let's wrap it up. I promised you'd be out of here by [time].*

Creating a paper trail

Notes from a meeting are called *minutes*. They recap the events of the meeting and detail who's responsible for what (and when). Minutes are the cure for future problems, so you won't hear, "I thought Jim was going to take care of that." If you're responsible for recording the minutes, here are some guidelines:

✔ **Record the date, time, place, and names of those who attended.** If you are unfamiliar with people at the meeting, ask how to spell their names or get a business card.

✔ **Sit near the presiding officer so you can hear clearly and accurately.** Don't be shy about asking for pertinent information to be repeated.

✔ **Remain constantly alert.** Each time a new motion is introduced, you must record the name of the person who introduced and seconded it.

✔ **Use your judgment about what should and shouldn't be included.** When in doubt, *don't* leave it out.

✔ **Have paper clips handy.** Clips help you tag any items you need to act on after the meeting.

✔ **Distribute the minutes.** Make sure all attendees get a copy of the minutes as soon after the meeting as possible. Ask if there are any corrections.

With Sensitivity and Justice for All

The hallmark of any good meeting is sensitivity to all who attend — those who are just like you and those who are different from you. Everyone has a valuable contribution to make.

Being sensitive to the customs of foreigners

Today's business is global, and meetings often include people from one or more foreign countries. When you conduct a meeting in a foreign country or host foreigners in your own country, be sensitive to cultural differences. Following are a few suggestions:

✔ **In addition to coffee, serve tea.** Think of the type of tea the guests may prefer and any formalities that go along with serving it. For example, do they drink from glasses instead of teacups?

✔ **Be sensitive to the food and alcohol you serve.** Foreigners generally enjoy sampling American food instead of their own cuisine. However, be aware of food and alcoholic beverages that may be inappropriate. (Check out Chapter 19 for tips on specific countries.)

✔ **Refer to your guests by their last names, unless you're asked to do otherwise.** Foreigners are typically more formal than Americans.

✔ **Don't be touchy-feely.** For the most part, foreigners dislike touching such as holding an arm, slapping a back, or poking a finger.

> ✔ **If a presentation requires an interpreter, make sure you have one on hand.** As the presenter, talk in your own language. The interpreter simultaneously translates. A good source for finding an interpreter is one of your own employees or the language department of a local college or university.

Being sensitive to people with special needs

When you meet people whose actions appear different, don't be quick to judge them. There are a number of hidden disabilities that have no (or little) immediate manifestation. For example, you may meet people with emphysema, arthritis, diabetes, epilepsy, a heart condition, Tourette's syndrome, psychiatric disorders, or early forms of multiple sclerosis, AIDS, or Alzheimer's. Always be respectful and understanding. Check out Chapter 23 to accommodate people with special needs. Here are a few highlights:

Making your space accessible

Following are ways to make space accessible for people with special needs:

> ✔ Be certain that ramps and walkways are free from snow and ice. (They should be free from these hazards for everyone, but disabled folks have a harder time getting around.)
>
> ✔ Allow at least one space in your waiting room for wheelchair users.
>
> ✔ Make sure lighting is appropriate for people who read lips, sign, or are visually impaired.
>
> ✔ Reserve seating in front for people with hearing and visual disabilities.

Allowing for personal differences

Here are some suggestions to help disabled people blend in:

> ✔ Use a microphone.
>
> ✔ When you serve beverages, provide straws for people with dexterity issues.
>
> ✔ Ask people to identify themselves for voice recognition.
>
> ✔ Refrain from presentations that have flickering lights or loud noises; they may trigger seizure disorders.

Videoconferencing

The new wave of technology has opened doors for electronic meetings — known as videoconferencing (VC) or teleconferencing. This requires dedicated audio, video, and communications networking technology. VC provides real-time interaction and often takes the place of face-to-face meetings. People from remote locations can "meet" without being physically together.

Because of the need for dedicated high-end equipment, the cost of VC is relatively expensive. If you have an extended need to videoconference, however, the cost can be offset by reduction in travel. To find out more about videoconferencing, check out the Internet and use *videoconferencing* as your search word.

Although videoconferencing has many advantages, there's no substitute for a face-to-face meeting. When people get together under one roof, they develop friendships and business relationships.

Lights, camera, action

Use a camera to see yourself as others see you. The camera mischievously captures you biting your nails, chewing gum, doodling, stroking your hair, or performing other little nervous habits. Perhaps you're the classic interrupter, the person who raises his voice, or the sourpuss whose traits jump out from the screen. Using a camera can help you identify these annoying habits and curb them the next time.

Here are some clothing tips when using a camera:

- ✔ **Don't wear clothing with thin stripes, checks, or loud plaids.** The camera tends to make those patterns look distorted.

- ✔ **Don't wear flashy jewelry.** It may cause glare and distract from what you're saying.

- ✔ **Don't wear stark white.** It offers too much of a contrast. There was a Goya commercial years ago that stressed you shouldn't wear anything close to your face that's whiter than your teeth.

Hold a meeting via the Net

Microsoft offers a neat way to use your computer to conduct a meeting in real time with two or more people in remote sites. Do an Internet search on *NetMeeting* to see how you can download conferencing tools to collaborate and share information, exchange text and graphics, have a face-to-face meeting, and record meeting notes — all via the Internet.

What's Hot on the CD-ROM

Here's what's available on the CD-ROM:

- ✔ 20-1: Determining When to Hold a Meeting
- ✔ 20-2: Distributing the Agenda
- ✔ 20-3: Determining the Location for a Meeting
- ✔ 20-4: The Structure of a Meeting
- ✔ 20-5: Taking Minutes
- ✔ 20-6: Being Sensitive to Meeting Attendees
- ✔ 20-7: Videoconferencing

Chapter 21

Presentations with Panache

· ·

In This Chapter

▶ Making a presentation with pizzazz

▶ Selecting visual aids

▶ Being a dynamic presenter

· ·

It usually takes me more than three weeks to write a good impromptu speech.

— Mark Twain

Presentations are an integral part of the business culture, but very few people can get up and speak off the top of their heads. People need to prepare. The way you present yourself and your materials may be the difference between a skyrocketing career and a dead-end job. Your goal is to prepare and deliver a presentation with panache, and not be just another talking head. The more you sweat in advance, the less you sweat during the presentation.

Getting from Point A to Point B

As a presenter, you must be clear, well organized, and show the audience how to get from point A to point B logically. Although this may seem like a big task, when you take one step at a time, it's quite manageable. Be sure to fill out the Start Up Sheet in Chapter 9. It walks you through the following critical issues:

✔ Knowing your audience

✔ Understanding your purpose

✔ Determining your key issue(s)

Learning all you can about your audience

The more you learn and understand about your audience, the better you'll relate to them. Here are some things to think about in addition to what's on the Start Up Sheet:

- ✔ What are the demographics of the audience?
- ✔ What is motivating your audience to be there for your presentation? Were they required to attend, or did they choose to on their own?
- ✔ Does the audience hold any emotional ties to the subject of your presentation (either positive or negative)?
- ✔ What is your audience's knowledge of the subject matter?
- ✔ What may your audience take away from the presentation that will make their jobs easier?
- ✔ What does your audience know about you?
- ✔ Will your audience view you as a credible presenter?

Knowing your purpose

The purpose of your presentation must be crystal clear in your own mind so you can relate it your audience. Here are some purposes you may relate to:

- ✔ You want to inform the audience about something near and dear to your heart (or theirs).
- ✔ You want to present your wonderful idea, service, or product.
- ✔ You want the glory — fame, money, personal commitment, or professional advancement.
- ✔ Your manager made you do it.

After you've identified your purpose, fashion the presentation strategically. For example, in Number 6 on the Start Up Sheet, do you really want to "present your wonderful product"? Or do you want to *convince* the audience to buy your product so you get a hefty commission? When you realize your purpose is to convince your audience to buy your product, you prepare a presentation that points out the benefits.

Identifying your key issue

Think of the key issue as a 10-second commercial. If your audience forgets everything else, what's the one issue you want them to remember? Let your presentation cascade from that issue.

> ✔ Start and end the presentation with your key issue.
>
> ✔ Arrange sub-issues (points) in a logical and understandable order.
>
> ✔ Be sure each point is clear and stands on its own.
>
> ✔ Tell your audience why each point is important *before* you make it.

The first part of your presentation attracts your audience's attention. The next part provides points to support the topic and offers a solution. The final part outlines how to implement the solution. Always leave time for a question-and-answer (Q&A) period at the end.

Checking out the environment

The environment in which you give your presentation is critical to your success. Some aspects of your environment may not be in your control, but you don't want any surprises. Here are some things to check out:

> ✔ Can you anticipate outside distractions that will interfere with your presentation? For example, does a railroad run alongside the building that blows a whistle to awaken the dead?
>
> ✔ Will there be a podium, table, microphone, audio/visual equipment?
>
> ✔ Is the room large enough or small enough to accommodate the audience so they can hear and see properly?

For Your Viewing Pleasure

Most people use some sort of visual aids that may include white boards (also called wipe boards), flip charts, transparencies, 35-mm slides, or a combination. Following is a list of issues to consider when deciding which visual aides to use for your presentation:

> ✔ Topic
>
> ✔ Company
>
> ✔ Industry
>
> ✔ Audience
>
> ✔ Budget
>
> ✔ Complexity of data
>
> ✔ Available resources

The overriding issue in selecting the right visual aid is your topic. For example, if you're trying to convince your manager that she should approve your budget, you wouldn't set up a projector in her office, you'd submit a report. Perhaps you'd enhance the report with a brief meeting, using a chalkboard or flip chart. However, if you're trying to convince a high-level committee that it should approve your budget, you'd undoubtedly opt for something more extensive.

White boards and flip charts

I clump these two visual aids together because they're similar in use and presentation. Both are appropriate for audiences of no more than 20 people. One advantage to using a flip chart is you can save the pages and have a record of what you write. However, there are high-tech white boards that print your text and graphics so you can save and distribute your pearls of wisdom at the end of the presentation. There are even white boards you connect to your PC so that you can convert the data into Microsoft Word files. Table 21-1 shows the pros and woes of white boards and flip charts:

Table 21-1 Pros and Woes of Using White Boards and Flip Charts	
Pros	*Woes*
Easy to get and use	Boring
Inexpensive	Low-visual impact
Informal	Difficulty in facing your audience and writing at the same time

When you write on a white board or flip chart, write so your back isn't facing your audience. Turn to the side and write.

Transparencies and slides

Most presentation software lets you create transparencies (also called viewgraphs or overheads) and 35-mm slides. But the software is only as good as its user. Give your visuals impact. Table 21-2 outlines the pros and woes of using transparencies; Table 21-3 outlines the pros and woes of using slides. The following pointers for preparing transparencies and slides will help you to wow your audience.

✔ **Use bulleted or numbered lists rather than sentences.** Doing this clarifies the points.

✔ **Convey one idea per visual.** The issue that relates to your topic may be a short list of who, what, when, where, or how much.

✔ **Use upper case and lower case, not all caps.** Upper case words are more difficult to read.

✔ **Limit each visual to between 5 and 7 double-spaced lines of text.** Otherwise, your visual is crowded and unreadable.

✔ **Use a 24-point font for headlines and an 18-point font for text.** Visuals must be easy to read, even from the back of the room.

Never apologize for any part of your visual presentation. If there's any part you're not proud of, *change it!*

Table 21-2	Pros and Woes of Using Transparencies
Pros	*Woes*
Quick to prepare	Don't display photographs well
Inexpensive	Projectors may block some audience members' view
Informal or formal	Switching visuals may be distracting
Easy to change	Good for no more than 75 to 100 people
Flexible for tailoring presentation	
Good interaction with audience	

We've all yawned our way through presentations in which the presenter got up and read her presentation from an overhead projector. She should have stayed home and mailed the presentation to the audience. *Don't subject your audience to "death by PowerPoint." Use transparencies only to emphasize key points.*

Table 21-3	Pros and Woes of Using Slides
Pros	*Woes*
Good for several hundred people	Expensive to prepare
Higher quality than viewgraphs	Darkened room prohibits interaction with audience

(continued)

Table 21-3 *(continued)*	
Pros	***Woes***
Formal	Can't be redone easily
Projectors are easy to carry	Inflexible
High visual impact	
Long shelf life	
Good for copying photographs	

When you make a computer-aided or slide presentation, use a remote mouse so you're free to move around and get close to your audience. Also, be prepared for technical glitches by having someone on hand to help out or bring handouts in the event that your equipment fails.

Thrill 'Em, Don't Chill 'Em

For many people, getting up to speak in front of a group is truly one of life's horrors. Many people would rather have a root canal than speak in public. If you feel stage fright, remember that you're perfectly normal and actually healthy. The sudden rush of the hormone *adrenaline* is a form of positive energy that will make you seem excited about your presentation. Famous entertainers talk of stage fright before each performance, yet they get up and thrill audiences. You can, too!

The audience will remember what you say first and what you say last. Don't waste either of those moments. Create a written outline that walks you through the entire presentation. Even if you've delivered the same presentation countless times and know it cold, you may get sidetracked and need to refer to it.

Opening do's

The audience makes a judgment about you within the first few minutes of your presentation. If you bore them with opening remarks, you lose them. Here are a few things to consider:

- ✔ **If you aren't introduced, introduce yourself.** You may say, *Good morning, I'm [name].*

- ✔ **Make a brief statement about your qualifications.** You do this to establish your credibility.

✔ **Make a strong statement that focuses on the audience's key issue —
the one discussed earlier in this chapter.** Tell the audience why this
presentation is worth their time and what they'll leave with that will
help them do their jobs better.

✔ **Address any concerns your audience may have.** If you expect opposi-
tion, build rapport.

Opening taboos

I always get a kick out of speakers who start with something like this: *For
those of you who don't know me, my name is. . . .* I've often wondered what
their names are "for those of you who *do* know me."

✔ Avoid weak statements, such as

- *I'll attempt to. . . .*
- *I'll be speaking on. . . .*
- *Today you'll be listening to. . . .*

✔ Avoid forecasts of doom and gloom.

✔ Don't share personal experiences unless they relate to the topic.

✔ Avoid overworked quotations or trite phrases.

✔ Avoid dictionary definitions. They're condescending and boring.

Expressions to leave at your desk

Following are tired phrases to leave at your
desk. Think about what they really mean and
how you would interpret them if they were said
to you:

If You Say . . .

I really don't know why I was asked
to speak here today.

As unaccustomed as I am. . . .

I won't take up too much of your time.

I don't want to offend anyone, but. . . .

Just give me a few more minutes.

Your Audience May Think . . .

Am I the victim of someone's bad
judgment? I should have stayed away.

Thanks for sharing that you're an amateur.

This is going to be a sleeper.

Look out. Here comes an insult.

It's already been too long.

Appearing natural

If you're more comfortable working with a script, that's fine. But be certain, you don't appear to be reading it. A wonderful way to hear how you sound is to talk into a tape recorder. Here are some tips for seeming natural:

- ✔ **Practice.** Practice before peers and/or a mirror to learn to maintain eye contact with the audience.

- ✔ **Tape your talk and listen to it.** If you stumble over any parts, rephrase them so you can say them more easily. If you talk in a monotone, vary the rise and fall of sentences.

- ✔ **Highlight the key statements.** Use a marker or other method to highlight your key words so that you remember to highlight them with your voice.

Be brief. Say what you need to say and stop talking. If we look back on inaugural addresses, we find that George Washington delivered his address in just 135 words. William Henry Harrison, on the other hand, ranted on for 9,000 words. He bored people for two hours on a freezing wintry day. He caught a cold the following day, and died of pneumonia a month later. Be brief.

Speaking to foreigners

This is a mighty small world, and it's shrinking all the time. International travel is commonplace, and you'll undoubtedly speak before an audience with people from other countries, here or abroad. Following are some do's and taboos:

Do's

- ✔ **Express your delight to be speaking.** Start your presentation by expressing how honored you are to address the group.

- ✔ **Open in your audience's language.** Learn a few words in the native tongue of your audience. For example, when John F. Kennedy delivered a speech in Germany, he started with *Ich bin ein Berliner!* (I am a Berliner.) It was a winning opening line.

- ✔ **Quote a person your audience admires.** Open with a quote from a well-known person from the country.

- ✔ **Use metrics.** If you deliver a technical presentation, use metrics.

Taboos

- ✔ **Avoid social blunders.** Don't make "cute" remarks that may be interpreted as social blunders. Be attuned to current events that are sensitive to your audience.

- ✔ **Refrain from using profanities.** Avoid off-color jokes or profanities.

- ✔ **Avoid using idioms.** A foreign audience won't understand them.

Delivering the heart of your presentation

As mentioned earlier, you don't want to be a talking head. Following are some suggestions for a lively presentation:

- ✔ **Make your presentation interactive.** Get the audience involved by preparing activities and asking questions.
- ✔ **Let your personality shine.** Try to be yourself as much as you can. When you start to relax, speaking will be a snap.
- ✔ **Identify with the audience.** Let the audience know you understand their needs and feelings.
- ✔ **Address people by names, if possible.** If you present to a small group, use name tags.

- ✔ **Keep your presentation current.** Be very careful when you deliver the same presentation or talk more than once. Your presentation must always seem crisp and current. If you have any time-sensitive material in your visuals, be sure to update it.

Ending on a high note: The grand finale

This is your last chance to persuade your audience to get behind whatever you've been talking about. Here are some suggestions:

- ✔ Repeat your recommendations or conclusions.
- ✔ Reiterate the call to action.
- ✔ Recap any major points you want them to walk away with.

Making a list, checking it twice

Regardless of the media you use for visuals, use the Checklist on your cheat sheet in Chapter 9 in addition to the one in Example 21-1. Pay special attention to proofreading all your visuals. Nothing can blow a dynamite visual presentation more than an error that's larger than life!

Arrive early to arrange the room and set up your equipment. And as they say in Hollywood — break a leg!

Checklist for Presentations

Before you deliver your presentation, here are a few points to double check:

❑ Is my objective is crystal clear?

❑ Did I learn all I can about the audience?

❑ Are my visuals informative and pleasing to look at?

❑ Have I organized my presentation into topics and sub-topics?

❑ Did I prepare an outline or script?

❑ Did I practice before my peers?

❑ Did I anticipate some difficult questions? Am I prepared to answer them?

❑ Did I confirm the date, time, and place of the presentation a week in advance?

Example 21-1:
Checklist for
presentations.

Why presentations fail

Following are the major complaints by people who view presentations. Make sure you keep them in mind so that no one is saying this about your presentation on the way out:

The speaker . . .

✔ Didn't focus on the key issue.

✔ Didn't take the time to "know" her audience.

✔ Tried to cram too much material into the presentation.

✔ Used humor inappropriately.

✔ Didn't introduce evidence to substantiate her key issue.

✔ The presentation was too long.

✔ The visual aids weren't effective.

What's Hot on the CD-ROM

Here's what you can find on the CD-ROM:

- ✔ 21-1: Learning All You Can about Your Audience
- ✔ 21-2: Developing a Purpose for Your Presentation
- ✔ 21-3: Identifying Your Key Issue
- ✔ 21-4: Checking Out the Environment
- ✔ 21-5: Using Visual Aids
- ✔ 21-6: Preparing Your Presentation Opening
- ✔ 21-7: Speaking Naturally
- ✔ 21-8: Delivering the Heart of Your Presentation
- ✔ 21-9: Ending on a High Note: The Grand Finale
- ✔ 21-10: Using a Checklist for Presentations

Chapter 22

Hosting a Special Event

· ·

In This Chapter

▶ Setting up a registration table

▶ Displaying your name badge properly

▶ Working with foreigners and interpreters

▶ Hosting and visiting a trade show

▶ Making accommodations for the disabled

· ·

There is no crisis to which academics will not respond with a seminar.

— Anonymous

*T*hroughout the course of your career, you're bound to attend or host an array of special events ranging from conferences to seminars to trade shows, not to mention various other kinds of events. When you host a special event, it's show time — your chance to display your products or services to large numbers of people. If you don't have a specialist on staff to manage special events, it's wise to bring in a professional to help you design and manage them.

Check your Yellow Pages Business-to-Business listings under "Special Event Coordinators." Here are a few popular coordinators. (They're not limited to doing business in their own regions.)

✔ **International Events Group,** Chicago, Illinois (phone 312-944-1727), for consulting and publications about global events.

✔ **Trade Show Exhibitors Association,** Springfield, Virginia (phone 703-941-3725), for information about trade shows in your industry.

✔ **Freeman Exhibit Co.,** Houston, Texas (phone 713-681-7722), to manage leads and coordinate domestic trade shows.

The Registration Table

When you sponsor an event, consider having one or more registration tables so people can check in quickly and easily. List the registrants alphabetically by last names, divisions, regions, countries, or some other system that's logical. Hand out a registration kit to each guest. The kit may include any or all of the following:

- A list of attendees with company names and phone numbers.
- The schedule (including the names of the speakers and a brief biography of each).
- Name badges (see the following section for more about badges).
- A map of the exhibit area, if any.
- Check-in and check-out instructions, if any.
- Listings of activities in and around the area and information about local transportation.

Your Badge of Honor

When you meet lots of new people, it's difficult to remember everyone's name. As much as people dislike wearing name badges, they let everyone know who you are at a glance. (They also save you embarrassment when you forget the name of someone you should recognize.) Name badges come in two basic flavors: the "hello-my-name-is" version and the plastic card holder kind.

Inviting spouses (or significant others)

If a seminar or conference will last three or more days, the sponsoring group may consider inviting spouses. It's a plus for any company to have a spouse share in activities and understand the company's business and its problems. Therefore, if there is an event that would be appropriate for spouses, by all means invite them.

A word of caution: The days of inviting the "little woman" to a makeup demonstration or fashion show went the way of high-button shoes. With so many women in professional roles, men are often the invited guests. Design activities that appeal to both sexes. Consider the theater, a sporting event, or tour of local attractions.

Wearing your badge proudly

Always wear your name badge on your right side — high enough to be seen. When you shake hands with someone, the person is looking at your badge. If you have the "hello-my-name-is" version, print your name clearly with a marker.

For all the world to see

Don't automatically let your business card serve as a name badge. Many business cards have people's names printed in such a small font that the name isn't visible without a magnifying glass. The lettering on your name badge must be large enough for everyone to read at arm's length. That's why a business card doesn't always work. Besides, no one looks at your chest to get your telephone number or e-mail address.

In Example 22-1 you see my business card with my name, rank, and serial number. That's what I hand out to people. In Example 22-2 you see how I modified my name and profession to create a very readable badge. (This is the brainchild of Jeffrey K. Schaffer, a business attorney in Wellesley, Massachusetts. Jeff is a member of my Business Network International [BNI] group and received an award for this wonderful idea.) Modify your card to reflect your profession or company name.

Example 22-1:
My business
card.

Sheryl Lindsell-Roberts

Nationally Known Author &
Business Writer

117 Sudbury Street, Marlborough, MA 01752
(508) 229-8209   jon-sheryl@worldnet.att.net

Sheryl
Lindsell-Roberts

Business Writer

Example 22-2:
My name
badge.

Native Tongues

With business being conducted globally, at some point you'll assemble with
people whose primary language isn't English. This may include people from
your own company who are foreign born, people from overseas offices of your
company, or people from other companies with whom you do business. You
must be sensitive to the needs of foreigners and make every effort to include
everyone in conversations and activities.

Lost in the translation

A bank in El Paso, Texas, hired a private investigator to track down a bank robber and get back the $150,000 the robber stole. The investigator chased the bank robber into Mexico. Because the investigator didn't speak Spanish, he looked through the Yellow Pages and found an interpreter to help him in his quest. When the robber was finally captured, the investigator drew his gun, and the interpreter asked him where he hid the money. "What money?" the robber responded. "Tell him," said the investigator, "if he doesn't tell us where the money is, I'll shoot him where he stands."

The robber started rambling: "Senor, I hid the money in a small canvas bag under the second floorboard of the San Pedro hotel men's room in Acapulco." "What did he say?" questioned the investigator. "He said he's prepared to die like a man."

The moral of this story is: Be certain your interpreter doesn't have a vested interest that may bias the translation.

English as a second language

Even though English is a second language in many foreign countries, it's not always easy for foreigners to converse freely in English. (Think of the years you studied a foreign language.) Following are a few suggestions for making yourself understood more easily:

- **Speak slowly.** When you speak too quickly, a foreigner may not understand all your words.

- **Avoid using idioms.** Idioms have meaning only in certain areas of the world. For example, if you tell someone to "eat their words," you're not going to provide them with a knife and fork. It's best to avoid idioms completely. Even in the United States, expressions may be regional.

I was at an office party in New York, and the cake for the occasion never arrived. Trying to be helpful, a colleague lifted a large block of cheddar and suggested (out loud), "Why don't we have the host cut the cheese?" Everyone rolled on the floor laughing. My colleague had no clue that "cut the cheese" is an expression that's an anagram of *raft*.

- **Avoid clichés like the plague.** In *The Play of Words*, Richard Lederer, has a wonderful explanation of clichés: "A girl was asked by her teacher to use the word *cliché* in a sentence. She responded with this statement: 'The boy returned home from the test with a cliché on his face.' When the teacher asked her to explain herself, the girl pointed out that the dictionary defines *cliché* as a 'worn-out expression.'"

- **Cater to the lowest common denominator.** Limit your language to words all attendees are likely to know. Technical terms usually aren't a problem if the audience is made up of your colleagues.

Using an interpreter

When you host an event, you may invite people who don't speak English. Hire an interpreter to translate. Check with colleagues in your office, graduate students, or the language department of a nearby university for an interpreter.

When you first hear your echo in a foreign language, you may be uncomfortable, but it becomes routine after a while. You can cut the clumsiness with a few simple guidelines:

- **Prepare a script.** Don't read from the script, just follow it closely. Give the interpreter as much time as possible to review the script. Go over technical terms. If you use charts, explain to the interpreter how you'll explain each one. If possible, have handouts prepared in the native language of the attendees.

> ✔ **Break your talk into manageable chunks of information.** Remember that the interpreter must paraphrase what you say. You can make his job easier if you speak in small chunks and wait for him to translate.
>
> ✔ **Talk to the audience, not the interpreter.** Resist the temptation to talk to the interpreter. Keep your voice at a normal level.

Using an interpreter doubles the time of your presentation. (Check out Chapter 21 to deliver presentations with panache.)

Tricks of the Trade Show

A trade show is a mega-event — an opportunity to increase your contact base, get information on the latest products and services, check out the competition, and just have fun. After all, where else would you find so many people from a single industry assembled under one roof?

If you host a trade show, remember that business isn't restricted to the booth. The social aspects of the show are just as important. Take a hot prospect to lunch or dinner or reserve a "hospitality room" to socialize.

Come one! Come all!

A trade show is the network of all networks. It's a great place to generate leads and improve the perception your current customers have of you. We've all wandered around trade shows or conferences. Some booths draw you in; others don't interest you. Following are some ways to lure visitors in:

> ✔ **Play music.** Music is a wonderful form of entertainment that attracts attention. It draws people to your booth and entices them to stay longer.
>
> ✔ **Use color.** Colorful banners, logos, curtains, balloons, and the like, are eye-catching. After you catch someone's eye, you can greet him and talk about your product or service.
>
> ✔ **Muster up activity.** When you see people congregate, it's natural to go see what's happening. Invite members of your organization to dress up in business suits (or whatever is appropriate for the occasion) and pretend to be interested consumers.
>
> ✔ **Hold a drawing.** Ask passersby to drop their business cards into a bowl and have a drawing every 15 minutes, half hour, hour, or whatever's appropriate. Tell people they must be present for the drawing. Display a cardboard clock letting everyone know when the next drawing will be.

✔ **Offer a unique giveaway with your logo or name.** Everyone likes to leave with a bag of tricks. I've gotten T-shirts, yo-yos, puzzles, pens, and other items I use. Every time I use the product, I think of the company that gave it to me. Check out Chapter 14 for trade show giveaways.

The next time you attend a conference or trade show, pay attention to what's around you. What attracts you? What detracts you? What's drawing people into the busy booths? What is keeping people away from the sleepers?

Staffing the booth

Staff your booth with people who are well versed in your product or service. These folks must be able to answer questions, know the competition, and have interesting tidbits to start conversations.

When a person approaches your booth, don't say, *Hello, may I help you?* That's just an invitation for the browser to say, *No thanks. I'm just looking,* which may cost you a hot contact. Be creative: Smile, extend your hand, and make an upbeat introduction. For example, take a peek at the attendee's name tag and say, *Good morning [name]. Isn't your company the one that just. . . ?*

Following up

You *must* follow up on all hot leads. I attended a trade show and gave my name to several vendors in whose products I was very interested. (I didn't just drop my card in the fish bowl; I spoke to a representative.) Only two ever bothered to send me information. The company I represented placed a very substantial order with one of the two vendors. The others lost out on a wonderful opportunity to be considered.

One way to endear yourself to customers is to send a follow-up letter. Example 22-3 is a sample of a follow-up letter to send to leads you got from a trade show. After you send the letter, remember to follow up with a phone call.

Walking the floor

Prepare your own agenda so you have a plan of action. For example, if you attend the trade show to check out trends or products, you may consider attending seminars that companies host. If you attend to increase your contact or customer base, you make better use of your time by chatting and socializing instead of sitting in a seminar room.

Dear [Name]:

 I enjoyed meeting with you at [name of trade show, location, and date] and thank you for your interest in [product or service]. I'm attatching our new brochure, which explains [what's hot]. [Give supporting details].

Next step

I look forward to helping you meet the needs of your customers and will call you next week to see how I may be of further help.

Sincerely,

Name and title

Example 22-3:
A trade show
follow-up
letter.

For the time you walk around the show, have a strategy in place so you don't just wander around collecting candy and yo-yos. Here are some tips:

- ✔ **Wear comfortable shoes.** You don't want to wind up with corns and calluses. Wearing sneakers with a business suit is appropriate for these events.
- ✔ **Outline a route.** With a route in mind, you're sure to meet the people you must see. Otherwise, you could easily get sidetracked.
- ✔ **Carry a notebook or a palm unit.** This makes it easy to make notes of information, ideas, and people to contact.
- ✔ **Bring lots of business cards.** Hand them out liberally.

Making Special Accommodations

Although the Americans with Disabilities Act (ADA) requires that facilities offer accommodations for people with disabilities, there are certain things you should check out before you sign on the dotted line. Choose a site that offers accessibility for the disabled in the following areas: entrance, meeting spaces, dining areas, parking, ramps, elevators, and the like. Also be aware that disabled people may need access to public transportation.

Before the event

✔ **Make sure that all materials are clear.** Registration packets and other related information will be read by a variety of people. Consider making audio tapes, printing in Braille, and offering large print.

✔ **Be aware of scents.** Some people are allergic or highly sensitive to perfumes, colognes, and heavily scented chemicals. Request that presenters and people hosting the conference stick to just soap and water for the duration of the conference. (I'm not allergic to the stuff, but I've been offended by some pretty awful whiffs.)

✔ **Offer alternate meals.** Offer options for people on special diets. Consider using the pre-registration material as an opportunity for special requests.

✔ **Prepare the site.** Be sure that table and chair arrangements allow room for walkers, wheelchairs, or guide dogs. Don't segregate disabled people to one area. Spread access throughout the room.

At the start of the event

✔ **Make an announcement pointing out key areas.** These include fire and emergency exits, accessible bathrooms, phones, and the like. You may also announce where the smoking areas are.

✔ **Ask speakers to identify themselves.** Ask speakers from the audience, the podium, and panel to identify themselves. Have only one person speak at a time.

During the event

✔ **Take regular breaks.** Provide a break every 1½ to 2 hours. Otherwise, you'll see people with bladders so full they'll float around the room. This is for everyone, not just the disabled.

✔ **Read all appropriate visual material on the spot.** If someone is presenting from an overhead or slide projector or is referring to written material, ask that it be read aloud.

At the end of the event

✔ **Provide extra time for questions.** People with cognitive disabilities, attention deficits, and learning disabilities, and other disabilities may need a little extra time.

✔ **Encourage feedback.** Many events conclude with an evaluation form. Ask for feedback on access issues.

What's Hot on the CD-ROM

Here's what you'll find on the CD-ROM:

✔ 22-1: Special Events Coordinators

✔ 22.2: The Registration Table

✔ 22.3: Wearing Your Name Badge

✔ 22-4: Dealing with Guests Who Speak English as a Second Language

✔ 22-5: Using an Interpreter

✔ 22-6: Drawing People into Your Booth

✔ 22-7: A Template for a Follow-Up Letter to a Trade Show

✔ 22-8: Walking the Floor of a Trade Show

✔ 22-9: Accommodating People with Disabilities

Part VII
The Part of Tens

The 5th Wave   By Rich Tennant

Disney Corp. vs. Diznee's Magic Kingpin Bowling Alleys

Okay, we'll change the name of the bowling alleys, but about our bowling ball caps, do these really look like mouse ears, your honor? I mean really now...

In this part . . .

No *For Dummies* book is complete without at least a couple of ragamuffin chapters that don't seem to fit anywhere else. In this part, I present information about accommodating people with disabilities and dressing to fulfill your career dreams.

Chapter 23

Ten Ways to Accommodate People with Disabilities

● ●

In This Chapter

▶ Knowing what's politically correct

▶ Interacting with people who are hearing, visually, or speech impaired

▶ Meeting with people with paralysis or loss of a limb

▶ Meeting with people with AIDS

▶ Dispelling fears of potential employers

● ●

When people begin to ignore human dignity, it will not be long before they begin to ignore human rights.

— G. K. Chesterton, English journalist and author

This chapter deals with people with disabilities and people who interact with them. (The key word is *people*.) People without disabilities are often uncertain how to act when they're around people with disabilities. The simple answer is: Treat them as you'd like to be treated. It's estimated that five out of every six people with disabilities weren't born that way. They acquired the disability later in life through natural causes or accidents. Therefore, each one of us is merely an incident away from joining the ranks. *"Do unto others. . . ."*

If you want to learn more about disability issues, the National Organization on Disabilities (NOD) is a great place to start. Visit the NOD Web site at www.nod.org, or write to the following address:

National Organization on Disabilities
910 16th Street NW, Suite 600
Washington, DC 20006

What's Politically Correct

Even the disabled haven't agreed on what's correct when it comes to certain terms. What everyone agrees on, however, is the importance of being respectful. For example, refer to the disabled as "people with disabilities," not "disabled people" or "handicapped people." This stresses that the disabled are people first and foremost, and their disability is secondary. Table 23-1 shows terminology with sensitivity.

Table 23-1	Terminology with a Focus on "People"
Correct	*Not Appropriate*
Person who uses a chair	Wheelchair bound, paraplegic, quadriplegic, cripple
Vision impaired or partially sighted	Blind
Person who's deaf or hearing impaired	Deaf
Person who doesn't use voice or person without speech	Dumb, mute, deaf & dumb
Person with AIDS	AIDS patient, AIDS victim
Cognitively disabled	Mentally retarded
Cancer survivor	Cancer patient
Emotionally disabled	Mentally ill or brain damaged
Functionally disabled	Physically handicapped

Working with People with Disabilities

People with disabilities feel that one of the biggest obstacles to integrating into the workforce is the attitudes of people without disabilities. Those of us who have disabled family members, friends, or coworkers are sensitive to their needs. But people who haven't had a lot of contact with the disabled are often uncertain how to behave when faced with the prospect of a disabled coworker.

There are many assumptions made about the quality of the lives of people with disabilities or their ability to function as contributing members of society. A person with disabilities is trying to live as normal a life as possible. We must do everything we can to honor and encourage that person's independence.

Do's

✔ If you notice that a person with disabilities is in any immediate danger, by all means intervene.

✔ Always encourage a person with disabilities to participate in business functions. They might tend to be withdrawn, and a little extra urging may make all the difference. Be sensitive to the person's reactions, and don't be too pushy.

✔ If a third party (server, salesperson, or others) responds to your disabled companion by speaking directly to you, don't answer and avoid eye contact. That will encourage the third person to speak directly to your companion. And you'll teach the third party a valuable lesson.

Taboos

✔ Never stare. It's rude to remind anyone that he's different in any way.

✔ Never ask a person about her disability, especially someone you've just met. Those who wish to share their experiences will volunteer to do so.

✔ Never assume that a person has multiple disabilities. For example, don't speak loudly to a person who's blind — she can hear you.

I worked with a woman who uses a chair. She says that one of the biggest complaints she has is that people often treat her as if she's cognitively disabled. She's just as intelligent as I am, perhaps more.

People who are vision impaired

People who are visually impaired are just like you in most ways. They can dial telephone numbers, use computesr, and perform a full range of activities. They learn to do much by touch, sound, and special equipment.

Do's

✔ Talk in a normal voice.

✔ Introduce yourself and those with you. For example, *Hi, Mr. Smith. It's Sheryl Lindsell-Roberts. With me to your left is Jon Allan. Shall we shake hands?*

✔ It's okay to use the word "see." A person who's visually impaired will use it.

✔ If you're giving directions, be as specific as possible. Use the terms *right* and *left* from the direction the person is standing. For example, *Walk about 100 feet and make a left at the corner.*

- If you go to a restaurant, read the menu and the prices. You can verbally locate the salt and pepper shakers and any other items on the table. When the meal is served, tell the person where the items are on his plate, using the clock. For example, *The potatoes are at three o'clock, the fish is at six o'clock.*

- If the person visits your home or office, lead her to a chair and then gently place your hand on her arm or back. If she's staying with you for any length of time, be certain to review the floor plan and identify where the furniture is.

- When taking a person who's visually impaired to a strange place, tell her where everything is and who's there.

- When there's a visually impaired person in a room you've entered, go over and identify yourself. When you're ready to leave, make sure that person knows you're leaving.

- Many elevators have Braille buttons identifying the floor numbers and a bell that rings at each floor. If an elevator is crowded, it's polite to say, *Which floor would you like?* And if the elevator is noisy and she can't hear the ring, it's polite to say, *We're at the [third] floor.*

Taboos

- Never grab the person's arm in offering assistance. Ask, *May I help you across the street?* If the person wants assistance, let her reach for your arm.

- Never play with a guide dog. The dog is there to be the *eyes* of the person and shouldn't be distracted. And don't feed a guide dog.

- Be careful not to leave doors partially ajar. (That can also be very dangerous for sighted people who aren't paying attention to where they're walking.)

SHERYL SAYS

Good for one, but not for another

I learned a few years ago that what's intended to help one disabled group may harm another. I was chatting with a business associate at a busy intersection in downtown Atlanta, Georgia. All of a sudden I heard horns honking and brakes squealing. I turned around and noticed a blind man in the middle of the intersection. He was in a panic. I ran toward him, took his arm, and brought him back to the sidewalk.

He explained that the down ramps intended for wheelchairs can be a nightmare to the blind. Their canes don't always let them know they're walking off the curb. What a frightening experience it was for this man, and what an enlightening one for me.

People with hearing disabilities

There are various degrees of hearing impairments, from a partial hearing loss to no hearing at all. If someone suffers from a partial hearing loss, you may need to speak a little louder or repeat a remark she may have missed. To attract the attention of someone who has moderate hearing, call the person by name. To attract the attention of someone who has little or no hearing, tap the person gently on the arm or shoulder. If someone suffers from a severe hearing loss, look at her when you speak. Many hearing-disabled people read lips.

Do's

- ✔ If you know American Sign Language (ASL), by all means use it.
- ✔ Look directly at the person and don't walk around while you converse. Your expressions and lip movements will help her *hear* you.
- ✔ Be patient and willing to repeat something the person may not have understood.
- ✔ If the hearing loss is in one ear, sit on the side of the person's good ear during times you can't face him.
- ✔ If you need to, write a note. (But don't talk while you write.)

Taboos

- ✔ Don't yell. A person with a total hearing loss won't be able to hear you, and a person with a hearing aid probably may hear as well or better than you.
- ✔ Don't use exaggerated mouth movements. Distorted lip movements can be confusing.

If you are the person who's hearing disabled, don't be ashamed to wear a hearing aid. It's no more a stigma than glasses. And remember that even people with normal hearing miss many remarks.

People with speech impairments

You may come across people whose speech is impaired for a wide range of reasons. Here are some ways to help:

Do's

- ✔ Give the speaker your full attention.
- ✔ Speak in a normal tone of voice. These folks don't have a problem hearing.

> ✔ Keep questions simple so the person you're speaking to can reply with short answers or a nod.

Taboos

> ✔ Don't fill in words unless you're asked to. Allow the speaker to finish her thoughts.

> ✔ Don't pretend you understand something you don't. Casually repeat what you thought you heard. If you phrase your uncertainty with a question in your voice, the person can nod or merely say "yes" or "no." *You'll be arriving at five and will be ready by six?*

People with paralysis or loss of a limb

A person who has lost a limb or suffers from paralysis may lead close to a normal life. Some embarrassing situations arise if you don't realize a person has a problem with an arm, for example. People with these types of disabilities have been criticized for not helping carry packages or lighting someone's cigarettes.

If you're the person who's disabled, there is nothing wrong with saying, *I'm sorry I can't help you. I have a bad arm.* If a person uses a wheelchair or has an artificial limb, he may need help in certain situations. Remember to ask, *May I help?*

When approaching someone who has lost his right hand or arm, you may feel some uncertainty during an introduction. If you know the person has lost his right hand or arm when you're being introduced, let her take the lead. Here are some clues: If the person who's disabled

> ✔ Smiles and says *Hello* without extending a hand, respond by smiling and saying *Hello.*

> ✔ Extends his left hand, shake the left hand.

> ✔ Extends an artificial limb, shake it as you normally would.

People with AIDS

If you're one of the growing number of people who knows someone infected with the AIDS virus, you need to have a special sensitivity to their problems. Unlike other disabilities, this one carries with it a stigma and a fear. Feel free to offer help to a person with AIDS without the fear of becoming infected. *You cannot get the AIDS virus through everyday contact.* The AIDS virus is transmitted only by sexual intercourse, sharing drug needles, or pregnant mothers to their babies. Most people with AIDS can lead active lives for long periods of time and the prognosis is getting better and better. Each person with AIDS is different and is affected by the disease in a different way.

Do's

✔ Above all, keep an upbeat attitude.

✔ Feel free to talk about the disease and gently encourage the person with AIDS to do the same. Often people need to talk about the disease to work it out in their own minds, especially those who have the illness.

✔ If the person has difficulty getting around, get her water from the cooler or lunch from the cafeteria.

✔ If you know the person with AIDS well, help the caregiver so that she does not feel isolated. She may need a break from time to time, a free afternoon, or someone to talk to.

Taboo

✔ Don't ignore your own emotions. Share your feelings and get support if you need it.

Dispelling Fears of Potential Employers

People with disabilities are often more conscientious, punctual, and reliable than their non-disabled counterparts. So, if you're looking to hire a great employee, Table 23-2 will disarm your fears.

Table 23-2	Getting Rid of Employment Fears
Fears	*Disarming the Fear*
If I hire this person, will my insurance increase?	No. Experts don't know of a single case where this has happened. Rates are based on the relative hazards of the work and the company's accident experience.
If I have to fire this person, am I opening myself up to a lawsuit?	No more so than with anyone else. The disabled are no more likely to be fired than the non-disabled.
Will the person get along with coworkers?	If you're disabled, defuse this thought at the beginning of an interview by saying, "I generally develop great rapport with my coworkers. We're all rooting for each other."

(continued)

Table 23-2 *(continued)*

Fears	*Disarming the Fear*
How will she get to work?	As an employer, that's not your problem. If the person is applying for the position, she's already figured out how to get there.
Will there be safety issues?	No. She'll figure out what she needs to do.

Set the person up with a "buddy" in case there's a fire or other emergency.

What's Hot on the CD-ROM

Here are the files on the CD-ROM:

- ✔ 23-1: Determining What's Politically Correct
- ✔ 23-2: Working with People Who Are Vision Impaired
- ✔ 23-3: Working with People with Hearing Disabilities
- ✔ 23-4: Working with People with Speech Impairments
- ✔ 23-5: Working with People with Paralysis or Loss of a Limb
- ✔ 23-6: Working with People with AIDS
- ✔ 23-7: Dispelling Fears of Potential Employers

Tireless traveler

Although the United States has recently awakened to the special needs of people with disabilities, many countries abroad have had the disabled in mind for a long time. There are many organizations that have devoted themselves to travelers with special needs. People you know who have disabilities and who travel often may want to contact the organization below:

Society for the Advancement of Travel for the Handicapped (SATH), 26 Court St., Brooklyn, NY; phone 212-447-SATH.

Chapter 24

Ten Hints to Conquer the Brave New World of Dress Codes

●●

In This Chapter

▶ Opening (but not pushing) the fashion envelope

▶ Getting specific: tips for men and women

▶ Dressing for success with foreigners

●●

> *Contrary to popular belief, it's often your clothing that gets promoted, not you . . . Always dress better than your peers so your clothes will be the ones selected for promotion. And make sure you're in your clothes when it happens.*
>
> — Scott Adams, *The Dilbert Principle*

Society as a whole is becoming more casual. Rigid dress codes among companies and industries are disappearing. When IBM — famous in the past for its starched white shirts and strict dress code — said workers could wear business casual, you know the times are changing. Even though today's dress code is often more relaxed than it used to be, there's a big difference between business casual and *oh-my-god*.

Opening the Fashion Envelope

All offices have a dress code, no matter how official or unofficial, no matter how conservative or casual. And everyone puts on a "uniform" to go to work. That uniform may be anything from a three-piece business suit, to casual business dress, or jeans and a T-shirt. This chapter is about how to dress like a professional, no matter what field you're in.

When you're at work, take the time to look around and see what other people wear. Also look at magazines that show fashion for business. If you see button-down shirts and blouses, plan to keep your sports jersey in your dresser until the weekend. Don't push the fashion envelope; it may push you back — right out the door. Here are some things everyone must keep in mind:

- ✔ Make sure your clothes fit properly. If you gain weight, either let your clothes out or buy new ones.

- ✔ If you wear running shoes or boots (for bad weather) be sure to keep a pair of shoes in your office and put them on as soon as you arrive.

- ✔ Never flaunt designer labels.

- ✔ Even though a type of clothing may be all the rage, adapt it to your build, your job, and your age.

Understanding Business Casual

The high-tech world has ushered in an entirely new ethos — *business casual*. This new world order includes Internet gurus who live life in the fast lane. They might never wear a tie, let alone a suit. The lawyers, accountants, and bankers who interact with the high-tech set often feel a little odd in their three-piece suits, so high-tech is now driving the way "the suits" of the world dress themselves.

An example is the prestigious New England law firm, Hale and Door. The firm has relaxed its dress code, and many lawyers show up for work in sport shirts and corduroys (known as *cords*). This is working well for Hale and Door's young, sought-after lawyers who are looking for a lifestyle that also includes child care, working at home, and flextime. However, the old-line attorneys view the suit as a symbol of their profession, and shun the business casual look.

It will be interesting to see how this plays out with other lawyers, bankers, and accountants. By the way, Hale and Door isn't abolishing the suited look entirely. The lawyers still keep suits on hand for court appearances and meetings with certain clients.

Even though we all talk about *business casual* and *dress-down Fridays,* there's a big difference between business casual and just plain casual. Business casual generally means something like a sport shirt (no tie) and khakis for men, or pants and a sweater for women. Save your ripped jeans and Grateful Dead T-shirts for the weekend.

Dealing with Jackets

Professionals wear jackets less often than they used to; however, there's still a certain etiquette involved:

- ✔ Men who usually work with their jackets off shouldn't wear short-sleeved shirts. If it's warm, it's more appropriate for men to roll long sleeves up to their elbows. However, it is appropriate for women to wear short-sleeved blouses. (If this seems sexist, I don't make the rules.)

- ✔ Men and women should put their jackets on when meeting with the head honcho of their company, with clients, or with anyone of importance.

- ✔ Keep double-breasted jackets buttoned; they aren't meant to hang open.

Tips for Men

Don't get into the habit of wearing the same thing every day. (I don't mean the same article of clothing, I mean the same colors and styles.) For example, try varied colors and fabrics. Buy pants and sports coats that coordinate with lots of items in your wardrobe so you can mix and match to add variety.

No matter how casual your working environment may be, you must own at least one suit. You'll need it when you eat in a fine restaurant or meet with a client. Your suit must fit properly, whether it's custom made or off the rack. Table 24-1 offers tips for suiting up.

Table 24-1	Suiting Up from Head to Toe
Item of clothing	*Tips for men*
Suit	Typical colors are black, brown, dark gray, or navy blue. The suits may be pinstriped or very muted plaid. In warm climates, you may wear light-weight fabrics, such as seer-sucker.
Shirts	Wear long-sleeved, conservative shirts. Buy them to coordinate with your suits. If you want to add a real touch of class, wear a shirt with French cuffs; these require cuff links. Make sure your shirt tails are long enough to tuck into your pants and your shirt is large enough so the buttons don't strain around the middle.

(continued)

Table 24-1 *(continued)*

Item of clothing	Tips for men
Ties	You can't go wrong with a silk or polyester tie. Keep ties conservative: solid, printed, or striped. Red ties are known as "power ties" and you may wear one when you want to make a bold statement about yourself. For example, you're the guest speaker at a conference. (Unless you're Peewee Herman, give your bow-ties to the Salvation Army.)
Shoes	Wing-tip shoes and loafers are favorites of businessmen. Wear black with black or gray suits and brown with brown suits.
Socks	Socks should be high enough so that when you sit with your legs crossed, you don't show your hairy (or hairless) legs between the tops of your socks and bottom of your trousers.

Cuffed pants and double-breasted suits fade in and out of fashion, so be careful. Also, double-breasted jackets look best on men who are tall and thin.

Tips for Women

Always wear clothing to compliment your body type. If you haven't figured out what looks well on you, consult a salesperson in a high-end department store. You can buy mix-and-match outfits and change their look with scarves and subtle jewelry.

Women have gotten away from the "female man's suit" and dress in a more feminine manner. Opt for skirts and blazers, silk dresses, and suits of feminine fabric. You may also wear tailored pants and bright (not loud) colors. Following are a few taboos for office clothes:

- ✔ Never wear spike-heeled shoes no matter how short you are. Instead wear heels that are medium to low.
- ✔ Save fur coats for the opera. They have no place in the office.
- ✔ Satins, brocades, lamés, and velvets are strictly for evening wear.
- ✔ Micro-miniskirts or anything see-through, low-cut, or too tight are for streetwalkers.
- ✔ Save noisy or outlandish jewelry for parties.

> ✔ Leggings with oversized sweatshirts are a no-no unless your office is moving and you're packing up your desk.
>
> ✔ Strapless tops and shorts belong on the beach.
>
> ✔ White shoes and pocketbooks are fine between Memorial Day and Labor Day. Otherwise, keep them in the closet.

Always keep an extra pair of pantyhose nearby (in your desk, car, briefcase, or pocketbook) to snag those runs.

Getting Clad for Business Meetings

Before you dive into your closet looking for just the right thing to wear, put on your reporter's hat and ask yourself the five Ws: Who? What? When? Where? Why?

Who'll be at the meeting?

> ✔ When you meet with people from your own company, you already know the culture.
>
> ✔ When you meet with people from outside your company, be guided by their culture. For example, young high-tech executives rarely show up in pinstriped suits.
>
> ✔ If you don't know the culture, err on the side of dressing up.

What's the meeting about? (**Why** are you meeting?)

> ✔ Are you trying to get someone's business? (Dress up.)
>
> ✔ Are you being pursued? (Dress as the pursuer.)
>
> ✔ Are you out to impress, or to put someone at ease?

When is the meeting?

> ✔ Is it a breakfast meeting? If so, you'll probably go straight to work and should dress accordingly.
>
> ✔ Is it an after-hours meeting? You can either wear your business attire or bring a change. It may merely mean changing a blouse or shirt.

Where is the meeting?

> ✔ Are you going to a ball game or a fancy restaurant? There's a big difference in how you dress.
>
> ✔ Are you meeting at a client's office? If so, dress appropriately for the culture of the client. If you don't know it, dress up.

If you work at home in your birthday suit, remember the words of Mark Twain: *Clothes make the man [or woman]. Naked people have little or no influence on society.*

Making a Good First Impression at an Interview

To set yourself above the competition, dress up. First impressions are important, so don't make your first impression your last.

- Take a look at the company's Web site. You often find annual reports or other literature that show how people dress.

- Discreetly ask the receptionist, who can be a wealth of information.

- Poke your head in the office, if that's appropriate. For example, if you're interviewing at a bank, stop by and see how people dress.

Meeting with Foreigners

Before you meet with foreigners (on your turf or theirs), know what's appropriate to wear. Check with a foreign counterpart or someone who's in the know. If you have any doubts about how to dress, err on the side of being formal. Here's a smattering of tips:

- Europeans and Americans have similar dress codes for both formal and casual. Remember, dress codes vary by industry.

- Asians tend to be more formal than Americans.

- In China, white is a symbol of mourning. Wear other colors.

- Women traveling to Arab countries shouldn't wear slacks or anything revealing. They should cover up as much of their bodies as possible.

- In Israel, people are very informal, so you may dress casually.

- If you visit the Far East or an Arab country, you may be asked to remove your shoes before entering a home (so don't have holes in your socks or stockings).

What's Hot on the CD-ROM

Here's what you can find on the CD-ROM:

- 24-1: Dealing with Jackets
- 24-2: Dressing Tips for Men
- 24-3: Dressing Tips for Women
- 24-4: Getting Clad for Business Meetings
- 24-5: How to Dress When Meeting with Foreigners

Appendix A

Geek Speak

● ●

Change is the one constant we can always count on. Changes in technology have ushered in a whole new language that many people find as foreign as French, Swahili, or Greek. But get with it, folks! The office of the future is here, and you must understand the lingo if you want to be successful in the business world.

Learning the Language of the Locals

A thousand years ago an anonymous bard composed *Beowulf* in Old English — a language that's barely recognizable to us. To read this epic, you need to put on your boar's-head helmet and serve up plenty of mead (an alcoholic drink of fermented honey and water). By the Middle Ages, something akin to modern English had evolved. All you need to read this type of English is a few aspirins, although mead is probably still a good idea. So grab your mead and continue to read.

@: In an e-mail message, the *at* sign separates the user name from the service provider. For example, sailaway@aol.com.

Asynchronous: A transmission in which each character or byte is synchronized by adding start and stop bits.

Bandwidth: A measurement of the amount of data a network connection can transfer at a given time. The greater the bandwidth, the faster data will transfer. You need a large bandwidth to transfer large files, graphics, or sound.

BBS (Bulletin Board System): An on-line area for posting messages. It's like an electronic version of a corkboard and tacks.

Bisynchronous: A transmission in which a block or group of characters moves together with a single start and stop.

Bit (short for Binary Digit): The smallest component of data in the binary number system; either a 0 or a 1.

Bot (short for robot): A little robot on the Internet that does comparison shopping, and makes you the bargain hunter of the century.

Bps (bits per second): Measures how fast a modem can send and receive data.

Browser (or Web browser): Software that translates HTML files, converts them into Web pages, and displays them on your computer screen. Some browsers access e-mail and newsgroups and play sound and video files.

Buffer: Temporary electronic storage.

Bug: A sticky wicket that prevents your software from operating properly.

Byte: A group of eight bits that the computer processes as one unit.

Chat room: An Internet location where you can "chat" with people around the world by typing messages and receiving responses in real time. Chat groups are often divided by special interests. They're a great way to meet people who share your personal and professional interests.

Cracker (or Hacker): Someone who breaks into a computer system to cause harm or steal data.

Cyberspace: The metaphorical space where electronic communications take place.

Decrypting: Decoding a message that's been coded (encrypted).

Downloading: Electronically copying a file to your computer from another computer. Think of it as loading something *down* from cyberspace. (The opposite is uploading.)

E-mail (Electronic mail): The main stop on the information superhighway. You can send and receive electronic letters and files in a flash.

Emoticons: Little faces made up of punctuation marks that add body language to your message. They're also called smileys or winkies. For example, :-) or ;~}.

Encrypting: Coding a message so only the recipient can read it.

FAQs (Frequently Asked Questions): A list of questions and answers on a specific subject.

File: A collection of categorized information, just as you find in a traditional file stuffed with papers.

Firewall: A software security mechanism that protects against unwanted access to a network.

Flaming: Using explosive (angry) language in an e-mail message.

FTP (File Transfer Protocol): The Internet service that transfers files from one computer to another.

G (for Gigabit): A computer's unit of capacity that's equal to 1,073,741,824 bits.

GIF (Graphics Interchange Format): A graphics-file format for displaying graphics on the Web. Another format is JPEG. (Pronounced *gif,* like *gift* without the *t.*)

GIGO (Garbage in, Garbage out): When you enter bad data, you get bad results. (Pronounced *guy-go.*)

Hard copy: A paper copy of a document.

Hardware: The physical components of a computer system, including the monitor, hard drive, printer, scanner, and anything else you can kick when it doesn't work properly.

Home page: The main page on a Web site. It gives folks on the Internet an overview of what the site has to offer.

HTTP (Hypertext Markup Language): The standard computer language in which Web pages are written and linked.

Hyperlink: A protocol to prepare Web pages for display when users click on hyperlinks.

Hypertext: Hidden codes that let you click on a word or phrase to give you various results.

Interface: Hardware or software that links your computer to other devices such as the printer.

Internet (also known as the Net): The "mother of all networks." A connection for hundreds of millions of computers. Learn all about the Internet in Chapter 5.

Intranet: A network of computers that can be accessed only by a set of users who have authorization. This is often set up for employees of a company.

ISP (Internet Service Provider): A business that provides a connection to e-mail and the Internet, such as AOL or AT&T.

JPEG (Joint Photographic Experts Group): A graphics file format for displaying graphics on the Web. It has a higher level of compression than GIF and as such has lower quality graphics. (Pronounced *jay-peg.*)

K (for Kilobyte): A measure of memory that equals 1024 bytes.

LAN (Local Area Network): A computer network that covers short distances and uses specialized computers to link small networks together.

Linux: An operating system which is based on several decades of Unix development. Linux supporters claim it's more reliable than the competition.

Logging off: Signing off from the Internet or your e-mail system.

Logging on: Signing onto the Internet or your e-mail system.

Mailing list: A list of people, groups of people, departments, or companies to whom you send messages.

Menu: A listing on your computer screen of the choices in a program.

Mg (Megabyte): One million bytes.

Modem: The modulator/demodulator gizmo that allows your computer's digital signals to travel through an analog phone line.

Mouse: A device you physically manipulate to move the pointer on the computer screen. Trackballs serve an identical purpose.

Net: Shortened version of *Internet.*

Netiquette: Etiquette guidelines for using e-mail and the Net.

Network: A system of two or more linked computers terminals connected by wires, cables, or a telecommunications system for the purpose of exchanging information.

Newbie: A new user of the Net.

Newsgroups: On-line forums where people with common interests can write messages back and forth. These are very popular with special interest groups (SIGs).

Offline: Working on your computer while not connected to a network.

Online: Working on your computer while connected to a network.

Password: A security measure that limits access to a network.

PDAs (Personal Digital Assistants): Handheld, wireless computers such as palm-held devices.

Peripheral: A device such as a printer or voice synthesizer that enhances your computer's capabilities.

RAM (Random Access Memory): A temporary storage system in your computer used for creating, loading, manipulating data, and running programs.

ROM (Read-Only Memory): A type of internal storage that holds instructions for the system.

Snail mail: A "geek speak" term that refers to traditional mail because it moves at a snail's pace — compared to electronic messages.

Spam: Electronic junk mail.

SSL (Secure Sockets Layer): Encryption that protects your e-mail messages from ogling eyes.

Surfing: Getting around the Net.

Synchronous: A transmission in which there's a constant spacing of time

Uploading: Sending a file from your computer to another computer. Think of it as loading something *up* into cyberspace. (The opposite is downloading.)

URL (Uniform Resource Locator): A string of information that creates the address to get you to a Web site. URLs normally start with *http://* (the Internet address of a Web page). Some start with *ftp://* (the network location of an FTP resource).

WAN (Wide Area Network): A computer network that covers a large distance and uses specialized computers to link smaller networks together.

World Wide Web (WWW): Affectionately referred to as the Web. In 1989, the Web was created by Tim Berners-Lee, of Switzerland, when he attempted to organize all the information on the Internet. When you use the Web, you normally start at your service provider's home page and surf from one place to another.

Virus: Definitely not a case of taking two aspirins and calling the doctor in the morning. Computer viruses are self-replicating codes written by people with devious minds who want to damage or destroy a computer system. A virus can be downloaded from the Internet, contained in an e-mail file, or transferred by a floppy disk. There are software "vaccines" such as Norton or McAfee virus checkers that will give you an early warning so you can avoid getting infected.

Zine: Cyberterm for magazine. (You sometimes see it written as *-Zine*.)

What's Hot on the CD-ROM

Here's what you can find on the CD-ROM:

- ✔ Document AppA-1: Geek Speak Terms from A to Z

Appendix B

Gulliver's Travel Terms

. . . .

*T*ravel terminology can often be daunting. Here are some definitions to help simplify your travel — covering airlines, hotels, and car-rentals.

Terms of Endearment for Airlines

Following are airline terms to help you become a savvy air traveler:

Airline club: Allows members to use airport facilities for making phone calls, sending faxes, photocopying, storing luggage, or just relaxing. Members pay an annual fee.

Blocked seats: Seats blocked for frequent flyers and passengers who wish to upgrade to business or first class. Sometimes travel agencies or tour groups purchase blocks of seats at a negotiated fare, allowing them to offer vacation or business packages at a discount rate.

Business class: Less expensive than first class, but you still receive free alcoholic beverages, above-average meals, roomy seats, and a quiet working atmosphere.

Coach class: Slightly better than being strapped to the wing. Coach is the least expensive form of air travel, and you get what you pay for. Seats are narrow and there's little leg-room. (If you're taller than four feet, your knees may touch your shoulders.) You pay for alcoholic beverages, meals are served from trays, and service is so-so.

Connecting flight: Requires that you change planes in one or more cities.

Direct flight: Stops in one or more cities, but you don't change planes.

Electronic ticketing: This isn't a real ticket; it's a ticket for a ticket. The advantage is that you don't have to pay for a replacement if you lose the e-ticket because it's not really a ticket. The disadvantage is that if your flight is canceled and you want to book on another airline, you can't. Check out Chapter 16 for a the full story of electronic tickets.

Fare wars: When one airline cuts fares and other major airlines jump on the bandwagon to stay competitive. To take advantage of these discount rates, be quick because seats are limited.

First class: Offers wider seats and more space than other classes. Includes quality food on dinner plates with tableware (not plastic), free alcoholic beverages, and lots of personalized attention.

Frequent flyer: Incentives encouraging you to fly a particular airline. After you accumulate a certain number of travel points, you may get free upgrades or free trips. Many airlines partner with credit card companies to offer frequent flyer points for all your purchases.

Group fares: A price quoted per person for ten or more people traveling together on the same flight.

Load: The number of available seats on a flight. This is important to know if you're traveling standby so you know what your odds are of getting on the flight. The higher the load, the better your chances. If you call the airline and ask for the load, here are the terms you need to know:

- *Excellent* means there are at least 50 seats available.

- *Good* means there are 20-49 seats available.

- *Fair* means there are 11-19 seats available.

- *Poor* means there are less than 10 seats available.

Matching fares: Airlines will often match fares other airlines offer. They do this to stay competitive, especially for frequent flyers.

Nonrefundable ticket: Has penalties attached if your plans change and you don't make the trip. You may lose either the entire cost of the ticket or a percentage of the cost. If you have to cancel because of a death in the family or medical emergency, you can present a doctor's letter and, perhaps, avoid the penalty. When you make reservations, check out the airline's cancellation policy and cancellation insurance options.

Nonstop flight: Has no stops between the departure and arrival cities.

Off-peak travel: Traveling during off-season when the number of passengers headed for a certain destination is low. This option can save you quite a bit of money. Take note that off-peak times vary with your destination. For example, Australia's off-season coincides with Europe's peak season.

One-way fares: Fares from one city to another with no return booked. These fares can be almost as expensive as roundtrip.

Open ticket: Valid between two cities, with no specific return reservation. This is a great option if you're not sure when you'll return.

Open-jaw trip: Routing that allows you to leave from one city, go to your destination, and return to another city. The departure and return cities must be within a certain distance of each other.

Peak travel: There are many passengers headed for the same destination (during peak season).

Promotional fares: Credit cards, long-distance phone carriers, hotels, and store chains often provide discount airline tickets as part of a promotion.

Red-eye flights: Flights that leave in an earlier time zone to arrive at your destination early in the morning. For example, an 11:30 p.m. flight from the West Coast gets you to the East Coast around 5:30 a.m. If you've ever taken one of these flights and have a hard time sleeping on the way over, you'll know why they call it a red-eye.

Round-trip fares: Fares for tickets from a city and back to the same city.

Standby: Gets you a seat on the plane if one is available at the last minute. Your name is placed on a numbered list, and if there's a seat within 24 hours of flight time, you get a confirmed seat. Or you may go standby at the gate and hope to get a seat. This is a little risky during peak-travel times such as Monday mornings, Friday evenings, and holidays.

Stopover: A planned stop when you spend more than 12 hours in a location. This is considered an interrupted trip.

Upgrade: When you fly in a higher class or service than the ticket you originally bought. For example, frequent flyers are allowed to buy upgrades to business- or first-class if seats are available. And if you're really lucky — and the person behind the ticket counter likes the color of your eyes — you may even get a free upgrade.

Hotel Lingo

Hotel rates and services vary. Be sure you know what you're getting.

American plan (AP): Offers a rate that includes breakfast, lunch, and dinner.

Budget hotel: Caters to the traveler on a limited budget. Rooms are adequate but there may be few amenities.

Club floor: You can go the exclusive route for about an additional 20 percent of your bill. Privacy and safety are the main draw. You need a special key to enter, and amenities may include complimentary drinks, hors d'ouerves, and other good stuff.

Concierge: Assists you with such needs as making flight arrangements, getting theater tickets, suggesting restaurants, and just about anything else to make your stay enjoyable.

Continental plan (CP): Includes coffee *and* . . . maybe rolls, muffins, juice, cereal, cheese, or cold meat. In many parts of the world (outside the U.S.) this term can denote a hearty breakfast.

Corporate rate: Is available to travelers on business. Some hotels have arrangements with companies to provide special rates.

European plan (EP): A room rate with no meals.

Frequent-stay benefit: Allows regular customers to received discounted rates or upgrades, just like frequent flyer points on airlines. Some hotels have incentive ties to frequent-flyer membership programs.

Government rate: Is available to travelers who are employed by the government. You may be asked for proof.

Hospitality suite: A room used to entertain. A hospitality suite is often booked at trade shows or conventions for people to socialize and do business.

Morning call: Also known as a wake-up call. Look on your phone to find out how to get a morning call.

Modified plan (MP): Also known as a modified American plan (MAP). Offers breakfast and dinner, but not lunch. This makes guests' mid-day schedule less restricted.

Preregistration: A procedure to register you before you arrive. This is often done for large groups, such as conventions, so each person doesn't have to register at the front desk. When you arrive, you give your name and get your key.

Automobile Terms

Following are terms specific to car rentals.

Compact: Describes a regular-size car.

Deluxe: Describes the largest and most expensive models.

Drop-off charges: Refers to the amount the car-rental agency collects when you return a car to a location other than the one from which you rented it.

Standard: Describes a full-size car.

Subcompact: Describes a small car.

Unlimited mileage: Refers to a set fee for a designated period of time. Payment isn't based on the number of miles you drive.

Don't accept rental-car insurance without checking with your auto insurance, credit card, or homeowner's insurance company before you leave home. Many of these companies provide coverage.

When you drive, remember that all interstate highways with even numbers (such as Route 80), run east and west. All with odd numbers (such as Route 95) run north and south. (Have you ever wondered how Hawaii has interstate highways?)

What's Hot on the CD-ROM

Here's what you'll find on the CD-ROM:

- ✔ AppB-1: Airline Terminology
- ✔ AppB-2: Hotel Terminology
- ✔ AppB-3: Car-Rental Terminology

Appendix C

About the CD

● ●

*H*ere's some of what you can find on the *Business Professional's Kit For Dummies* CD-ROM:

- Files with lots of useful tips and toll-free numbers. A complete listing comes later in this appendix under "Chapter files."

- A listing of all the hyperlinks featured in the book.

- Microsoft Internet Explorer, Netscape Communicator, and Adobe Acrobat Reader – for Mac and Windows. (Acrobat Reader enables you to read the PDF documents on this CD.)

- Punctuation and grammer guidelines.

System Requirements

Make sure your computer meets the minimum system requirements listed below. If your computer doesn't match up to most of these requirements, you may have problems in using the contents of the CD.

- A PC with a 486 or faster processor, or a Mac OS computer with a 68040 or faster processor.

- Microsoft Windows 95 or later, or Mac OS system software 7.55 or later.

- At least 16MB of total RAM installed on your computer. For best performance, we recommend at least 32MB of RAM installed.

- At least 50MB of hard drive space available to install all the software from this CD. (You'll need less space if you don't install every program.)

- A CD-ROM drive – double-speed (2x) or faster.

- A sound card for PCs. (Mac OS computers have built-in sound support.)

- A monitor capable of displaying at least 256 colors or grayscale.

- A modem with a speed of at least 14,400 bps.

If you need more information on the basics, check out *PCs For Dummies,* 7th Edition, by Dan Gookin; *Macs For Dummies,* 6th Edition, by David Pogue; *iMac For Dummies,* by David Pogue; *Windows 95 For Dummies,* 2nd Edition, or *Windows 98 For Dummies* both by Andy Rathbone (all published by IDG Books Worldwide, Inc.).

Using the CD with Microsoft Windows

1. **Insert the CD into your computer's CD-ROM drive.**

   Give your computer a moment to take a look at the CD.

2. **Open your browser.** If you do not have a browser, we have included Microsoft Internet Explorer on this CD.

   Click File⇨Open (Internet Explorer) or File⇨Open Page (Netscape).

3. **Double-click the file called License.txt.**

   This file contains the end-user license that you agree to by using the CD. When you are done reading the license, close the program, most likely NotePad, that displayed the file.

4. **Double-click the file called Readme.txt.**

   This file contains instructions about installing the software from this CD. It might be helpful to leave this text file open while you are using the CD.

5. **In the dialog box that appears, type** D:\START.HTM **and click on OK.**

   Replace the letter D: with the correct letter for your CD-ROM drive, if it is not "D."

   This action will display the file that will walk you through the content of the CD.

6. **To navigate within the interface, simply click on any topic of interest to take you to an explanation of the files on the CD and how to use or install them.**

7. **To install the software from the CD, simply click on the software name.**

   You'll see two options — the option to run or open the file from the current location or the option to save the file to your hard drive. Choose to run or open the file from its current location and the installation procedure will continue. After you are done with the interface, simply close your browser as usual.

To run some of the programs, you may need to keep the CD inside your CD-ROM drive. This is a Good Thing. Otherwise, the installed program would have required you to install a very large chunk of the program to your hard drive space, which would have kept you from installing other software.

Using the CD with Mac OS

To install the items from the CD to your hard drive, follow these steps.

1. **Insert the CD into your computer's CD-ROM drive.**

   In a moment, an icon representing the CD you just inserted appears on your Mac desktop. Chances are, the icon looks like a CD-ROM.

2. **Double-click the CD icon to show the CD's contents.**

3. **Double-click the Read Me First icon.**

   This text file contains information about the CD's programs and any last-minute instructions you need to know about installing the programs on the CD that we don't cover in this appendix.

4. **Open your browser.**

   If you don't have a browser, we have included Microsoft Internet Explorer and Netscape Navigator on the CD.

5. **Click File⇨Open and select the CD entitled Business Professional's Kit. Double-click the Links.htm file to see an explanation of all files and folders included on the CD.**

6. **Some programs come with installer programs — with those you simply open the program's folder on the CD and double-click the icon with the words "Install" or "Installer."**

   Once you have installed the programs that you want, you can eject the CD. Carefully place it back in the plastic jacket of the book for safekeeping.

What You'll Find on the CD

The CD-ROM contains business software as well as example files, reference information, and other documents that relate to specific chapters in the book.

Software Tools

Acrobat Reader 4.0 from Adobe Systems *(For Mac and Windows; evaluation version).* This program lets you view and print Portable Document Format (PDF) files (like the ones on this CD). To learn more about using Acrobat Reader, choose the Reader Online Guide from the Help menu, or view the Acrobat.pdf file installed in the same folder as the program. You can also get more information by visiting the Adobe Systems Web site at www.adobe.com.

Internet Explorer from Microsoft *(Version 5.0 for Windows and Version 4.5 for Mac; commercial product)*. Microsoft Internet Explorer provides the best support to date for Dynamic HTML and CSS. This browser from Microsoft enables you to view Web pages and perform a host of other Internet functions, including e-mail, newsgroups, and word processing. Keep an eye on the Microsoft Web site at www.microsoft.com. This program is updated frequently!

Netscape Communicator *(Version 4.7 for Mac and Windows)*. This suite of Internet applications from Netscape allow you to browse the Web, send and receive e-mail, and much more.

MindSpring Internet Access from MindSpring *(for Mac and Windows)*. MindSpring is a complete Internet service provider package that you can use to open an account for access to the Internet. You need a credit card to sign up for MindSpring Internet Access.

WinZip from Nico Mak Computing *(Version 7 for Windows)*. WinZip is a utility for compressing and decompressing ZIP files. Almost all large files available on the Internet (for Windows) are compressed in the ZIP format, and WinZip is an indispensable part of any netizen's tool kit.

StuffIt Lite Version 3.6 and Drop Stuff with Expander Enhancer Version 5 from Aladdin Systems (for Mac). These utilities allow you to compress and decompress StuffIt files, the most common file format for compressed files in the Macintosh universe.

Aladdin Expander from Aladdin Systems (for Windows). This utility allows Windows users to decompress StuffIt files, a common compression format for Macs.

Eudora Light from QUALCOMM *(Version 3.13 for Mac and 3.06 for Windows)*. Eudora Light is a powerful, full-featured e-mail program.

Reptile, SilverThingy, and HotDog Professional from Sausage Software (for Windows). These utilities enable you to easily build your own cool-looking Web pages.

Chapter files

What follows is a list of all of the documents on the CD. All of these files appear as both PDF documents and plain-text files. Use Adobe Acrobat Reader to view the PDFs. The plain-text files are for those of you who'd like to carry some of the information on this CD in your hand-held computer. See the next section for more details.

Document Number	*Document Name*
2-1	Dealing with a Grumpy Caller
2-2	Putting Someone on Hold
2-3	Cutting a Caller Short
2-4	Getting Rid of Telemarketers
2-5	When You Dial the Wrong Number
2-6	Screening Calls
2-7	Placing a Call
2-8	Saving Money on Calls
2-9	Selecting a Long-Distance Carrier
2-10	Superb Outgoing Voice-Mail Messages
2-11	Refreshing Incoming Voice-Mail Messages
2-12	International Calling Codes
3-1	What to Do When Your Computer Crashes
3-2	Waking up a Sluggish Computer
3-3	Searching for a Missing File
3-4	Protecting Against Power Surges
3-5	Avoiding Viruses
3-6	Speeding Up Internet Access
3-7	A Survival Kit for Your PC or Mac
3-8	Getting Help Online
3-9	Protecting Your Laptop
3-10	Dealing with Photocopiers
3-11	Solving Fax Problems
3-12	Using a Palm Computer
4-1	Keeping Your E-Mail System Safe
4-2	Eliminating Spam
4-3	Using Emotion
4-4	Minding Your E-Manners

(continued)

Document Number	Document Name
4-5	Creating an Electronic Filing Cabinet
5-1	Country-Specific Internet Extensions
5-2	Using Search Engines
5-3	Web Sites for Cyberlearning
5-4	Web Sites for Shopping
5-5	Web Sites for Safe and Secure Surfing
6-1	What to Do Before You Leave Your Current Job
6-2	Do What You Love
6-3	Selecting a Name
6-4	Deciding Whether to Incorporate
6-5	What You Need to Get Your Home Business Started
6-6	Leading a Balanced Work and Home Life
6-7	The Web Site
6-8	Keeping the IRS at Bay
6-9	Buying Insurance
6-10	Saving for Retirement
6-11	Expanding Your Sphere of Contacts
7-1	Ergonimics and the Human Factor
7-2	Choosing the Ideal Chair
7-3	Avoiding Aches and Pains When Spending Too Much Time in Your Car
7-4	Desktop Comfort
7-5	Adjusting Your Computer Monitor
7-6	Mousing Around
7-7	Keyboarding with Safety
7-8	Exercises for Keeping Limber and Relieving Tension
8-1	Putting the Parts of a Letter Together
8-2	Letter Styles
8-3	Multi-Page Letters

Document Number	Document Name
8-4	Writing Memos
9-1	Six Steps to Effective Business Writing
9-2	Start Up Sheet
9-3	Proofreading Tips
9-4	Proofreading Checklist
10-1	Web Sites for Carriers
10-2	Keeping Costs Down
11-1	Retaining Valuable Records
11-2	Recycling Info
12-1	Introducing Yourself and Others
12-2	Shaking Hands Properly
12-3	Becoming a Good Speaker and Listener
12-4	Reading Body Language
12-5	Working a Room
13-1	Making Reservations
13-2	Checking Your Coat
13-3	Greeting Guests
13-4	Using Your Napkin, Not Your Sleeve
13-5	The Pecking Order at a Restaurant
13-6	Placing an Order
13-7	Minding Your Table Manners
13-8	Paying the Check
13-9	Eating Different Kinds of Food
13-10	Going "French"
14-1	Web Sites for Creative Gifts
14-2	Gifts for Supervisors
14-3	Gifts for Administrative Assistants
14-4	Baby Gifts

(continued)

Document Number	Document Name
14-5	Gifts for Weddings
14-6	Giving Gifts to Foreigners
14-7	Trade Show Giveaways
15-1	Tips for Men Only
15-2	Tips for Women Only
15-3	Gender-Neutral Terms
15-4	Sticky Wickets
15-5	Appropriate Behavior for Supervisors and Assistants
15-6	The Good Old Girls' Network
16-1	Getting the Best Deal when Flying
16-2	Web Sites for Airlines and Booking Services
16-3	Toll-Free Numbers for Airlines and Car Rental Agencies
16-4	Special Services for the Disabled
16-5	Avoiding the Perils of Electronic Tickets
16-6	Avoiding Getting Bumped
16-7	Dealing with Flight Delays and Cancellations
16-8	Exercises to Work Out the Kinks
16-9	Reducing Earaches from Changes in Air Pressure
16-10	Overcoming Jet Lag
16-11	Getting Free Flights
16-12	Navigating International Airports
17-1	Hotel Star Ratings
17-2	Toll-Free Numbers for Popular Hotels
17-3	Shopping for Safety Before You Book a Hotel Room
17-4	Staying on the Club Floor
17-5	What's Important in a Room
17-6	Minimizing Telephone Expenses
18-1	Papers You Need to Get a Passport
18-2	Information on Visas

Document Number	Document Name
18-3	Getting an International Driving Permit
18-4	Information on Vaccinations
18-5	Phone Numbers for Major Credit Cards
18-6	Phone Numbers for Traveler's Checks
19-1	General Do's and Taboos When Travelling
19-2	Handbag Tips for Women
19-3	Shopping Tips
19-4	Enjoying Europe
19-5	Amazing Asia
19-6	Loving Latin America
19-7	Mingling in the Middle East
19-8	Going Through U.S. Customs
20-1	Determining When to Hold a Meeting
20-2	Distributing the Agenda
20-3	Determining the Location for a Meeting
20-4	Knowing the Structure of a Meeting
20-5	Taking Minutes
20-6	Being Sensitive to Meeting Attendees
20-7	Videoconferencing
21-1	Learning All You Can about Your Audience
21-2	Developing a Purpose for Your Presentation
21-3	Identifying Your Key Issue
21-4	Checking Out the Environment
21-5	Visual Aids
21-6	Preparing Your Presentation Opening
21-7	Speaking Naturally
21-8	Delivering the Heart of Your Presentation
21-9	Ending on a High Note The Grand Finale

(continued)

Document Number	Document Name
21-10	A Checklist for Presentations
22-1	Special Events Coordinators
22-2	The Registration Table
22-3	Wearing Your Name Badge
22-4	Dealing with Guests Who Speak English as a Second Language
22-5	Using an Interpreter
22-6	Drawing People into Your Booth
22-7	A Template for a Follow-Up Letter to a trade Show
22-8	Walking the Floor of a Trade Show
22-9	Accommodating People with Disabilities
23-1	Determining What's Politically Correct
23-2	Working with People Who Are Vision Impaired
23-3	Working with People with Hearing Disabilities
23-4	Working with People with Speech Impairments
23-5	Working with People with Paralysis or Loss of a Limb
23-6	Working with People with AIDS
23-7	Dispelling Fears of Potential Employers
24-1	Dealing with Jackets
24-2	Dressing Tips for Men
24-3	Dressing Tips for Women
24-4	Getting Clad for Business Meetings
24-5	How to Dress When Meeting with Foreigners
AppA-1	Geek Speak Terms from A to Z
AppB-1	Airline Terminology
AppB-2	Hotel Terminology
AppB-3	Car-Rental Terminology

Bonus Files

We didn't have enough room to put some information in the book, so we tossed it on the CD. Here's what you get:

Document Number	Document Name
Bonus 01	Editing for Excellence
Bonus 02	Charts and Tables

Using the CD Files with a Handheld Computer

If you use a Palm or Windows CE computer, you can carry some of the files on the CD with you. We have placed plain-text (.TXT) versions of the PDF chapter files on the CD. After you copy these text files to the hard drive of your main computer, simply hook up your Palm or Windows CE device to your computer and copy the files that interest you. Cool, no? Remember that your handheld has a limited amount of memory. All of the text files add up to about 5.4 megabytes, so you should probably load only the files you find most useful.

If You've Got Problems (Of the CD Kind)

I tried my best to compile programs that work on most computers with the minimum system requirements. Alas, your computer may differ, and some programs may not work properly for some reason.

The two likeliest problems are that you don't have enough memory (RAM) for the programs you want to use, or you have other programs running that are affecting installation or running of a program. If you get error messages like Not enough memory or Setup cannot continue, try one or more of these methods and then try using the software again:

- ✔ **Turn off any anti-virus software that you have on your computer.** Installers sometimes mimic virus activity and may make your computer incorrectly believe that it is being infected by a virus.

- ✔ **Close all running programs.** The more programs you're running, the less memory is available to other programs. Installers also typically update files and programs. So if you keep other programs running, installation may not work properly.

> ✔ **Have your local computer store add more RAM to your computer.** This is, admittedly, a drastic and somewhat expensive step. However, if you have a Windows 95 PC or a Mac OS computer with a PowerPC chip, adding more memory can really help the speed of your computer and allow more programs to run at the same time. This may include closing the CD interface and running a product's installation program from Windows Explorer.

If you still have trouble installing the items from the CD, please call the IDG Books Worldwide Customer Service phone number: 800-762-2974 (outside the U.S.: 317-572-3342).

Index

• A •

AAA (American Automobile
    Association), 236
Addressing letters, 110–111
Administrative assistants
  gifts for, 188–189
  relationship with supervisor, 206–209
AIDS, people with, 306–307
Air travel, 213–224
  airlines
    toll-free numbers, 214–215
    Web sites, 216
  booking flights, 213–215
  cancellations, 218–219
  delays, 218–219
  disabled travelers and, 217
  earaches, avoiding, 222
  electronic ticketing, 217
  executive lounges, passes for, 219
  exercising and, 220–221
  flight etiquette, 219–220
  frequent flyer clubs, 222–223
  getting bumped, 218
  glossary of terms, 323–325
  international airports, 223–224
  overcoming jet lag, 221–222
  safeguarding tickets, 216
  saving money on, 215–216
Alcoholic drinks, ordering, 173–175
Algorithms, 60
AltaVista (search engine), 63
American Automobile Association
    (AAA), 236
American Bar Association, 73
American Express, 239
American Paper Institute, 153
Answering machines, 19–21
AO mail, 143
Applications, computer, 28
  low memory and, 29

Archive files, 149
Asia, 253–257
  conversation topics, 254
  dining tips, 255–256
  dress codes, 254
  general business practices, 256–257
  greetings, 253–254
  shopping tips, 254–255
  tipping, 256
Auctions, on-line, 77

• B •

Baby showers, gifts for, 189–190
Block letter style, 117, 120
BNI (Business Network International),
    41, 94
Body language, 167–168
Books, as gifts, 186
Bots, 72
Buffets, 183
Bulk mail postage, 140
Business casual dress code, 310
Business meals, 171–183
  buffets, 183
  check, paying the, 178–179
  coats, checking, 172
  cocktails, ordering, 173
  guests, greeting, 172
  messy foods, tips for eating, 179–182
  napkin etiquette, 172–173
  ordering tips, 173
  reservations, making, 171–172
  table manners, 175–177
  tipping, 178–179
  toasts, proposing, 175
  wine, ordering, 174–175
Business Network International (BNI),
    41, 94
Business travel. *See* Travel issues

Business writing, 127–137. *See also* Letters
  drafts, 132
  headlines, 131–132
  planning process, 128–131
  proofreading documents, 134–136
  strategic sequencing, 131–132
  tone, 133–134
  visual impact, designing for, 133
  writer's block, 131

• C •

Cable Internet access, 33
Car travel
  American Automobile Association
    (AAA), 236
  glossary of terms, 326–327
  rentals, toll-free numbers, 215
Carpal tunnel syndrome, 103
CD-ROM, 329–339
  chapter files, 332–338
  software tools, 331–332
  system requirements, 329
  troubleshooting, 339
  using with handheld computers, 339
  using with Mac OS, 331
  using with Microsoft Windows, 330
Cell phones, 23–26
  driving and, 25
  etiquette, 25–26
  rates, 25
  selecting, 24
Centers for Disease Control, 237
Certificates of mailing, 141
Certified mail, 141
Chairs, choosing, 99–100
Change, 9–12
Chopsticks, 256
Circadian rhythm, 221
Close corporations, 83
Club floors (hotels), 231
Coats, checking at restaurant, 172
Cocktails, ordering, 173
COD (cash on delivery) mailings, 142

Compliments, accepting, 165
Computer vision syndrome (CVS), 101
Computers, 28–35
  applications, 28
  crashes, 28–29
  defragging hard drives, 30
  e-mail. *See* E-mail
  glossary of terms, 317–321
  hackers, 50, 67
  help, finding, 34–35
  home offices and, 85
  Internet. *See* Internet
  laptops, 35
  missing files, finding, 31
  operating systems, 28
  palm units, 40–41
  power outages, 32
  protecting data, 34
  repetitive action injuries, avoiding, 101–103
  saving work, 34
  speed, increasing, 29–31
  translation software, 242–243
  viruses, 32–33
Concierges, 231
Conferences, 289–298
  coordinators, 289
  foreign participants, 292–294
  name badges, 290–292
  registration table, 290
  special accommodations, 296–298
  spouses and, 290
Conversation, art of, 162–167
  in Asia, 254
  compliments, accepting, 165
  in Europe, 250
  listening tips, 165–167
  rating skills, 163
  speaking tips, 163–165
Copy machines, 36–38
Cordless telephones, 85
Corporations, 83
CP mail, 143
Crashes, computer, 28–29
Cumulative trauma disorder, 98

Currencies, foreign, 238
European, 250–251
Middle Eastern, 260
Customs regulations, 261
CVS (computer vision syndrome), 101

• *D* •

Date, writing, 110
Dating (office romances), 205–206
Defragging hard drives, 30
DHL Worldwide Express, 146
Digital subscriber line (DSL), 33
Dinners, 171–183
buffets, 183
check, paying the, 178–179
coats, checking, 172
cocktails, ordering, 173
guests, greeting, 172
messy foods, tips for eating, 179–182
napkin etiquette, 172–173
ordering tips, 173
reservations, making, 171–172
table manners, 175–177
tipping, 178–179
toasts, proposing, 175
wine, ordering, 174–175
Disability insurance for home-based
businesses, 92
Disabled people. *See* People with disabilities
Domestic mail, 140–143
bar codes, 143
certificates of mailing, 141
certified letters, 141
express mail, 142
first class, 140
priority mail, 142
registered mail, 141–142
Dress codes, 309–314
in Asia, 254
business casual, 310
for business meetings, 313–314
in Europe, 251
jacket etiquette, 311
for job interviews, 314
meeting with foreigners, 314
tips for men, 311–312
tips for women, 312–313
Driving permits, international, 236
DSL (digital subscriber line), 33

• *E* •

EC (European Community), 249
E-commerce, 71–76
bots, 72
cybermerchant, becoming a, 73–75
refunds, 76
security, 72
shipping costs, 76
shopping tips, 75–76
taxes, 75
Electronic commerce. *See* E-commerce
Electronic Communication Privacy Act
(ECPA), 49
Electronic mail. *See* E-mail
Electronic ticketing, 217
E-mail, 45–58
advantages, 49
disadvantages, 49
information overload, reducing, 51–53
messages, 46–48
addresses, 47–48
attachments, 47
electronic filing systems, 57
emoticons, 53–54
encrypting, 50
etiquette, 54–57
flames, 55
libel and copyright laws, 55
priority options, 48
spam, 50–51
outsourcing services, 54
security, 49–50
uses, 46
Emoticons, 53–54
EMS (Express Mail International
Service), 144
Enclosure notations, 115–116
Encryption, 50

Ergonomics, 98
  computer equipment and, 101–103
  furniture, choosing, 98–100
Esperanto, 242
EU (European Union), 249
Euro, the, 250
Europe, 249–253
  conversation topics, 250
  currencies, 250–251
  dress codes, 251
  greetings, 250
  table manners, 252
  tipping, 250
  Value Added Tax (VAT), 252–253
European Community (EC), 249
European Union (EU), 249
Excite (search engine), 63
Exercise, 104–105
  air travel and, 220–221
Express mail, 142
Express Mail International Service (EMS), 144

• F •

FAQs (frequently asked questions), 35
Fax machines, 38–39
Federal Express, 145
Federal Trade Commission (FTC), 73, 76
Firewalls, 33, 64
Flames (e-mail), 55
Flip charts, 280
Flowers, as gifts, 186
Foreign currencies, 238
  European, 250–251
  Middle Eastern, 260
Foreign language issues, 242–243
  common key words, 243
Freeman Exhibit Co., 289
Freeware, 61
Frequent flyer clubs, 222–223
Frequently asked questions (FAQs), 35
FTC (Federal Trade Commission), 73, 76
Full block letter style, 117–118
Furniture, ergonomically sound, 98–100

• G •

Gender issues, 199–210
  gender-neutral terms, 202–203
  office romances, 205–206
  sexual harassment, 204–205
  stereotypes, 200–202
  sticky situations, handling, 203–204
  tips for men, 200–201
  tips for women, 201–202
Gifts, 185–196
  for administrative assistants, 188–189
  for baby showers, 189–190
  books, 186
  finding on–line, 186
  flowers, 186
  for foreigners, 192–194
  gift certificates, 186–187
  homemade, 186
  inappropriate, acknowledging, 196
  magazines, 186
  mailing, 191
  plants, 186
  refusing, 194
  for supervisors, 188
  thank-you notes, 195–196
  for travelers, 187
  unwanted, exchanging, 191–192
  for wedding showers, 190
Global Priority Mail (GPM), 144
Gossip, 205
GPM (Global Priority Mail), 144
Greeting guests at business meals, 172

• H •

Hackers, 50, 67
Handicapped people. *See* People with
  disabilities
Handshakes, 161–162
Headsets, 85
Health Information for International
  Travel, 236

Health insurance
  for home-based businesses, 91
  while traveling, 237
Health issues while traveling, 237
Hearing impaired, the, 305
Heimlich maneuver, 184
Holidays, in foreign countries, 247–249
Home pages (World Wide Web), 64
Home-based businesses, 79–95
  business plans, 81
  computer issues, 85
  incorporating, 83
  insurance policies and, 91–92
  multifunction devices (MFDs), 86
  naming, 82–83
  networking, 93–94
  retirement plans, 92–93
  tax deductions for, 90–91
  telecommuting, 80
  telephone issues, 85
  Web sites, 87–90
  work space, setting up, 84
Hotels, 225–232
  bargain shopping, 227
  club floors, 231
  concierges, 231
  glossary of terms, 325–326
  personalizing rooms, 231
  ratings, 225–226
  reservations, getting room without, 227
  safety tips, 228–229
  telephone calls, 231–232
  toll-free numbers, 226
Hyperlinks, 62

● *I* ●

IAMAT (International Association for
    Medical Assistance to Travelers), 237
Incorporating, 83
Information overload, 51–53
Insurance
  for home-based businesses, 91–92
  while traveling, 237
International airports, 223–224

International Association for Medical
    Assistance to Travelers (IAMAT), 237
International driving permits, 236
International Events Group, 289
International mail, 143–145
International time zones, 21–22
Internet, 59–77. *See also* Intranets
  access, speeding up, 33
  conferencing tools, 276
  e-commerce, 71–76
    bots, 72
    cybermerchant, becoming a, 73–75
    refunds, 76
    security, 72–73
    shipping costs, 76
    shopping tips, 75–76
    taxes, 75
  freeware, 61
  gifts, finding, 186
  on-line auctions, 77
  search engines, 63
  surfing, 60–61
  URLs (uniform resource locators), 48, 62
  virtual colleges, 66
  viruses, 61
  World Wide Web, 61–64
Interpreters, 293–294
Interviews (job), dress codes for, 314
Intranets, 64–66
Introductions
  first versus last names, 160
  introducing others, 157–160
  introducing yourself, 161
  memory lapses, 160
  names, remembering, 159
  nicknames, 160
  titles, 160
Israel, 260
IT (Information Technology), 28

● *J* ●

Jet lag, overcoming, 221–222
Job interviews, dress codes for, 314
Junk mail, reducing, 152

• K •

Keogh plans, 92–93
Knowledge management, 11
Kosher food, 260

• L •

Languages, foreign, 242–243
  common key words, 243
Laptops, 35
Latin America, 257–259
  border crossings, 258–259
  confirming appointments, 258
  dining tips, 259
  names, 257
  transportation within, 258
LC mail, 143
Letters, 109–126
  components, 109–117
    attention line, 112
    body, 114
    complimentary closing, 114
    copy notation, 116
    date, 110
    enclosure notation, 115–116
    in-house notations, 110
    inside address, 110–111
    mailing notation, 110
    postscript, 116
    reference initials, 115
    salutation, 113
    signature line, 115
    subject line, 113
  multi-page, 123
  styles, 118–122
Life insurance, for home-based
      businesses, 92
Linux operating system, 32
Lithium ion (Li-ion) batteries, 24
Luncheons, 171–183
  buffets, 183
  check, paying the, 178–179
  coats, checking, 172
  cocktails, ordering, 173

guests, greeting, 172
messy foods, tips for eating, 179–182
napkin etiquette, 172–173
ordering tips, 173
reservations, making, 171–172
table manners, 175–177
tipping, 178–179
toasts, proposing, 175
wine, ordering, 174–175

• M •

Magazine subscriptions, as gifts, 186
Mail
  bar codes and, 143
  certificates of mailing, 141
  certified, 141
  costs, reducing, 143
  express, 142
  first class, 140
  gifts, sending, 191
  international, 143–145
  junk mail, reducing, 152
  non-USPS carriers, 145–146
  postage meters, 144
  priority, 142
  registered, 141–142
Mail merge, 123
Mailing notations, 110
Malpractice insurance, 91
Manners, table, 175–177
  in Europe, 252
McAfee Virus Checker, 33
M-commerce, 25
Meals, 171–183
  buffets, 183
  check, paying the, 178–179
  coats, checking, 172
  cocktails, ordering, 173
  guests, greeting, 172
  messy foods, tips for eating, 179–182
  napkin etiquette, 172–173
  ordering tips, 173
  reservations, making, 171–172
  table manners, 175–177

tipping, 178–179
toasts, proposing, 175
wine, ordering, 174–175
MedicAlert, 237
Meetings, 265–276
agendas for, 267–268
disabled participants, sensitivity to, 274
dress codes for, 313–314
facilitating a productive environment, 270–271
foreign participants, sensitivity to, 273–274
introducing participants, 270
length of, 266
locations for, 268–269
minutes, recording, 272–273
planning, 266–269
reasons for, 266
recapping, 271
thanking participants, 271
videoconferencing, 275
Memos, 124–126
Men and women in the workplace
gender-neutral terms, 202–203
office romances, 205–206
sexual harassment, 204–205
stereotypes, 200–202
sticky situations, handling, 203–204
Messages
e-mail messages
addresses, 47–48
attachments, 47
electronic filing systems, 57
encrypting, 50
etiquette, 54–57
flames, 55
libel and copyright laws, 55
priority options, 48
spam, 50–51
telephone messages, 19–21
MFDs (multifunction devices), 86
Microsoft Windows. *See* Windows (Microsoft)
Middle East, 259–261
currencies, 260
dining tips, 259–260
general business practices, 261

Minutes (for meetings), 272–273
Modems, high-speed, 33
Modified block letter style, 117, 120
Multifunction devices (MFDs), 86
Musculoskeletal disorders (MSDs), 97–98

• *N* •

Name badges (special events), 290–292
Names, remembering, 159
National Association for Women Business Owners (NAWBO), 95
National Consumer League, 73
National Organization on Disabilities (NOD), 301
NAWBO (National Association for Women Business Owners), 95
Netiquette, 54–57
NetMeetings, 276
Nickel Cadmium (NiCd) batteries, 24
Nickel Metal Hydride (NiMH) batteries, 24
NOD (National Organization on Disabilities), 301
Norton AntiVirus, 33
Norton Utilities, 30

• *O* •

Office equipment, 27–41
computers, 28–35
crashes, 28–29
e-mail. *See* E-mail
help, finding, 34–35
Internet. *See* Internet
laptops, 35
missing files, finding, 31
palm units, 40–41
power outages, 32
protecting data, 34
saving work, 34
speed, increasing, 29–31
viruses, 32–33
fax machines, 38–39
palm units, 40–41
photocopiers, 36–38
Office gossip, 205

Office romances, 205–206
On-line auctions, 77
Operating systems, 28
  Linux, 32
  startup disks, 36
Overhead transparencies, 37, 280–282

• P •

Palm units, 40–41
Paperless offices, 67–71
Paperwork, reducing, 147–153
  archive files, 149
  electronic media and, 153
  in-boxes/out-boxes, emptying, 152
  life cycles of records, 150–151
  magazines, 152
  recycling, 153
  reference files, 149
  rough drafts, 152
  sources of clutter, identifying, 151–152
  working files, 149
Passports, 233–235
PCs (personal computers). *See* Computers
People with disabilities, 301–308
  AIDS, 306–307
  fears of employers, dispelling, 307–308
  hearing impaired, 305
  National Organization on Disabilities
    (NOD), 301
  people with paralysis/loss of limb, 306
  politically correct terminology, 302
  sensitivity to during meetings, 274
  speech impaired, 305–306
  vision impaired, 303–304
Phone calls. *See* Telephone calls
Photocopiers, 36–38
Plants, as gift, 186
Politically correct terminology, 302
Post office
  costs, reducing, 143
  domestic mail, 140–143
    bar codes, 143
    bulk mail postage, 140
    certificates of mailing, 141

    certified letters, 141
    express mail, 142
    first class, 140
    priority mail, 142
    registered mail, 141–142
  helpful brochures, 139
  international mail, 143–145
  non-USPS carriers, 145–146
  postage meters, 144
  state abbreviations, 111–112
Postage meters, 144
Postscripts, 116
Power outages, computers and, 32
Presentations, 277–287
  appearing natural during, 284
  audience, knowing, 278
  checklist for, 285–286
  closing remarks, 285
  complaints about, 286
  environment for, 279
  foreign participants and, 284
  key issue, identifying, 278–279
  opening remarks, 282–283
  purpose, understanding, 278
  viewgraphs, 37
  visual aids, 279–282
Priority mail, 142
  GPM (Global Priority Mail), 144
Processes, knowledge management and, 11
Professional associations, 93
Professional liability insurance, 91
Proofreading documents, 134–136

• R •

Recycling paperwork, 153
Reference files, 149
Reference initials, 115
Registered mail
  domestic, 141–142
  international, 144
Registration tables (special events), 290
Rental cars, toll-free numbers, 215
Repetitive action injuries, 98
Reservations (business meals), 171–172

Restaurants, 171–183
  in Asia, 255–256
  buffets, 183
  check, paying the, 178–179
  coats, checking, 172
  cocktails, ordering, 173
  guests, greeting, 172
  in Latin America, 259
  messy foods, tips for eating, 179–182
  in the Middle East, 259–260
  napkin etiquette, 172–173
  ordering tips, 173
  reservations, making, 171–172
  table manners, 175–177
  tipping, 178–179
  toasts, proposing, 175
  wine, ordering, 174–175
Retirement plans for home-based
    businesses, 92–93
Romances, office, 205–206

● *S* ●

Safety, hotels, 228–229, 230
SBA (Small Business Administration), 82
Screening telephone calls, 17
Search engines, 63
self-employment, 79–95
  business plans, 81
  computer issues, 85
  incorporating, 83
  insurance policies and, 91–92
  multifunction devices (MFDs), 86
  naming businesses, 82–83
  networking, 93–94
  retirement plans, 92–93
  tax deductions for, 90–91
  telephone issues, 85
  Web sites, 87–90
  work space, setting up, 84
Semiblock letter style, 117, 121
SEPs (Simplified Employee Pensions), 92
Service clubs, 93
Sexual harassment, 204–205
Signature lines, 115

Siminars. *See* Special events
Simplified Employee Pensions (SEPs), 92
Simplified letter style, 117, 122
Small Business Administration (SBA), 82
Society for the Advancement of Travel for
    the Handicapped (SATH), 217
Sommeliers, 174
Spam e-mail messages, 50–51
Speaker telephones, 85
Special events, 289–298
  coordinators, 289
  foreign participants, 292–294
  name badges, 290–292
  registration table, 290
  special accommodations, 296–298
  spouses and, 290
  trade shows, 294–296
Speech impaired, the, 305–306
State abbreviations, 111–112
Subchapter S corporations, 83
Supervisors
  gifts for, 188
  relationship with administrative
    assistant, 206–209
Surfing the Internet, 60–61
Surge protectors, 32

● *T* ●

Table manners, 175–177
  in Europe, 252
Tape disks, 34
Taxes
  on e-commerce, 75
  home-office deductions, 90–91
  Value Added Tax (VAT), 252–253
Technology, knowledge management and, 11
Telecommuting, 80
Teleconferencing, 275
Telemarketers, getting rid of, 15–16
Telephone calls, 13–26
  answering for someone else, 17–18
  cell phones, 23–26
  chatty callers, 15
  from hotel rooms, 231–232

Telephone calls *(continued)*
international country codes, 22–23
irate callers, 14
money-saving tips, 18–19
placing, 18–19
first impressions, 13–14
placing caller on hold, 15
screening, 17–18
telemarketers, getting rid of, 15–16
voice mail guidelines, 19–21
wrong numbers, 16
Tendinitis, 103
Thank-you notes, 195–196
35-mm slides, 280–282
Time zones, international, 21–22
Tipping (for food and drinks), 178–179
in Asia, 256
in Europe, 250
Toasts, proposing, 175
Trade Show Exhibitors Association, 289
Trade shows, 294–296
attracting visitors, 294–295
following up leads, 295
staffing the booth, 295
walking the floor, 295–296
Translation software, 242–243
Travel agents, 214
Travel issues
Air travel, 213–224
booking flights, 213–215
cancellations, 218–219
delays, 218–219
disabled travelers and, 217
earaches, avoiding, 222
electronic ticketing, 217
executive lounges, passes for, 219
exercising and, 220–221
flight etiquette, 219–220
frequent flyer clubs, 222–223
getting bumped, 218
glossary of terms, 323–325
international airports, 223–224
overcoming jet lag, 221–222
safeguarding tickets, 216
saving money on, 215–216
toll-free numbers, 214–215
Web sites, 216

American biases, 241
Asia, 253–257
conversation topics, 254
dining tips, 255–256
dress codes, 254
general business practices, 256–257
greetings, 253–254
shopping tips, 254–255
tipping, 256
credit cards, 238–239
customs regulations, 261
directions, asking for, 246
Europe, 249–253
conversation topics, 250
currencies, 250–251
dress codes, 251
greetings, 250
table manners, 252
tipping, 250
Value Added Tax (VAT), 252–253
foreign currency, 238
glossary of terms, 323–327
health issues, 237
holidays, 247–249
international driving permits, 236
language issues, 242–243
Latin America, 257–259
border crossings, 258–259
confirming appointments, 258
dining tips, 259
names, 257
transportation within, 258
Middle East, 259–261
currencies, 260
dining tips, 259–260
general business practices, 261
passports, 233–235
representing the United States, 243–246
taboos, 245–246
tips, 243–244
traveler's checks, 239
vaccination certificates, 236–237
visas, 236
Traveler's checks, 239

• U •

United States Postal Service. *See* Post office
UPS (uninterruptable power supply), 32
UPS (United Parcel Service), 146
URLs (uniform resource locators), 48, 62

• V •

Vaccination certificates, 236–237
VAT (Value Added Tax), 252, 253
VC (videoconferencing), 275
Videoconferencing, 275
Viewgraphs, 37, 280–282
Virtual colleges, 66
Viruses, computer, 32–33
Visas, 236
Vision impaired, the, 303–304
Voice mail, 19–21

• W •

Web, the, 61–64
  air travel, booking flights, 214
  airline sites, 216
  country-specific address extensions, 63
  error messages, 65
  gifts, finding, 186
  home offices and, 87–90
  home pages, 64
  hyperlinks, 62
  search engines, 63
  travel-related bargains, 217
  URLs (uniform resource locators), 62

Wedding showers, gifts for, 190
Western Union, 240
White boards, 280
Windows (Microsoft)
  low memory and, 29
  using the CD with, 330
Wine, ordering, 174–175
Wipe boards, 280
Women's issues
  dress codes, 312–313
  gender-neutral terms, 202–203
  networking, 209–210
  office romances, 205–206
  sexual harassment, 204–205
  stereotypes, 200–202
Workers' compensation, for home-based
  businesses, 92
Working files, 149
Working the room, 168–170
World Wide Web. *See* Web, the
Writer's block, 131
Writing. *See* Business writing

Y

Yahoo (search engine), 63

Z

Zip disks, 34

Notes

Notes

IDG Books Worldwide, Inc., End-User License Agreement

READ THIS. You should carefully read these terms and conditions before opening the software packet(s) included with this book ("Book"). This is a license agreement ("Agreement") between you and IDG Books Worldwide, Inc. ("IDGB"). By opening the accompanying software packet(s), you acknowledge that you have read and accept the following terms and conditions. If you do not agree and do not want to be bound by such terms and conditions, promptly return the Book and the unopened software packet(s) to the place you obtained them for a full refund.

1. **License Grant.** IDGB grants to you (either an individual or entity) a nonexclusive license to use one copy of the enclosed software program(s) (collectively, the "Software") solely for your own personal or business purposes on a single computer (whether a standard computer or a workstation component of a multiuser network). The Software is in use on a computer when it is loaded into temporary memory (RAM) or installed into permanent memory (hard disk, CD-ROM, or other storage device). IDGB reserves all rights not expressly granted herein.

2. **Ownership.** IDGB is the owner of all right, title, and interest, including copyright, in and to the compilation of the Software recorded on the disk(s) or CD-ROM ("Software Media"). Copyright to the individual programs recorded on the Software Media is owned by the author or other authorized copyright owner of each program. Ownership of the Software and all proprietary rights relating thereto remain with IDGB and its licensers.

3. **Restrictions on Use and Transfer.**

   (a) You may only (i) make one copy of the Software for backup or archival purposes, or (ii) transfer the Software to a single hard disk, provided that you keep the original for backup or archival purposes. You may not (i) rent or lease the Software, (ii) copy or reproduce the Software through a LAN or other network system or through any computer subscriber system or bulletin-board system, or (iii) modify, adapt, or create derivative works based on the Software.

   (b) You may not reverse engineer, decompile, or disassemble the Software. You may transfer the Software and user documentation on a permanent basis, provided that the transferee agrees to accept the terms and conditions of this Agreement and you retain no copies. If the Software is an update or has been updated, any transfer must include the most recent update and all prior versions.

4. **Restrictions on Use of Individual Programs.** You must follow the individual requirements and restrictions detailed for each individual program in the "About the CD" appendix of this Book. These limitations are also contained in the individual license agreements recorded on the Software Media. These limitations may include a requirement that after using the program for a specified period of time, the user must pay a registration fee or discontinue use. By opening the Software packet(s), you will be agreeing to abide by the licenses and restrictions for these individual programs that are detailed in the "About the CD" appendix and on the Software Media. None of the material on this Software Media or listed in this Book may ever be redistributed, in original or modified form, for commercial purposes.

5. **Limited Warranty.**

    (a) IDGB warrants that the Software and Software Media are free from defects in materials and workmanship under normal use for a period of sixty (60) days from the date of purchase of this Book. If IDGB receives notification within the warranty period of defects in materials or workmanship, IDGB will replace the defective Software Media.

    (b) IDGB AND THE AUTHOR OF THE BOOK DISCLAIM ALL OTHER WARRANTIES, EXPRESS OR IMPLIED, INCLUDING WITHOUT LIMITATION IMPLIED WARRANTIES OF MERCHANTABILITY AND FITNESS FOR A PARTICULAR PURPOSE, WITH RESPECT TO THE SOFTWARE, THE PROGRAMS, THE SOURCE CODE CONTAINED THEREIN, AND/OR THE TECHNIQUES DESCRIBED IN THIS BOOK. IDGB DOES NOT WARRANT THAT THE FUNCTIONS CONTAINED IN THE SOFTWARE WILL MEET YOUR REQUIREMENTS OR THAT THE OPERATION OF THE SOFTWARE WILL BE ERROR FREE.

    (c) This limited warranty gives you specific legal rights, and you may have other rights that vary from jurisdiction to jurisdiction.

6. **Remedies.**

    (a) IDGB's entire liability and your exclusive remedy for defects in materials and workmanship shall be limited to replacement of the Software Media, which may be returned to IDGB with a copy of your receipt at the following address: Software Media Fulfillment Department, Attn.: *Business Professional's Kit For Dummies,* IDG Books Worldwide, Inc., 10475 Crosspoint Blvd., Indianapolis, IN 46256, or call 800-762-2974. Please allow three to four weeks for delivery. This Limited Warranty is void if failure of the Software Media has resulted from accident, abuse, or misapplication. Any replacement Software Media will be warranted for the remainder of the original warranty period or thirty (30) days, whichever is longer.

    (b) In no event shall IDGB or the author be liable for any damages whatsoever (including without limitation damages for loss of business profits, business interruption, loss of business information, or any other pecuniary loss) arising from the use of or inability to use the Book or the Software, even if IDGB has been advised of the possibility of such damages.

    (c) Because some jurisdictions do not allow the exclusion or limitation of liability for consequential or incidental damages, the above limitation or exclusion may not apply to you.

7. **U.S. Government Restricted Rights.** Use, duplication, or disclosure of the Software by the U.S. Government is subject to restrictions stated in paragraph (c)(1)(ii) of the Rights in Technical Data and Computer Software clause of DFARS 252.227-7013, and in subparagraphs (a) through (d) of the Commercial Computer–Restricted Rights clause at FAR 52.227-19, and in similar clauses in the NASA FAR supplement, when applicable.

8. **General.** This Agreement constitutes the entire understanding of the parties and revokes and supersedes all prior agreements, oral or written, between them and may not be modified or amended except in a writing signed by both parties hereto that specifically refers to this Agreement. This Agreement shall take precedence over any other documents that may be in conflict herewith. If any one or more provisions contained in this Agreement are held by any court or tribunal to be invalid, illegal, or otherwise unenforceable, each and every other provision shall remain in full force and effect.

Installation Instructions

The *Business Professional's Kit For Dummies* CD offers valuable information that you won't want to miss. To install the items from the CD to your hard drive, follow these steps (which are for computers using Windows):

1. **Insert the CD into your computer's CD-ROM drive.**

   Give your computer a moment to take a look at the CD.

2. **Open your browser.** Click on File⇨Open (Internet Explorer) or on File⇨Open Page (Netscape).

3. **Double-click the file called License.txt.**

   This file contains the end-user license that you agree to by using the CD. When you are done reading the license, close the program, most likely NotePad, that displayed the file.

4. **Double-click the file called Readme.txt.**

   This file contains instructions about installing the software from this CD. It might be helpful to leave this text file open while you are using the CD.

5. **In the dialog box that appears, type** D:\START.HTM **and click on OK.**

6. **Replace the letter D: with the correct letter for your CD-ROM drive, if it is not "D."**

   This action will display the file that will walk you through the content of the CD.

7. **To navigate within the interface, simply click on any topic of interest to take you to an explanation of the files on the CD and how to use or install them.** You will see Install buttons that will install the software for you. When you select that option, instead of installing directly from the CD, select Open this file when the Download File dialog box pops up. After you are done with the interface, simply close your browser as usual.

If you use a Macintosh computer, you can also use the documents on this CD. Simply insert the CD into your computer's CD-ROM drive, double-click the CD icon when it appears on the desktop, read the Read Me file, and then open the file start.htm to see the contents of the CD.

For more information, please see the "About the CD" appendix in this book.

YOUR ONLINE RESOURCE

WWW.DUMMIES.COM

Discover Dummies Online!

The Dummies Web Site is your fun and friendly online resource for the latest information about *For Dummies*® books and your favorite topics. The Web site is the place to communicate with us, exchange ideas with other *For Dummies* readers, chat with authors, and have fun!

Ten Fun and Useful Things You Can Do at www.dummies.com

1. Win free *For Dummies* books and more!
2. Register your book and be entered in a prize drawing.
3. Meet your favorite authors through the IDG Books Worldwide Author Chat Series.
4. Exchange helpful information with other *For Dummies* readers.
5. Discover other great *For Dummies* books you must have!
6. Purchase Dummieswear® exclusively from our Web site.
7. Buy *For Dummies* books online.
8. Talk to us. Make comments, ask questions, get answers!
9. Download free software.
10. Find additional useful resources from authors.

Link directly to these ten fun and useful things at
http://www.dummies.com/10useful

SURF THE NET

WWW.DUMMIES.COM

For other technology titles from IDG Books Worldwide, go to
www.idgbooks.com

Not on the Web yet? It's easy to get started with *Dummies 101*®: *The Internet For Windows*® *98* or *The Internet For Dummies*® at local retailers everywhere.

IDG BOOKS WORLDWIDE

Find other *For Dummies* books on these topics:

Business • Career • Databases • Food & Beverage • Games • Gardening • Graphics • Hardware
Health & Fitness • Internet and the World Wide Web • Networking • Office Suites
Operating Systems • Personal Finance • Pets • Programming • Recreation • Sports
Spreadsheets • Teacher Resources • Test Prep • Word Processing

IDG BOOKS WORLDWIDE BOOK REGISTRATION

Register This Book and Win!

We want to hear from you!

Visit **http://my2cents.dummies.com** to register this book and tell us how you liked it!

✔ Get entered in our monthly prize giveaway.

✔ Give us feedback about this book — tell us what you like best, what you like least, or maybe what you'd like to ask the author and us to change!

✔ Let us know any other *For Dummies*® topics that interest you.

Your feedback helps us determine what books to publish, tells us what coverage to add as we revise our books, and lets us know whether we're meeting your needs as a *For Dummies* reader. You're our most valuable resource, and what you have to say is important to us!

Not on the Web yet? It's easy to get started with *Dummies 101*®: *The Internet For Windows*® *98* or *The Internet For Dummies*® at local retailers everywhere.

Or let us know what you think by sending us a letter at the following address:

For Dummies Book Registration
Dummies Press
10475 Crosspoint Blvd.
Indianapolis, IN 46256

...FOR DUMMIES™

BESTSELLING BOOK SERIES